THE JEWISH COMMUNITY IN POLAND

Historical Essays

The Vienna Divorce: History of a Dispute on the Validity of Conditional Divorce in the 17th Century. Lwów, 1931.

The Jewish Excommunication in Lithuania in the 17th and 18th Centuries. Lwów, 1932.

The Right of the Dissolution of Parliament. Lwów, 1933.

Contributions to the History of Jews in Poland. Lwów, 1935.

History of the Bar in Ancient Poland. Lwów, 1936.

Past and Present. Studies in historical and literary problems. Lodz, 1939.

The Protection of Jewish Religious Rights by Royal Edicts in Ancient Poland. New York, 1943.

Religious Freedom: The Right to Practice Shehitah. New York, 1946.

The Destruction of Europe. New York, 1948.

After the Destruction. New York, 1950.

Religious Jewry and the United Nations. Addresses before the United Nations. New York, 1953.

In the Struggle Against Discrimination. Addresses before various organs of the United Nations and of the Congress of the United States. New York, 1957.

In Defense of the Shehitah. Statement and Testimony before the Committee on Agriculture and Forestry of the U.S. Senate. New York, 1958.

Late Summer Fruit. Essays. New York, 1960.

The Jews in Old Poland. Historical studies. Buenos Aires, 1962.

To the History of Agudath Israel. Essays and Speeches. New York, 1964.

War on War. New York, 1969.

Ten Years of Hope. Addresses before the U.N. New York, 1971.

Shall the Sword Devour Forever? New York, 1974.

Unto the Mountains. Essays, New York, 1975

Personalities and Events. Essays and Speeches, New York, 1978.

Towards International Guarantees for Religious Liberty. Addresses Before the United Nations. New York, 1981.

From the Morning Till Eve. Jerusalem, 1981.

From the History and Tradition. Warsaw, 1983.

THE JEWISH COMMUNITY
IN POLAND

Historical Essays

by
Isaac Lewin

A POLISH INSTITUTE OF ARTS
AND SCIENCES OF AMERICA BOOK

Philosophical Library
New York

A POLISH INSTITUTE OF ARTS
AND SCIENCES OF AMERICA BOOK
Ludwik Krzyżanowski and Gerard T. Kapolka, editors

The publication of this volume was made possible with the
assistance of the Lucius N. Littauer Foundation and the
Research Institute of Religious Jewry, Inc., in New York.

Library of Congress Cataloging in Publication Data

Lewin, Isaac, 1906-
    The Jewish community in Poland.

    1. Jews—Poland—History—Addresses, essays, lectures.
2. Poland—Ethnic relations—Addresses, essays, lectures.
I. Title.
DS135.P6L4966   1985   943.8'004924   84-16705
ISBN   0-8022-2477-6

Published 1985 by Philosophical Library, Inc.,
200 West 57th Street, New York, New York 10019.

This volume is dedicated to the memory
of my beloved parents, Rabbi Aaron and Dora Lewin,
and my dear sister, Dr. Paula Blatt,
who were murdered by the Nazis during World War II.
May their memory be a blessing.

PREFACE

Noble Jewish people, you are in Europe
Like a statue shattered in the East.
Scattering your fragments everywhere
You carry on each an eternal hieroglyphic
(*Cyprian Norwid*)

Dr. Isaac Lewin has brought together in this volume a variegated collection of the Jewish experience in Poland over a period of a thousand years. Serious and humorous, often sad and moving, social and political, the stories paint a rich and authentic picture of a segment of Poland's population now irretrievably lost.

Following the holocaust, Dr. Isaac Lewin has saved from oblivion a treasure of genuine Jewish folklore which is part of the universal Jewish heritage.

"To Israel, our elder brother, respect and equal rights in

everything." This principle enunciated by Poland's national poet, Adam Mickiewicz, has guided the Polish Institute of Arts and Sciences of America in extending its sponsorship to the publication of this book.

Ludwik Krzyżanowski
Vice-President, The Polish Institute of Arts and Sciences of America

CONTENTS

INTRODUCTION

Some things exceed even the wildest reach of the human imagination. What seemed inconceivable yesterday becomes reality today. One's eyes, ears, and senses can no longer be trusted.

Who could have believed that a community of three and one half million people could be completely annihilated? How could that have been imagined?

But it happened in our time. The Jewish community of Poland—the most vibrant and flourishing segment of the world's Jewish population—was eradicated in cold blood by the German Government, which occupied Poland in September 1939 and implemented, over a two-year period, the worst program of genocide the world has ever seen. In July 1942 the massacre began. By the middle of 1943, the grisly work was finished.

No one had ever imagined such bestiality, such mass murder of innocents, including a half million children, whose only crime was that they belonged to the Jewish people, which the Germans preferred to identify as a "race." No normal human could have anticipated the acts of cruelty by which this genocide was accomplished.

The *Endziel* of the German rulers was that no single Jew should survive. Their leader proclaimed this horrifying intention openly, in advance, and it was a sheer miracle that he could not bring it to fruition. Germany lost its war before the small remnants of European Jewry could be put to death in the extermination camps of Auschwitz, Treblinka, Majdanek, Dachau, Buchenwald, and elsewhere. Fragments of destroyed Jewish communities fled to the United States, England, Switzerland, and to other countries beyond the reach of the Germans. And through it all, the world watched, with only an occasional cry of protest.

Those who survived have been trying to rebuild what was lost and to preserve a record for future generations. One phase of their reconstruction requires telling the story of the past glory of the destroyed European Jewish communities, to pass on to future generations the legacy that was so savagely wiped away.

It was my privilege to edit a seven volume collection of essays called *Eleh Ezkra* ("These Will I Remember"), containing the biographies, in Hebrew, of 368 religious leaders of European Jewry whose deaths were attributable to the German persecution of the Jews. That collection, however, tells only of the recent past. We must go farther back into the thousand-year history of Polish Jewry, which grew from small beginnings to become the great Jewish spiritual center of the first part of the twentieth century. Polish Jewry became, as it were, the staff of life which nourished the world's Jews in the eighteenth, nineteenth, and early twentieth centuries.

Today this nourishment is gone. When we forage for what is left in the pages of history, we find only crumbs. They are, however, golden crumbs.

nized that better results could be expected from leaders elected by the Jews themselves.

However, once the right to be governed by elected leaders (rabbis and laymen) was established, the cornerstone was laid for the autonomy of the Jewish community. Although, even before 1551, the Jewish leadership was occasionally represented by persons of high caliber—such as Rabbi Shalom Shachna of Lublin, who was appointed in 1541 as "general rabbi" of a large province of Poland—the leadership could now become the real mirror of Polish Jewry. Leaders were elected not because of their ability to collect taxes, but because of their distinction in Jewish learning or in other traits of personality or character. The system of elections was, to be sure, far from democratic in a modern sense; it favored the rule of an oligarchic group which was perpetuated in office for generation after generation. Elections were not direct; only those members of the community who shared in the budget of the expenses of the *Kehilla* were permitted to participate in the selection of the so-called *borrerim* (electors). The actual election was similar to a lottery. Various names were put into a box, and the electors were drawn from it. Sometimes the names were divided into more than one box. After several electors were drawn from one box, the remaining names were transferred to a second box. The same procedure followed the drawing of names from the second box; several additional electors were drawn, and the remaining names were then mixed in with those in a third box. Often "miracles" occurred on the way from one box to another. The group of electors which were finally to appoint the leadership of the community was, for all practical purposes, an organ of the outgoing leaders. Nevertheless, the communal life of Polish Jews was, in fact, administered soundly.

The most important aspect of Jewish public life in Poland was the establishment of a central body which functioned for about 200 years, until 1764. We do not know exactly when this

Map of the "Four Lands" (Greater Poland, Little Poland, Red Russia, Wołyń) with their capitals—and Lithuania.

body, called in Hebrew *Vaad Arba Aratzot* (Synod of Four Lands), began to function. Some scholars, like Abraham Elijah Harkavy, are inclined to believe that it began about 1530. Others thought that there was proof of its existence in a royal decree of 1540 which had been quoted in another source. I obtained the original decree, written in Latin, and am convinced that the decree has been misinterpreted. Heinrich Graetz thought he had even found the individual who was the father of the central Jewish communal organization in Poland, Rabbi Mordecai Yaffe (1530-1613), and he fixed the birth of this organization at the reign of King Stefan Batory (1576-1586). But this historian appears to have been moved more by intuition and emotion than by evidence. He did not like Polish Jews (although he was himself born on former Polish territory near Poznań) and could not bring himself to believe that Polish Jews could have invented a form of self-government unique in the history of the Diaspora. Since Rabbi Mordecai Yaffe had traveled in Germany and Italy, Graetz considered him capable of dealing with communal problems using "a German sense of order or German exactness" (*deutscher Ordnungssinn oder deutsche Pedanterie*), without "the Polish lack of form" (*polnische Formlosigkeit*). Other modern historians, such as Moses Schorr, Meyer Bałaban, and Simon Dubnow, feel that the central organization of Polish Jews became a reality about 1580.

As we have said, this organization was known as the Council of Four Lands. The "Four Lands" were: (1) "Little" Poland with Cracow as its capital, (2) "Greater" Poland with Poznań as capital, (3) Red Ruthenia with Lwów as capital, and (4) Wołyń (Volhynia) with Włodzimierz (Ludmir) as capital. Lithuania was initially part of the Council as well, but in 1623 it separated and formed the Council of Lithuanian Communities.

The *Vaad Arba Aratzot* was a real parliament. It met twice a year, in Lublin and Jarosław. It had its speaker, called *Parnas Bet Israel d'Arba Aratzot*, and treasurer, called *Neeman Bet*

Israel D'Arba Aratzot. The activities of the *Vaad Arba Aratzot* extended to all aspects of Jewish life. The Council not only allocated the head tax, for which it was responsible to the King, among individual communities, but also regulated the entire economic life of the Jewish population. It issued important regulations, such as the procedure governing bankruptcy, issued in 1624, and the prohibition against entry into various business fields. The Council regularized acquisition of rabbinical positions by prohibiting bribery of the electorate. It assumed responsibility for the content of printed books by issuing special permissions (*Haskamot*) for their publication. It appeared as the official representative of all Jews in Poland through a special delegate called a *Shtadlan*. The *Shtadlan* had a monopoly in this respect; no other individual was permitted or authorized to intervene with the Polish parliament (*Sejm*), High Court (*Trybunał*), or other offices.

Jewish autonomy was, of course, recognized by the Polish state, which lent its assistance to the decisions of the Council of Four Lands and of the Council of the Lithuanian *Kehillot*. The decisions of the Councils had an effective means of internal enforcement—excommunication (*Herem*). If an individual did not opt to be released from excommunication within thirty days by performing the deed which the Council had ordered, the State intervened by confiscating the property of the disobedient Jew, sometimes even threatening the death penalty. The State had an interest in enforcing Jewish excommunication because the *Herem* was used for the collection of taxes and its effectiveness was, therefore, of paramount interest to the State.

Under the leadership of the Council of Four Lands, the Jewish community in Poland rose to great heights. Jews not only acquired material wealth but were also able to dedicate their energies to the study of the Torah. The Code *Shulhan Aruch,* written by the great Sephardic scholar Rabbi Joseph Caro, was adapted to the needs of Western European Jewry by the Rabbi of Cracow, Moses Isserles. Only with his *Mappa* did the *Shulhan Aruch* achieve the recognition it deserved. The principal commentaries to this Code were written by Polish rabbis. The section dealing with daily ritual problems (*Yore Deah*) was authoritatively explained by two Polish rabbis, David Halevy (in a commentary entitled *Turey Zahav*) and Shabtai Cohen (in a commentary entitled *Siftei Cohen*). The best commentaries on the civil code (*Hoshen Hamishpat*) were written by the Polish rabbis Joshua Falk Cohen (entitled *Sefer Meirat Eynayim*) and Shabtai Cohen (entitled *Siftei Cohen*). The two best commentaries on the section dealing with the laws of marriage and divorce (*Even Haezer*) were written by the Polish rabbis Moses Lima (entitled *Helkat Mehokek*) and Samuel-ben-Phoebus (entitled *Bet Shmuel*). Finally, the accepted commentaries to *Orah Hayim*, the section of the *Shulhan Aruch* which deals with prayers and with the laws of the Sabbath and festivals, were authored by the Polish rabbis David Halevy (entitled *Turey Zahav*) and Abe Gombiner (entitled *Magen Abraham*). The leading Talmudic commentaries written in the sixteenth and seventeenth centuries were the works of the Polish rabbis Salomon Luria (known as *Maharshal*), Meir-ben-Gedalia (known as *Maharam*), and Samuel Eidels (known as *Maharsha*). Authoritative responsa were also written during this period by Polish rabbis, among them Benjamin Aaron Solnik (whose collection is called *Masat Benjamin*), Joseph Katz (whose collection is entitled *Sheerit Joseph*), and many others. A commentary of exceptional value to the code of Jacob Asheri (*Tur*) was written by the Polish rabbi Joel Serkes (entitled *Bayit Hadash*). A book which became synonymous with Jewish ethics was authored by Isaiah Hurvitz, a rabbi who was educated in Poland and functioned in several Polish communities (entitled *Shney Luhot Habrit*).

An attempt at codification of Jewish law was made by Rabbi Mordecai Yaffe (collectively entitled *Lvush*). Due to the works of these and many other Talmudic scholars in Poland in the sixteenth and seventeenth centuries, this country became the same kind of center for Jews in the Diaspora as Babylonia had been in the time of the creation of the Talmud, France in the time of Rashi, Germany in the time of the "Tossafists," and Spain in the time of Rabbi Salomon-ben-Adreth (known as *Rashba*).

This period of glory lasted until the middle of the seventeenth century. In 1648 Polish Jewry suffered a great calamity—the massacres of Chmielnicki.

II

The *Geserot Tah—Tah* is equivalent in Hebrew to [5] 408, which year in the Hebrew calendar corresponds to 1648—was called by Rabbi Sheftel Hurvitz (the son of Rabbi Isaiah, the author of *Shney Luhot Habrit*) the third *Hurban*. It constitutes one of the great catastrophes in Jewish history. The prosperous Jewish center in Poland—probably the best organized since Spanish Jewry was destroyed in 1492—was suddenly devastated as if by a tornado.

It is difficult to describe all the atrocities committed on the Jews of Poland by Chmielnicki, his Tatar associates, and the Swedish conquerors of the Polish State. A contemporary, Nathan Hanover, in his book, *Yevein Metzula*, recorded the story of Jewish suffering in the years 1648-1655, and an examination of that story shows that it was surpassed only by Auschwitz and Treblinka in our time.

Had Polish Jewry not been as well organized as it was at the time Chmielnicki appeared with his hordes, it would have been totally destroyed. Fortunately, however, the *Kehillot*, the *Vaad Arba Aratzot*, and the *Vaad Medinat Lita* immediately assumed the burden of rescue and relief work.[1]

The protocols of the *Vaad Medinat Lita* tell us how this work was done. The refugees were systematically distributed among the communities which had not been reached by Chmielnicki and his hordes. The Council adopted the rule that every group of ten Jews was required to maintain one refugee. A special tax was imposed on the Jews who had not been immediately attacked, and the money collected was used for the redemption of prisoners (the Tatars, who came with Chmielnicki, took many Jewish prisoners and sent them to Constantinople, where they were offered for ransom). A kind of "United Jewish Appeal" of the seventeenth century was established to lend constructive assistance to those Jews who had to start from scratch in their new environments. In order to give expression to the grief and sorrow of the entire Jewish community of Poland and Lithuania, a period of mourning was declared, and no one was permitted to put on jewels or luxurious clothes at this time. The period was initially fixed at three years, but it was later extended for another three years when the massacres continued. Music was banned from weddings, and the number of guests at any such affair was limited to forty or fifty. The date of the twentieth of *Sivan*, when the first Chmielnicki pogrom took place, was declared a fast day. It coincided with the date declared a fast day at the time of the Crusades, 1171, by the famous "Tossafist" Rabbenu Jacob Tam.

It is quite clear that, notwithstanding the rescue and rehabilitation efforts of the *Vaad Arba Aratzot* and the *Vaad Medinat Lita*, the position of the Jewish communities in Poland became very critical after the massacres. The funds collected were insufficient. The loss of one third of the population was too great to be made up. The communities and the *Vaadim* began to borrow a lot of money from the Polish clergy and nobility. Very soon the once-flourishing communities stood on the verge of bankruptcy. The State needed money and looked toward increasing the taxes of the impoverished Jews. The successors of Jan Kazimierz, the two kings of Polish origin, Michał Wiśniowiecki (1669-1673) and Jan III Sobieski (1674-

1696), were friendly toward Jews but could not halt the wave of pogroms. Pogroms occurred in Brześć in 1680, in Cracow in 1682, in Wilno in 1681 and 1687, and in Poznań in 1687. They were usually begun by students, who were subsequently joined by the mob.

Poland became disorganized. The nobility and the clergy liked the chaos because their influence grew in inverse proportion to the weakening of the authority of the King and his administration. Real chaos developed under the two kings from Saxony, August II (1697-1732) and August III (1732-1763). Jews suffered most in this anarchical period. Ritual murder accusations were openly encouraged by these two kings, who had stated that they believed that "Jews and heretics are killing Christian children." In 1698 a Catholic priest in Sandomierz accused the leader of the local Jewish community of murdering a Christian child in order to get its blood for *Matzot*. The innocent man was tortured and, of course, confessed his guilt. The King then ordered the expulsion of all Jews from Sandomierz. Similar incidents followed.

How could the Jews defend themselves? Indeed there was one way which offered some hope of success—bribery of officials. Everything cost money. The Jews knew it and the Poles knew it too. Noblemen took it for granted that they were to get something from "their" Jews. One of them, a member of the distinguished Radziwiłł family, even ordered the Jews of one of his villages to bring fifty pounds of wax to the church to exonerate him for a sin he had committed.

In 1764 a new king—Stanisław August Poniatowski—took over the reins of Poland; he was destined to preside over the dismemberment of his country. On three occasions, in 1772, 1793, and 1795, Poland's neighbors, Russia, Prussia, and Austria, shaved off slices of this country, until nothing remained. In this last period of Polish independence, the Jewish community had to dance the "*salto mortale*" of its material life. Even before the beginning of the new king's administration, the *Sejm* had decided that the Council of Four Lands and the Council of Lithuanian Communities should be dissolved. The head tax that the Jews had heretofore paid by agreement of the Councils with the Treasury was transformed into a direct duty on every Jew, consisting of two złoty per annum. In 1768 the bloody tradition of Chmielnicki was revived by two rebels, Gonta and Żeleźniak, who murdered several thousand Jews assembled in the Ukrainian town of Humań.

After the first partition of Poland in 1772, the Polish nation awoke and made several attempts to stop the rapidly approaching complete annihilation of its independence. Money was desperately needed, and in 1775 the Jewish head tax was increased from two to three złoty per capita per annum. However, apart from the need for Jewish money, individual Polish thinkers and politicians made some attempts to solve the Jewish problem in Poland. The fact that more than 600,000 Jews still lived in Poland, even after its territory had shrunk considerably in 1772, demanded some consideration.

It cannot be said that the attempts to regulate the Jewish position in this period were fortunate. One proposal, presented in 1778 by Andrzej Zamojski, was deeply reactionary. It envisaged Jewish ghettos in the towns and restricted the economic activities of the Jews. A more liberal proposal was presented in 1782, printed anonymously and later authenticated by Mateusz Butrymowicz, a member of the *Sejm*, who suggested that it be adopted by the so-called Quadrennial *Sejm* in 1789. It recommended Jewish emancipation, but at a high price: cultural assimilation with the Polish nation. The Jews would have had to abandon their language, to ban Hebrew printing and even the importing of Hebrew books from abroad, to curtail their religion, and to abstain from some business activities such as selling liquor. Neither proposal was adopted by the reform *Sejm*.

The constitution of May 3, 1791, prepared by two great Polish thinkers, Stanisław Staszic and Hugo Kołłątaj, did not even mention Jews. After the new constitution was adopted, a new debate took place on the solution to the Jewish problem, both in the *Sejm* and in the press. The proposal which appealed most to the legislators and the public was that Jewish marriages be limited in order to cause a gradual decrease in the number of Jews—or at least curb any further increase. However, the discussion was already meaningless; the angel of death had seized the Polish State. In 1793 the second partition took place. Russia and Prussia (this time without Austria) seized the provinces of Wołyń, Podole, and Greater Poland from Poland. About half of Polish Jewry suddenly found itself outside of Poland.

The final struggle was approaching. Kościuszko, the great national hero, who had earlier played a role in America, led the Poles' battle for independence. Polish Jews joined with him in this fight. A Jewish regiment of cavalry under the command of Colonel Berek Joselewicz fought together with the Poles on November 4, 1794 against the Russians in Praga, a suburb of Warsaw. The entire regiment was wiped out by the overwhelming power of the Russians under Suvarov. Berek Joselewicz escaped and fled abroad, where he waited for another occasion to fight the occupiers of Poland. This occasion came a few years later, when in 1807 Napoleon Bonaparte established the Grand Duchy of Warsaw. Berek lost his life in 1809 when his newly organized regiment fought against the occupiers in a battle near the town of Kock.

III

The sad conditions of life for Polish Jewry from 1648 to 1795 were not reflected in their spiritual life.

True, there was no new code of Jewish law authored or authoritatively interpreted during the eighteenth century in Poland. But the great rabbinical scholars of this century rank with those of the previous period. One of them even stands higher—a conclusion proven by the title he received from the Jewish people at large, an honor granted neither Maimonides nor Jacob Asheri nor Joseph Caro, the three greatest codifiers of the Diaspora. I am speaking of the Gaon of Wilno, Rabbi Elijah (1720-1797). Folk tradition bestowed this title, "Gaon" (Excellency), which no scholar had possessed for nearly seven hundred years. It had once been used in Babylon and disappeared in 1038, with the death of Rabbi Hai ben Sherira. It was revitalized for Elijah, whose Talmudic genius was so unequalled that with no formality he is remembered in Jewish history as the "Gaon of Wilno."

When he was seven years old, Elijah ben Shlomo Zalman delivered a sermon in the synagogue. He had no teacher past the age of ten, and he studied not only the Talmud, but also mathematics and other sciences. He used to say that the lack of knowledge of mathematics and the natural sciences severely hinders the study of the Torah. His way of life was ascetic. During the day he always dressed in his *Tallith* and *Tefillin*. His fifty-four books reflect almost the entire world of the Talmud and the Jewish law. His books are only a small portion of what his encyclopedic mind generated. He became a legend in his own time, and in our time he stands for unsurpassed mastership of Jewish law.

His contemporary was Israel ben Eliezer (1700-1760) of Międzybór in Podole, known as "*Baal Shem Tov*" or "Bearer of the Good Name." He began a trend of life which exists to this day and has influenced the Jewish people as practically no other movement had ever done before. This great Polish Jew originated Hasidism, the movement which educated millions. He left no books, and his teachings are known to us mostly from the writings of his student, Rabbi Jacob Joseph of Połonne, and from some anonymous writings of his followers. The *Baal Shem Tov* taught that God reveals Himself in nature. According to his philosophical system, every human being can and should find God near himself, in his most intimate surroundings, and grows close to Him with the help of man's intellect. This closenesss is called *Dveikut* in Hebrew. In his very being, man possesses sacred sparks (*nitzotzot kedoshim*), which the intellect (*mahshava*) transmits to God. In this way we gain peace of mind. We ought to be optimists because there is no absolute wrong in the world. The wrong is only a lower grade of the good. If a just man sees something wrong, he feels good that he is not doing wrong himself. Consequently a man should always live in joyfulness (*b'simha*), because God is omnipotent and can change what is depressing us at any moment. Man is so close to God that every moment, even the most tragic, can bring change for the better, if we only direct our spiritual sparks towards Him. Prayers and the study of the Torah are the channels through which these sparks flow. The creator of Hasidism built the intricate structure of a philosophy of life which responded to, and reflected the mood of, the Jewish masses in Poland. Hasidism was accepted almost instantaneously. It is the most popular current in Jewish Orthodoxy to the present day.

According to the *Baal Shem Tov*, there are two ways to reach God, prayer and study of the Torah. Prayer removes the curtain between God and man. Therefore our prayer has to be very thorough and enthusiastic. During this prayer we have to rise from this material world into the world of God, and to this end we may use all means: dance, songs, etc. We may disregard the reaction of other people to our behavior during prayer, just as a man who finds himself in deep water and makes desperate moves to save himself will not pay any attention to other men's reactions to his movements.

The second way of reaching God is the study of the Torah. The *Baal Shem Tov* recommended the use of the same thoroughness and enthusiasm in studying the Torah as in prayer.

The founder of Hasidism hated sorrow. He believed that man should know that God cannot be reached through misery and sadness. He explained this as follows: Satan (the *Yetzer*

Hara) sometimes tells an individual that he has committed a great sin, even though his sin is not so great. His evil intention is to make the individual feel bad and consequently not serve God. The man should answer Satan: "I do not care what you say. I will serve God with joy because in this way I will satisfy the will of God."

The *Baal Shem Tov* opposed asceticism and preached the joy of life. No matter how the outside world reacts, whether our actions cause praise or condemnation, we should conduct ourselves the same way. He has explained verse 8 in Psalm 16, "*Shiviti Hashem lnegdi tamid* (I have set the Lord always before me)" in the following way: When "*Hashem lnegdi tamid*"—then "*Shiviti*." In other words: "When I have God always before me—I am always the same, I do not differ, I do not change my reaction."

The *Baal Shem Tov* further taught that if a man achieves contact with God, and he elevates his intellect to God, then he is a *Tzaddik*, a just man. God finds pleasure in the *Tzaddik*'s actions.

Unfortunately, the *Baal Shem Tov*'s teachings were not understood at the beginning. The Gaon of Wilno stood up against Hasidism. A great fight began to shatter the Jewish community, not only in Wilno but in all of the territories which once belonged to Poland. Jewry was divided into the "*Hasidim*" and the "*Mitnagdim*." This division has now lasted for 200 years.

But the glory of Polish Jewry was not diminished by this division. There is a saying among Jews which characterizes such discussions: *Ele ve-ele divre Elokim hayim*. These as well as these are the words of the living God.

Note

[1] A detailed study of this very interesting chapter in the history of Polish Jewry can be found in my book *Hurban Europa* [The destruction of Europe], New York, 1948, pp. 268-281.

CHAPTER II
One Thousand Years of Jewish Life in Poland

I

The origins of Jewish settlement in Poland are enveloped in clouds of uncertainty. When the "Polan" tribe began to construct its state in the tenth century in the Warta River basin, it made contact with newcomers. Whether it was Piast or his son Ziemowit or grandson Leszek who greeted them is difficult to determine. This period is veiled in mystery. But once Leszek's son Ziemomyśl and his successor Mieszko firmly established themselves on "Polan" soil, they opened the gates wide to strangers.

Jews from the West began to seek a market for their commodities. They moved through the lands of the Polan state, journeying as far as the Caspian Sea.[1] Similarly, in the opposite

17

direction, from Khazaria in the Volga basin, where in the ninth and tenth centuries a state professing the Jewish faith had existed, the Khazars moved westward.[2]

The sources do not tell us how the Polans received the Jews from the West and East. But the silence is itself significant. We are told that in a somewhat later period, during the First Crusade in 1096, Poland's southern neighbors—the Czechs—witnessed a pogrom, during which Jews fled from Prague to Poland.[3] Apparently the Polans—already called Poles by this time—were more hospitable. Had Jewish blood been shed over the Warta or Wisla Rivers, as it had been over the Voltava, it would probably have been mentioned.

There is some evidence of a permanent Jewish settlement in Poland as early as the twelfth century. A document of 1150 refers to a Jew as the proprietor of a rural village near Wrocław[4], and there is a tombstone dated 1203 of a Jew in Wrocław.[5] Wincenty Kadłubek notes in his *Chronicle* that Mieszko III (1173-1209) imposed heavy punishment on those who attacked Jews.[6]

How the Jews earned a living is not difficult to reconstruct. There is indisputable evidence that Jews fulfilled important economic functions. The silver coins, the so-called *brakteaty*, which circulated in Poland at the end of the twelfth century and in the beginning of the thirteenth century, bear Hebrew letters.[7] This unquestionably attests to the fact that, as in other neighboring countries such as Saxony and Wuerzburg, the Princes' mints were in Jewish hands. The inscriptions were characteristic. One coin dating from the beginning of the thirteenth century bears the words *Mesko bracha*, meaning "the blessing of Mieszko." Mieszko had evidently given his blessing to the efforts of this unknown Jewish minter. And there is evidence that the Prince of Greater Poland in the second half of the twelfth century, Mieszko the Elder (Mieszko Stary), leased his mint in Gniezno to Jews.[8]

A picture of Jewish activities in thirteenth-century Poland is provided by the Statute of Kalisz, a historic document of rights granted to the Jews in 1264 by Bolesław Pobozny (Bolesław the Pious). This document, modeled on charters of privileges issued by Frederick Babenberg of Austria in 1244, Bela IV of Hungary in 1251, and Ottokar II of Bohemia in 1254, became the legal foundation for the rights of Polish Jewry for centuries.[9]

The Statute conferred upon the Jews the status of *servi camerae*, which described their linkage to the Prince's treasury or, with the reemergence of the Polish Kingdom in the fourteenth century, to the Royal Treasury.[10]

According to the Statute of Kalisz, a Jew was guaranteed full protection for his life and property. He was free to conduct his business activities. He was protected against discrimination in court. His oath was recognized as evidence in legal proceedings. Synagogues and cemeteries were to be secure against attacks. It was prohibited to accuse Jews of ritual murder. Neighbors of Jews were instructed to help them if someone attacked the Jews during the night.

The Statute of Kalisz is a great document of human rights.[11] But it must be emphasized that it was only the first of several documents asserting the human rights of Polish Jews. Casimir the Great (Kazimierz Wielki) thrice reaffirmed its contents. Other Polish kings, in particular Kazimierz Jagiellończyk in the year 1453, extended the rights of Jews in Poland by affixing their signatures to reconfirmations of the Statute of Kalisz. Decrees of Zygmunt II August, Stefan Batory, Zygmunt III, Jan Sobieski, and others expressed care for the Jews, made their material well-being possible, and guaranteed their religious rights and free practice of religious laws.

In a decree of 1580, for example, Stefan Batory condemned some customs which were followed when an oath was administered to Jews in court. The German *Schwabenspiegel* and other collections of German laws, like the *Statute of Dortmund* or the *Schlesisches Landrecht* of 1422, prescribed that a Jew reciting an oath must stand with one leg raised on a three-legged stool. He was not permitted to move during the pronouncement of the oath, nor was he permitted to alter the order of a series of curses pronounced against those who did not speak the truth. Sometimes a Jew was required to stand on the skin of a pig while taking an oath. This is how the oath *more judaico* was practiced in Germany. The Statute of Kalisz specified that a Jew's oath was to be *supra rodale*, i.e., on the Torah. Influenced by a Western trend, however, Poles began to interpret *rodale* as either "pigskin" or "tripod." Stefan Batory then authoritatively clarified the fact that *rodale* meant the Ten Commandments. In another decree in the year 1585, the King declared it unjust to have anyone lose a case because of a technical error in the administration of the oath, and he forbade such a result.

The problem of coexistence between people professing diverse beliefs, but inhabiting the same land, was regulated in ancient Poland in an extremely liberal manner. It could serve as a model of legislation for more modern times. Polish kings demonstrated in the charters of privileges issued to the Jews more understanding for the principles of religious freedom than many European legislators did in the twentieth century.

II

One of the most glorious chapters of Polish history concerns the granting of self-government to the Jews.

Beginning in 1551, Polish kings recognized the Jews' right to freely select their own leaders. Jewish communities elected their own mayors and community governments. The communities convened meetings, and late in the sixteenth century a nationwide institution was formed known as *Vaad Arba Aratzot*. The authority the *Vaad* possessed was enormous. It operated an active tribunal which issued decisions based on Jewish law on matters of importance.[12] A seventeenth-century chronicler, Nathan Hanover, compared this tribunal to the San-hedrin in Jerusalem. The distinguished historian Heinrich Graetz said in his *Geschichte der Juden* that the *Vaad Arba Aratzot* was a "unique event in the history of the Jewish Diaspora."[13]

The Polish authorities not only recognized this Jewish parliament as the legitimate representative of the Jews in Poland and Lithuania, but they endowed it with great power. Disobedience of a decision of the *Vaad* meant a possible *Herem* (anathema), which was enforced by the State's *bracchium secu-lare* (secular power). The analogous institution of the Catholic Church—excommunication—also invoked *bracchium secu-lare*, but of a weaker nature.[14]

Under the leadership of the *Vaad Arba Aratzot* the spiritual life of Polish Jewry late in the sixteenth and during the seventeenth century attained an uncommonly high level. Thanks to the works of Polish rabbis, Jewish ritual and the religious laws governing civil and matrimonial life have been accepted by European Jews to the present day. Indeed, without a doubt, the sixteenth and seventeenth centuries were the period of spiritual hegemony of Polish Jews in world Jewry.

This period of unusual glory, however, was interrupted by a series of pogroms committed by Bohdan Chmielnicki at the time of the Cossack Wars in 1648-1655. One third of all Polish Jews perished at the hands of the Cossack-Tatars amid untold torture and suffering. It was a time when the Polish nation experienced the greatest crisis in its history, and when it was subjected to partition. Heavy blows were dealt to Poland from the East by the army of Czar Alexis Mikhailovich and from the West by the Swedish King Charles Gustav, and Poland seemed almost to disappear from the map of Europe. Plans for the partitioning of Poland had been included in a series of treaties, such as that of December 1656 in Radnot (Hungary), when Sweden, Brandenburg, and Siebenbuergen divided Poland among themselves and gave the Ukraine to the Cossacks and the voievodship of Novogródek to Bogusław Radziwiłł.[15] In a treaty concluded that same year, Charles Gustav gave Warmia and Greater Poland to Brandenburg. Blood was flowing in Poland, and the Polish Jews did not suffer alone. They had occasional protectors, such as Jeremy Wiśniowiecki during the Cossack Wars.

Michał Korybut Wiśniowiecki and Jan III Sobieski followed the tradition of helping the Jews. Conditions deteriorated, however, under the kings of the Saxon dynasty in Poland. This period was characterized by the popular motto "Poland stands on its disorder" (*Polska nierzedem stoi*). No steps could then be initiated to help the Jews. Similar conditions prevailed under the last king. Stanisław August Poniatowski. But one interesting fact emerges. Despite anti-Jewish trends which appeared in the contemporary literature, despite the difficult economic situation and the enormous debts of the Jewish communities, and despite persecution on the part of the clergy, the Jews loved Poland. When it became clear that Poland was on the verge of collapse, when Tadeusz Kościuszko led the nation into action, the "Jewish Legion" of Berek Joselewicz was formed. Approximately 500 Jews fought in it voluntarily in order to rescue Poland.

Some excerpts from two documents of the time illustrate the Poles' understanding for the Jews, and also prove the Jews' attachment to Poland. First is the proclamation of September 17, 1794, by Tadeusz Kościuszko, which granted permission for the formation of a Jewish Corps in the struggle for Poland. Second is the proclamation of Berek Joselewicz of October 1 of the same year, urging Jews to join his regiment. In his proclamation, Kościuszko proved he was an excellent judge, not only of Jewish history, but of Jewish character as well. He first declared that "nothing can convince the most remote nations more of the sacredness of our struggle and the righteousness of our present revolution than the fact that those distanced from us by religion and custom have by their own will sacrificed their lives in support of our uprising." Kościuszko then cited the heroism of King David and other Biblical figures such as Jephtha, Abner, and Joab, as well as the heroism of Deborah and Judith. He continued: "Out of such valiant men a nation was constituted. Albeit meager in itself, it terrified its invaders. With a small handful it dispersed the numerous armies of great Eastern powers. The rebuilding of Jerusalem offers a most splendid display of the character of this nation. While holding a cutlass in one hand and a trowel in the other, the people restored their native walls and fought for their native land."

Of the war of the Jews against the Romans, Kościuszko wrote:

The Romans, who fought the most powerful nations, could destroy the government of the Jews in no way other than by taking advantage of its discord. But when the Jewish nation perceived that it would remain imprisoned by this ambitious power, it immediately declared a fierce war on the tyrant. There has never been a war which surpassed this persistence. While the numerous assembled nations gathered around the walls of Jerusalem, which they had previously been unable to reach, the besieged were almost completely annihilated in a demonstration which will be remembered in human history. Amid the sad images of discord and atrocity, it was obvious that the attachment to freedom and to the laws of their fathers was greater than the attachment to life itself. This warrior nation filled even their vanquishers with awesome wonder.

After this characterization of the Jewish people—a unique specimen of modern diplomatic flattery—Kościuszko said of the sacrifice of the Jewish people:

And now, in the year 1794, on the seventeenth and eighteenth of April, when Warsaw waged a bloody battle on the Muscovite invaders, the Jews residing in this city took up their arms and battled bravely with the enemy, proving to the world that where humanity is at stake, they disregard their own lives.

Based on such premises, Tadeusz Kościuszko granted permission for the formation of a special Jewish light cavalry regiment. Berek Joselewicz, identified as a "colonel of the light cavalry," called upon his fellow Jews immediately to gather arms in defense of Poland. He began:

> Listen, you successors of the tribes of the Israelites. All who have the Eternal and the Almighty inscribed on their heart and wish to fight for our country. Now is the time for us to turn our powers to this task. My true and faithful brothers! The love of your country must inspire you to do this, in order that you gather new blood, which for years has been sucked from you by the venomous serpents.

He then cited Kościuszko's invitation and wrote:

> Now it comes to us easily, for our guardian and leader Tadeusz Kościuszko, being indeed a messenger of the Eternal Almighty, has ventured to pull all his efforts towards the creation of a Jewish regiment. He possesses all the capabilities, a good mind and a merciful heart. He is the chosen leader. It is from him, dear brothers, that we take our example. A man as great as he, together with other men who already have much freedom, still long for more freedom and for the liberation of their country. Should not we, the downtrodden and oppressed, take up our arms, if it is we who are more downtrodden than all other people on this earth?

Berek then continued with a fiery appeal, which ranks among the most powerful pleas on behalf of freedom:

> So prepare yourselves and call upon the Almighty God for help, and our protector will be He, who has liberated us from the most terrible and largest shackles and who will now assist us. Rise up! Open your closed eyes! Should we not strive to attain freedom, which has been so assuredly and so honestly promised to us as it has to the other people of this earth? But first we must deserve it.

The colonel of the "Jewish light cavalry regiment" went on to say:

> Beloved brothers, I expect of the Eternal Almighty, nor do I doubt, that the propitious time has come for us to humble our enemy. The Eternal in heaven wants this, already there are signs of this. We need only be honorable and have a valiant and heroic heart. God Almighty be with you and I shall lead you! Where the greatest danger is present, there shall I go, and you will follow me. My beloved brothers, I have had the good fortune to be appointed your Colonel by command of the highest leader. Awaken, help us to retrieve a hitherto down-trodden and oppressed Poland. Faithful brothers! Let us fight for our country to the last drop of our blood. Even if we do not live to see it, our children will live freely and safely, and they will not roam about like wild beasts. Beloved brothers! Awaken as lions and leopards.

Notwithstanding these proclamations and the noble thoughts expressed in them, it was too late. On November 4, 1794, the decisive battle took place near the Warsaw suburb of Praga. Suvorov was victorious. Poland was soon wiped off the map of Europe.

Berek did not give up. He left Poland, but returned to it twelve years later, this time to the Duchy of Warsaw (Księstwo Warszawskie), where, in the Constitution of July 22, 1807, equality for all inhabitants had been proclaimed by law. Based on Napoleon's notorious decree of 1808, however, equal rights for Jews were deferred even in the Duchy of Warsaw for a period of ten years. But this did not deter Berek. Once again he organized his legion and fought for Poland, sacrificing his life in 1809 in a battle near Kock.[16]

III

In financial straits, fighting many enemies, Polish Jewry of the eighteenth century nevertheless rose on eagles' wings to the highest peaks of spiritual creativity. Let it suffice to note two luminaries of this period, who not only graced Polish Jewry of that time but who continue to shine in the firmament of world Jewry to the present day. These two luminaries are Elijah ben Salomon Zalman, known as the "Gaon of Wilno," and the founder of Hasidism, Israel ben Eliezer, known as the *Baal Shem Tov*. Both of these men have been discussed in the previous chapter.

One of the elements of the *Baal Shem Tov's* philosophy was the principle that man should not rebel against turns of fate, but should accept agreeably all that befalls him. This gave peace of mind to even the most poor and abused individuals. Polish Jews were in special need of this consolation. After the partitioning of Poland at the end of the eighteenth century, bad times befell the hundreds of thousands of Jews who were in the grasp of the invaders.

The foreign governments confronted the problem of the Jewish minority with one overriding objective—to suppress the Jews' development. Weddings were permitted to only one descendant in each family—i.e., only one son could marry. The Jews in the Austrian sector were shamelessly told that "Empress Maria Teresa wants to avoid by all means possible the growth of Galician Jewry."[17] Married couples were subjected to additional taxes. Only those owning 500-1,000 florins could marry, and they were required to pay ten percent of their possessions as a marriage tax. The Prussian Government relegated the majority of the Jews to a category of "the tolerated," who were given no essential human rights. The Czarist Government imposed other brutal measures on the Jews. Young boys were inducted into the army for a period of twenty five years, thereby destroying the Jewish population by removing its young. The wearing of traditional Jewish robes was prohibited, and kosher meat was specially taxed. In the Austrian sector, a special tax was levied on Sabbath candles. Any attempt to avoid payment of this tax was punished as a revolutionary act on the following unique reasoning: since religion requires that Sabbath candles be lit, anyone not paying the tax for this religious function must be a revolutionary.[18]

The attitude of the occupying powers towards the Jewish population drove the Jews and the Poles closer together. The common enemy would occasionally try to generate resentment between the groups, and shortsighted leadership of either the Jews or the Poles would then cause both the Jews and the Poles to suffer.

At critical moments, however, leaders emerged who proved equal to the task. On the Jewish side, one recalls the Rabbi of Warsaw, Ber Meisels, who, prior to the period of the 1863 uprising, stood together with the Poles and summoned the Jews to support Polish interests, which ulitmately culminated in his arrest. In a manifesto of April 9, 1862, "to our co-religionists," published anonymously but perhaps inspired by Rabbi Meisels, we find a profound attachment to Poland, "who cleaved us to her breast at a time when all other nations were still breathing murder and destruction." This manifesto recalls the granting of rights to the Jews "in the noble intent of Casimir the Great, who strove to alleviate our misery and to embody us with feeling and understanding for the Polish people."[19]

A Polish leader who promoted a close relationship between Poles and Jews was Joachim Lelewel. He recalled that, "when despair besieged the capital in 1794, the Jews were not afraid of death. Mixing with the army and with the people, they showed that danger did not frighten them, but that their Native Land was dear to their hearts."[20]

There were, of course, many disagreements between the Jews and the Poles. But how could friction not exist in a society which was the center of a hurricane and which was beset by an enemy who constantly incited one community against the other?

After Meisels' demonstrative participation in a funeral

honoring the victims of a police attack on Polish youth on February 27, 1861, he issued an appeal to Poland's rabbis, in which he wrote: "Would you like to discern the true spirit of the Polish nation? Behold. Barely does Poland breathe a bit easier, and already the priests in the local churches respond with words of love and brotherhood towards us, recognizing us as children of the country which we have inhabited for eight centuries. Israelite brothers! Be courageous and valiant! We shall eagerly accept every brotherly hand proffered to us."[21]

Meisels' appeal characterized Warsaw's chief of police, Sergei Mukhanov, as "Haman." The authorities then alleged to the Austrian Consul in Warsaw that Meisels (who was an Austrian citizen) was participating in the Polish revolutionary movement. The Consul sent Meisels' appeal to Vienna and termed it an "open declaration of war." The Russian Government surely did not overlook the affront contained in this proclamation.[22]

In the territory occupied by Austria, Franciszek Smolka, one of the most prominent Polish political leaders of the nineteenth century, worked for full equal rights for Jews. On September 30, 1868, the Galician Legislature (*Sejm*) debated the Jewish question, and many urged that equal rights for Jews must wait "until the time when they become Poles." Smolka then declared: "They will not be Poles and, in the first place, they cannot become Poles before we give to them all that belongs to them, and on this score they are absolutely correct.... Let us remember that the Jews have been persecuted, and let us understand that they cannot overflow with love for us. The effects of persecution are absorbed into the blood, they transform the human organism. It is, therefore, impossible to demand that in a single moment all be changed for the good. What has been festering for centuries must take generations to heal. For the healing process to begin, we must show justice towards the Jews, unhampered and total justice. In the meantime I say to you gentlemen, if not they, then certainly their

children will be Poles. Before that, let us not make demands of
the Jews, for we have no right to do so."[23]

Several other statements made by Smolka at a session of the
Sejm of October 8, 1868, when the debate on the Jewish
question was concluded, deserve to be noted. These words have
not lost their relevance, even though more than a century has
passed since they were uttered. Smolka said then:

> On their surface the most complex problems may be quickly
> and simply resolved. The book of history, the book of nature lie
> open before us, but we are unable to read them. The most
> important questions resolve themselves simply, and the most
> difficult questions may often be resolved with one word. This
> magic word is 'Freedom.' Freedom and equal rights can favor-
> ably and most happily resolve the whole Jewish question.[24]

At the end of the nineteenth century, there were two million
Jews living on the land which had once been Poland. In 1918,
when the lines between the partitioned sections disintegrated
and an independent Poland was reborn, the final period of the
thousand-year existence of Polish Jewry began.

IV

Was Smolka's prediction fulfilled? After the "healing of the
wounds" did the Jews become Poles?

When Poland became independent, Smolka's prediction
took on another meaning. Anyone who lived in Poland and
qualified as a citizen was, of course, a Pole. But did the two
million Jews—who after twenty years of independence numbered more than three million—become emotionally attached
to Poland?

The history of Polish Jewry in the period between the World
Wars reveals an extraordinary spiritual blossoming. It marked
consolidation of Jewish society and the increased importance
of the role it played in national political life. It also brought

about a critical economic situation for Polish Jewry. All this requires a careful analysis of the Jews' relationship to the Poles.

Spiritual growth presented a truly extraordinary image. Polish Jews developed their own schools of every variety—religious and secular, Hebrew, Yiddish, and Polish. They created a network of elementary schools, as well as schools of higher learning and professional schools, in which vast numbers of male and female students were educated. Jewish youth studied at State Universities, demonstrating resistance to attempts of certain departments to impose a *numerus clausus*. By 1921-2, the percentage of Jewish students reached 24.3 percent. Ten years later, in the academic year 1930-1, it had been reduced by quotas to 18.5 percent. Nonetheless, the number of Jewish students in law faculties rose during this ten-year period from 22.1 to 26 percent. In medicine, however, the percentage of Jewish students decreased from 34 to 18.9 percent.[25]

Judaic institutions of higher learning (*Yeshivot*) enrolled vast numbers of students and set extremely high standards. The greatest authority was enjoyed by intellectual institutions in the Eastern borderlands—Mir, Kamieniec, Kleck, Raduń, Baranowicze, Grodno, Białystok, Łomża, Pińsk, Ostróg, Słonim, and Wołożyn. The Talmudic school of Lublin spread its learning far and wide.[26] These institutions attracted great masses of students from all over the world.

Distinguished rabbis and deans of these schools lived in Poland. The leader of the *yeshiva* of a small town in the eastern sector of Poland, Raduń, was Rabbi Israel Meyer Hacohen Kagan, universally recognized then as the leading Talmudic authority in the world. He was first known for his short work, *Hofetz Haim*, which was published anonymously in his early years. The work contained observations on the importance of maintaining high standards of speech and the obligation to avoid idle talk and slander. Rabbi Kagan was a scholar of the highest rank, whose commentary to the first book of the ritual Code *Shulhan-Aruch*, entitled *Mishna Berura*, was accepted by Jews all over the world as the most definitive supplement to the Code. He also became a legend in his time.

There also lived in Poland many other internationally renowned scholars of Jewish law. The Hasidic movement was represented by *Tzadikim*, including Abraham Mordecai Alter from Góra Kalwaria, Isaac Menahem Dancygier from Aleksandrów near Łódź, Aaron Rokach from Bełz, Benzion Halberstam from Bobowa, and many others. Their words became the beacon for hundreds of thousands of Jews.

Other scholars left their marks with published works. Moses Schorr, Meyer Bałaban, Ignacy Schiper, Maurycy Allerhand, and Szymon Askenazy were learned experts in fields of history or law.

The Jewish press was also highly developed in Poland. Newspapers appeared in Polish and in Yiddish in metropolitan centers such as Warsaw (*Hajnt*, *Moment*, *Togblat*, *Folks-Cajtung*, *Unzer Ekspres* in Yiddish; *Hatzefira* in Hebrew; *Nasz Przegląd* [Our View] in Polish), Łódź (*Lodzer Togblat*, *Folks-Blat*), Cracow (*Nowy Dziennik*), Lwów (*Chwila*, *Der Morgen*), Wilno (*Cajt*, *Wilner Tog*), and Lublin (*Lubliner Togblat*). These daily journals had circulations in the tens of thousands. Innumerable weekly and monthly papers were also published.[27] This testifies to the unusual vitality of the Polish Jews, who participated vigorously in all aspects of Jewish life.

Soon after the creation of independent Poland in 1918, Jewish society entered a phase of consolidation. Jews took an active part in parliamentary and municipal elections, as well as in campaigns for Jewish community leadership positions. Every *Sejm* and Senate, every city council was a proving ground for Jewish representatives. They presented the needs and demands of their constituency. The Jewish parliamentary group (*Koło Żydowskie*) at the first ordinary *Sejm* numbered thirty four representatives, and there were Jewish representatives who did not belong to the *Koło Żydowskie* such as the representative of the Folkist Party and the Jewish members of the PPS (Polish Socialist Party). The struggle among the various active Jewish groups for power—particularly within the Jewish communities of towns and villages—was very intense.

A major problem, however, was the impoverishment of the Jewish masses. Economic problems in Poland were severe and they had a major impact on merchants and craftsmen, many of whom were Jews.

Serious conflicts between Jews and Poles began to arise. They led to complications in the country's political situation, and in 1926 to a coup. Before the overthrow of the government, however, a so-called "Polish-Jewish Agreement" had been concluded by the government of Aleksander Skrzyński with the Jewish parliamentary representatives. The agreement did not last long. The government of Kazimierz Bartel announced that it would not implement agreements with particular segments of Polish society. Later governments took more drastic steps against the Jewish minority. *Shehita* (ritual slaughter) was curtailed, and before the catastrophe of 1939, a legislative resolution banning it altogether had reached its final stages.

In view of such shifts of mood in the country, could there be amicable coexistence between the Jews and the Poles?

An answer to this question requires differentation between specific manifestations and an overall view. In addition, the attitudes of those in leadership positions have to be distinguished from the events which occurred.

On November 12, 1918, Józef Piłsudski received various delegations at the Kronenberg Palace in Warsaw. He then declared to the members of organizations which had been invited by him that "he would be ashamed to be called a Pole if anti-Jewish pogroms could find a place in Poland."[28] This was the announced view of the leading figure of free Poland, which was reborn after 120 years of captivity. The then Minister of Internal Affairs, Stanisław Wojciechowski (who later became

President), issued a statement (published on February 2, 1919) to all his subordinates in which he emphasized that the Jewish population had the same rights as the Poles, that in free Poland all were equal before the law, and all illegal acts committed against the Jewish population would be severely punished.

At the *Sejm*, representatives of the Polish population categorically condemned anti-Jewish excesses. By way of example, on June 12, 1919, the *Sejm* emphasized the urgency of three resolutions. The first was introduced by Representative Ignacy Daszyński and comrades of the PPS and concerned "attempts undertaken in various parts of the country to incite turmoil and outbreaks directed against Jewish citizens." The second was introduced by Representative Maciej Rataj and comrades of the Peasant Group *Wyzwolenie* "in the matter of sporadic transgressions incurred against the Jewish population." The third was introduced by Representative Thon and concerned "the matter of a pogrom in Cracow on the 6th and 7th of June 1919." Representative Ignacy Daszyński said at this session of the *Sejm*: "A significant portion of serious Polish opinion perceives the hand of a provocateur in these anti-Jewish outbreaks, with a great deal of validity." This serious statesman and Polish champion of socialism stressed the importance of Poland's relationship to eleven percent of the country's inhabitants. In the words of Daszyński, "Thrusting the crowd on the Jews will defer the question of internal troubles for no longer than a few weeks or months." The *Sejm* nodded in agreement.[29]

From the Jewish vantage point, the community's view of Poland was positive, even at the critical moment when blood was being shed. The Jewish Representative Dr. Osias Thon, delegate of Cracow's Jews, who had himself experienced difficult times only days earlier, said at this same session of the *Sejm*: "No one had expected this of Poland with her illustrious past...of a resurrected Poland, of a Poland possessing such a mighty impulse and impetus to rebuild itself. ...Poland should be a great and noble power. What is possible elsewhere should not happen here."[30] With visible feeling for Poland, Thon continued, "Poland will be the mainstay of nobility and justice on earth. The world is convinced of this, and I too am still convinced, in spite of everything, that it will come to pass, that so it will be, that the conscience of society will rouse itself and awaken."

Despite the sense of injustice felt by the Jewish population shortly after the rebirth of an independent Poland Thon clung to the motherland with all his heart. Addresses by other representatives of Polish Jewry echoed these feelings. And these words were uttered at a time when the country's borders were still in a state of flux, and when Poland was under fire abroad from, among others, the American press. This kind of statement regarding Poland could only mean that the speaker loved his country.

The period of Polish independence was brief. From the end of 1918 to September 1939 there was too little time to develop an image of a Jew who was a Polish citizen, consistent with the land's thousand-year historical tradition and with the new trends of the twentieth century.

The German onslaught then befell Poland, and the primary aim of the German hordes was the extermination of the Jews. What a tragedy it is that on this Polish land, which had witnessed many years of Polish-Jewish coexistence, the abhorrent murder of millions of innocent people was perpetrated.

Such was the will of the Providence. We now gaze upon the vacuum created in Poland, and it is hard to describe it more aptly than Antoni Słonimski did in his "Elegy for the Jewish Villages:"

> They are gone, no longer do you have Jewish villages in Poland
> In Hrubieszow, Karczew, Brody, Falenica.
> In vain would you search in candle-lit windows,
> And to overhear a song in a wooden synagogue.
> Gone are the last vestiges, the tattered Jewish clothes,
> The blood has been sprinkled with sand, the traces wiped away,
> And cleanly white-washed with blue lime are the walls....

No longer are there such villages, where the cobbler was a poet,
The watchmaker a philosopher, the barber a troubadour.
Such villages are no longer, where the wind joined
Biblical songs with a Polish tune and the Slavic passion,
Where old Jews in orchards under the shade of cherry-trees
Would bewail the holy walls of Jerusalem.
No longer are there such villages, although poetic mists,
The moons, winds, ponds, and stars over them
Have recorded with the blood of centuries tragic histories,
The events of the two saddest nations on earth.

Notes

[1] See M. Bałaban, *Kiedy i skad przybyli Żydzi do Polski?* [When and whence came the Jews to Poland?], *Miesięcznik Żydowski*, Warsaw, 1930.

[2] D.M. Dunlop, *The History of the Jewish Khazars*, New York, Schocken Books, 1954, pp. 198 and 262.

[3] S. Dubnow, *Weltgeschichte des juedischen Volkes*, vol. IV, Berlin, 1926, p. 285.

[4] B. Weinryb, *The Jews of Poland*, Philadelphia, Jewish Publication Society, 1973, p. 23.

[5] M. Brann, *Geschichte der Juden in Schlesien*, vols. I-V, Wrocław, 1896-1918.

[6] B. Weinryb, *op. cit.*, p. 23.

[7] M. Gumowski, *Monety hebrajskie za Piastów* [Hebrew coins under the Piasts], "Biuletyn Żydowskiego Instytutu Historycznego," 1962, no. 41, pp. 3-19, and no. 42, pp. 3-44.

[8] G. Łabuda and J. Bardach, *Utrwalenie i wzrost rozbicia dzielnicowego w XII i na początku XIII w.* (in) *Historia Polski* [Consolidation and augmentation of regional break-up in the XIIth and beginning of the XIIIth c. in The History of Poland], vol. I, Warsaw, Państwowe Wydawnictwo Naukowe, 1958, p. 310.

⁹Text in P. Bloch, *Die General-Privilegien der polnischen Judenschaft*, Poznań, 1892, pp. 12, 31.

¹⁰An attempt to explain the concept of a *servus camerae* in Poland was made by me in a lecture delivered at the Congress convened by the Polish Institute of Arts and Sciences in New York honoring the Millennium of Poland on November 27, 1966. The lecture is included in this book as Chapter III.

¹¹See the lecture printed in my book *Late Summer Fruit* (New York, 1960, pp. 99-108), delivered on the occasion of the acceptance by the Jewish Museum in New York of a series of drawings by Arthur Szyk under the combined title "Statute of Kalisz."

¹²Text (in original Hebrew) in *Acta Congressus Generalis Judaeorum Regni Poloniae (Pinkas Vaad Arba Aratzot)*, pub. I. Halperin, Jerusalem, Mosad Bialik, 1948, pp. 45-50.

¹³Graetz, *Geschichte der Juden*, vol. IX, Leipzig, 1866, p. 483 and LXXIX.

¹⁴I. Lewin, *Klątwa żydowska na Litwie w XVII i XVIII wieku*, [Jewish Anathema in Lithuania in the XVII and XVIII centuries], Lwow, 1932, pp. 12-15.

¹⁵K. Piwarski, *Wojny połowy XVII wieku i nieudane próby reformy państwa* (in) *Historia Polski* [The wars of the mid-XVIIth century and unsuccessful attempts at state reform, in The History of Poland], vol. I, Warsaw, 1957, p. 693.

¹⁶*Album pamiątkowy ku czci Berka Joselewicza*, edited by M. Bałaban [Commemorative album in honor of Berek Joselewicz], Warsaw, 1934, pp. 163-165.

¹⁷Declaration of Governor Hadik at the enforcement of the Emperor's decree of 1776.

¹⁸M. Bałaban, Dzieje *Żydow w Galicji i w Rzeczypospolitej Krakowskiej*, [A history of the Jews in Galicia and the Cracow Commonwealth], Lwów, 1914, p. 77 and on.

¹⁹Text of proclamation in Jacob Shatzky, *Geshichte fun Yidn in Warshe*, vol. II, New York, Yiddish Scientific Institute YIVO, 1948, p. 289.

[20]F. Kupfer, *Ber Meisels i jego udział w walkach wyzwoleńczych narodu polskiego* [Ber Meisels and his participation in the liberation struggles of the Polish people], Warsaw, Żydowski Instytut Historyczny, 1953, p. 77; W. Feldman, *Dzieje polskiej mysli politycznej*, [A history of Polish political thought], pp. 410-412.

[21]F. Kupfer, *op. cit.*, p. 9.

[22]N.M. Gelber, *Die Juden und der polnische Aufstand von 1863*, Vienna and Leipzig, 1923, p. 166 (document no. II 3 of March 17, 1861, also no. 16 of March 26, 1861).

[23]The address of F. Smolka concerning the Jews was published in 1889 by the Jewish Congregation in Lwów. Quote from M. Bałaban. *Dzieje Żydow w Galicji*, Lwów, 1914, pp. 208-210.

[24]M. Bałaban, *op. cit.*

[25]S. Bronsztein, *Ludność Żydowska w Polsce w okresie międzywojennym* [The Jewish population in Poland in the interwar period], Wrocław, Warsaw, Cracow, Zaktad Narodowy im. Ossolińskieb, 1963, pp. 192-195.

[26]Concerning this institution see I. Lewin, *Wyższa Uczelnia Talmudyczna w Lublinie*, "Miesięcznik Żydowski," Warsaw, 1931, p. 455; also by the same author *Yeshivat Hackmej Lublin* (in Hebrew) in *Yearbook I. World Federation of Polish Jews*, Tel Aviv, 1967, p. 381.

[27]A detailed description of the Jewish press (in all languages) in Poland in the collective work *Itonut Hayehudit Shehayta* (in Hebrew) edited by David Flinkier, M. Canin, and S. Rozenfeld, Tel Aviv 1973, pp. 10-338, and in Marian Fuks, *Prasa Zydowska w Warszawie 1823-1939*, Warsaw, 1979.

[28]At a meeting with representatives of "Agudas Haortodoksim." Printed in *Der Moment*, November 13, 1918, no. 211.

[29]Stenographic report of the 48th meeting of the legislative *Sejm* of June 12, 1919, columns 62-67.

[30]*Ibid.*, column 71.

CHAPTER III
The Historical Background
of the Statute of Kalisz

I

On August 16, 1264, Duke Bolesław of Kalisz, the son of
Władysław Odonic, signed a document which thereafter won
great fame and importance. The document granted privileged
status to the Jews living in the province called Greater Poland.[1]
After the death of Władysław Odonic in 1239, Bolesław
became the ruler of the territories surrounding the towns of
Kalisz and Gniezno. His brother, Przemysł, inherited Poznań.
Jews had obviously been living in the territory ruled by
Bolesław for some time, and it was necessary for him to clarify
their basic rights and duties. The Duke of Kalisz (who was later
known as Bolesław the Pious) was not obligated to be original;
Jews had been accorded royal privileges in three neighboring

countries—Bohemia, Hungary, and Austria—only a few years earlier. King Premysł Ottakar II of Bohemia signed two privileges for his Jews: on March 29, 1254, and on March 8, 1255.[2] So did King Bela IV of Hungary: on December 5, 1251, and on March 22, 1256.[3] Duke Frederick II Babenberg of Austria signed his privilege on July 1, 1244.[4] These documents were almost identical. Duke Bolesław of Kalisz joined the three rulers who had previously issued similar privileges. No one knows whether he was aware that this document was a copy of others, because none of the privileges refers explicitly to any other foreign decree of this kind.

The privilege signed by Frederick II Babenberg in 1244 is the first known document in this series of identical decrees specifying the rights and duties of Jews in Austria, Hungary, Bohemia, and Poland. It is possible, however, that even this privilege was not original. Premysł Ottakar II refers to a privilege issued by his father, King Václav I, to the Jews of Bohemia, and this document has never been found. The Václav privilege could have been the prototype for the Austrian document of 1244.[5]

It is generally accepted that the series of privileges signed by the rulers of Austria, Hungary, Bohemia and Poland during the twenty years from 1244 to 1264, as well as subsequent documents in the same vein (like that of King Premysł Ottakar II for the Jews of Moravia, August 23, 1268,[6] or of Duke Bolko I for the Jews of Silesia, August 7, 1295[7]), conferred upon the Jews the status of *servi camerae*. This term is, however, not found *expressis verbis* in any of the documents, from the privilege of Frederick II Babenberg up to the statute of Kalisz.[8] Although the *camera* of the Duke or King was mentioned in these documents as the beneficiary of fines to be levied against those who harmed Jews or their property, the expression *servi camerae* was not applied to Jews.

This chapter will attempt to explain the absence of the term *servi camerae* in the Statute of Kalisz and its chronological predecessors in Austria, Hungary, and Bohemia. That explanation depends, however, on a clear understanding of the meaning of this term in the documents in which it appears. We must, therefore, first analyze privileges granted to Jews by German Emperors.

II

In the year 1090, Emperor Henry IV issued a privilege to the Jews of Worms wherein he stated that in all legal questions the Jews of Worms were to depend on the Emperor alone, unless they would elect their own leaders, subject to confirmation by the Emperor. In this document, after the stipulation concerning the elected Jewish leaders (*"nisi tantum ille, quem ex eleccione ipsorum...ipse imperator eis prefecerit"*), a clause was added reading: "particularly since they belong to our chamber" (*"praesertum cum ad cameram nostram attineant"*).[9] The privilege was later confirmed by Emperor Frederick I Barbarossa, in 1157,[10] and by Frederick II, in 1236.

Frederick I Barbarossa also granted a privilege to the Jews of Ratisbon (Regensburg) in September 1182. His stated basis was that he, the Emperor, was providing for "all Jews in our empire who are distinguished because they belong to our imperial chamber" (*"qui speciali prerogativa dignitatis nostre ad imperialem cameram dinoscuntur pertinere"*).[11] These words were, incidentally, misunderstood and misinterpreted by Berthold Altmann, in his *Studies in Medieval German Jewish History*,[12] to mean that Barbarossa "demanded the guardianship of all the Jews of the empire in virtue of his imperial dignity and position...and, thus, connected the supreme office of the emperor with the 'immediacy' of the Jews and with the imperial protection resulting from these direct relations to the Crown." The text of the decree contains no trace of such a demand by the Emperor. Barbarossa simply included the Regensburg Jews among all other Jews who "belonged to the imperial chamber." He was obviously referring to the Jews who were granted special peace protection in his land peace of 1179 ("*Judei, qui ad fiscum imperatoris pertinent*").[13] The use of the words *fiscus* and *camera* in two documents by the same emperor within three years is very significant. It shows, I believe, to what kind of "ownership" the Emperor was referring.

In granting a privilege to the church of Arles in 1177, Frederick I described it as "belonging to our chamber" ("*camere nostre pertinentes*").[14] That must have meant that the Emperor considered himself to be the protector of the church. It was clearly so explained by Frederick I in a document of 1155 concerning the monastery of Salem. Berthold Altmann, in his *Studies in Medieval German Jewish History*, writes that in the time of Frederick II "to belong to the Empire meant liberty and independence.... The 'pertinence' to the Empire did not lead to serfdom, to loss of rights and privileges, but became a guarantee of right and peace, and expressed immediacy as well as special protection by the Emperor."

I would agree fully with Altmann, who examined the expressions used in the privileges granted to the Jews in light of the documents referring to the churches, and reached the conclusion "that it is impossible to base upon these phrases a theory of stages and different steps leading to Jewish Chamber-Serfdom. The phrases which express 'pertinence to the chamber' or to the empire describe only the immediate relations to the Empire, that is to say a high, advantageous, and privileged position, and assurance of special royal protection."

When commenting on the privilege of Barbarossa for the Jews of Regensburg, Julius Aronius stated that "*Kammerknechtschaft* is undoubtedly not a real serfdom; it meant only that the Jews were bound to pay taxes to the imperial chamber and got in exchange a special protection of the emperor."[15] The "theory of stages and different steps leading to Jewish Chamber-Serfdom," mentioned by Altmann, was originated by Eugene Taeubler, who divided the historical development of *Kammerknechtschaft* into three stages: (1) the entire Jewish community (2) individual communities and (3) individual Jews.[16] Taeubler's theory falls, however, if one agrees with Aronius' proposition denying real serfdom in the position of Jews in Germany during the twelfth century.

George Caro went even further than Aronius in explaining the word *Kammerknechtschaft*. He stated that "it is not improbable that the expression *Kammerknechte* originates with the Jews themselves; they described themselves, possibly in overflowing modesty, as serfs, and a writer added, for better understanding, the chamber" (to such description).[17] Taeubler saw the seeds of destruction of his own theory in this hypothesis and he added, while quoting Caro, "One does not believe his eyes."

A careful analysis of the first document which uses the term *servi camerae* (and not only *ad cameram nostram attineant*, *ad imperialem cameram dinoscuntur pertinere*, *ad fiscum imperatoris pertinent*) hardly confirms the suggestion that it meant a certain legal status. In July 1236, Frederick II reaffirmed the privilege granted by Henry IV to the Jews of Worms. He explained thereon that "because all *servi camerae* of Germany made this request of our graciousness" ("*quod universi Alemannie servi camere nostre celsitudini supplicarunt*"), he decided to extend the privilege of Henry IV, confirmed by Frederick I, to cover all Jews in Germany "directly relating to our chamber" ("*omnibus judeis ad cameram nostram immediate spectantibus*"). The obvious question is: who were all the "*servi camerae* of Germany" who made the request of Frederick II? They could not have been the Jews themselves, because the request was made on behalf of the Jews of Germany. Had *some* Jews made the request for others, the emperor would undoubtedly have mentioned that "*Judei*" *universi* (or *singuli*) *Alemannie servi camere nostre* were instrumental in obtaining the new privilege. The word *Judei* does not appear. It seems probable, therefore, that the confirmation of the old privilege for the Jews of Worms and its extension to include *all* Jews of Germany was done at the request of all those who "belonged" to the chamber, Jews and non-Jews alike.

Richard Schroeder noted that, as a result of the feudal concepts of the Middle Ages, the Jewish *regalia*, like other imperial rights, were not considered as obligations toward the state but as financial sources of income.[18] Could not the expression *servi camerae*, at least as used in its early form, be the equivalent of "taxpayer"? The "direct" taxpayers could easily have approached Frederick II with a request that he include all Jews of Germany in the same fiscal category. Such an extension would have been beneficial to other taxpayers. The broader the group of taxpayers contributing to the emperor and his "chamber," the less need was there for heavier taxes.

This also serves to explain the reference to Jews "directly relating to our chamber" ("*ad cameram nostram immediate spectantibus*") which appears in the document of 1236. Some Jews had been paying taxes not to the emperor's chamber but to other individuals such as bishops or lay dignitaries. Those Jews were, of course, not *servi camerae*. They were the *servi* (i.e. "payers") of the recipients of their taxes.

Interpreting *servi camerae* as taxpayers would also explain the content of the privileges of Frederick II and those of his predecessors. They regulated principally the business activities of the Jews and had legal jurisdiction over them. In providing for payment of taxes for the imperial chamber the decrees established the protection necessary to enable the taxpayers to carry on their activities.

III

Two years after the extension of the privilege of Worms to the Jews of the entire country, Frederick II signed, in 1238, a special privilege for the Jews of Vienna.[19] In this document, the Emperor declared that "he accepted his Vienna Jews, the *servi camerae nostrae*, under his and the imperial protection and grace."

If the expression *servi camerae nostrae* signified a special legal status, one might ask why it was necessary to grant special protection and grace to the Jews of Vienna? If, however, *servi camerae nostrae* meant only that the Jews of Vienna were obliged to pay taxes to the Emperor's chamber (and not to any local authority, particularly not to the Austrian Duke, who had just been removed by Frederick II), the special protection became meaningful and important.

Further support for this definition of *servus camerae* emerges from the contents of the privilege of Frederick II for the Jews of Vienna. This privilege should be compared to the privilege granted to the Jews of Speyer, in 1090, by Emperor Henry IV; the same privilege, with small changes, was repeated in the same year for the Jews of Worms. These two documents begin with four articles dealing with important economic rights. These articles specified the rules governing the business activities of the Jews of Speyer and Worms. As a result of later confirmations by Frederick I and Frederick II, all the Jewish communities in the Holy Roman Empire of the Germans were regulated by the documents of 1090. These clauses provided as follows:[20]

(1) Nobody may dare to disturb or attack the Jews.
(2) Nobody may dare to take away from them what they inherited in real estate, land, slaves, or other property. Whoever acts violently against them must pay a fine to the Emperor's chamber (and also to the Bishop's chamber in Speyer) and refund double the value of the damage.
(3) Jews have the right to exchange their goods with anyone in legal commercial activity.
(4) Jews have freedom of movement within the borders of

the country, to do business, buy and sell, without the obligation of paying any duties.

Following the introductory regulations on economic rights, additional articles dealt with specific problems of great importance to Jews:

(1) No one may demand hospitality in Jewish homes without their consent.

(2) If stolen goods are found in Jewish homes and the Jews claim that the goods were purchased, the amount paid by them must be refunded when the goods are returned to their owner.

(3) Jewish children may not be forcibly baptized. Violations are punishable by a fine of twelve pounds in gold to the Imperial Treasury. Any Jew who asks to be baptized voluntarily must wait three days so that it can be determined whether his reason is preference for the Christian faith or desertion of his own law caused by some harm. Who deserts the law of his fathers must also relinquish his inherited property.

(4) Pagan slaves owned by Jews may not be taken from them by being baptized. Violations are punishable by a fine of three pounds in silver and the return of the slave to his owner.

(5) In litigations between Jews and Christians each party must prove its rights according to its law.

(6) No one may force a Jew to trial by battle with hot irons or to trial by ordeal in ice water or to imprisonment; rather, the Jew must take an oath after forty days in accordance with his law. Proof may be offered by witnesses only if they are both Jewish and Christian. Appeals to the Emperor himself are permitted in all such cases.

(7) Whoever causes the death of a Jew, be he the conspirator or the perpetrator of the murder, must pay twelve pounds in

gold to the Treasury of the Emperor. If he inflicts a wound only, without causing death, the fine is one pound. If a slave kills or wounds a Jew, his owner must pay the fine and deliver the slave for punishment.

(8) Litigation among Jews must be judged by their leaders. Whoever conceals the truth may be forced by his leader to confess. Accusations of major crimes must be judged by the Emperor.

(9) Jews may sell their wine, herbs, and medicines to Christians.

Significantly, the privilege of 1238, granted to the Jews of Vienna, *servi camerae nostrae*, omitted the four introductory articles of the privileges of 1090 for Speyer and Worms. It included only the nine subsequent articles. It also omitted two other articles of the 1090 privileges (granting Jews the right to hire Christians for work, except on Sundays and holidays, and prohibiting the purchase of Christian slaves). Why were the four introductory articles of Henry IV eliminated in the 1238 decree of Frederick II?

The reason, I believe, was that the general status of the Jews belonging (or paying direct taxes) to the Emperor's chamber was sufficiently clear in 1238. The general clauses of the earlier privileges were simply unnecessary.

Such basic provisions could not, however, have been omitted entirely from the decree of Frederick II without any implicit recognition of them. That recognition appears in the introductory phrases of the decree which state that the Emperor had "accepted the Jews of Vienna, the servants of our chamber, under our and the imperial protection and grace" ("*Per presens scriptum Notum fieri volumus universis, quod Nos Judeos Wienne seruos camerae nostrae sub nostra et Imperiali protectione recipimus et fauore*"). This was the equivalent of the four introductory clauses of the two decrees of Henry IV. What followed was obviously *not* understood to be part of the concept of *servi camerae nostrae*. Consequently, it was tied to the introductory clause by the word *Praeterea*, which means *in addition*.

IV

The validity of the decree of Frederick II concerning the Jews of Vienna was abruptly terminated in 1238 when his namesake, Frederick II Babenberg (The Warlike), recaptured the government of Austria, from which he had been forced three years earlier. After several years, Frederick II Babenberg, who lived the title "Duke of Austria and Styria and Land of Carniola," decided to modify the official status of the Jews in his country. On July 1, 1244, a decree regulating the status and conditions of the life of the Jews was signed by him in the Castle of Starkenberg. This decree is the prototype of the Statute of Kalisz. We do not know whether Frederick the Warlike was really the first to regulate the status of the Jews in the manner done in the decree of July 1, 1244, but so long as the decree of the Bohemian King Václav I—which may have been the model for Frederick Babenberg's legislation—has not been found, we must accept the originality of the decree of July 1, 1244.

Frederick Babenberg did *not* call his Jews *servi camerae nostrae*. Was this intended to change the legal status of the Jews? Were they no longer "serfs" (if, indeed, that was the meaning of *servi camerae*)?

A comparison of the decree of 1244 and of the earlier decree shows that the status of the Jews was not substantially altered. The major differences were: (1) in the structure of the decrees themselves; (2) in the protected occupations of the Jews; and (3) in the provisions regarding the inner organization of the Jewish community.

So far as the "chamber" of the Duke was concerned, it was mentioned in the decree of Frederick Babenberg only in connection with the fines which a Christian inflicting a wound upon a Jew was required to pay (Article 9); a Christian who devastates a Jewish cemetery was condemned to death and his property forfeited to the chamber of the Duke (Article 14); a Christian who takes a pledge from a Jew by force was to be punished as a plunderer of the ducal chamber (Article 29). Without mentioning the chamber, the decree stated that if a Christian were to kill a Jew he was to be punished with death "and all his movable and immovable property shall pass into the power of the Duke" (Article 10).

Comparing the decree of 1244 with the decrees of Henry IV we find that out of the four introductory clauses only the fourth was adopted by Frederick II Babenberg. It corresponds to Article 12 of Frederick's decree, which guaranteed to the Jews freedom of movement within the borders of the country. The first clause of the decrees of Henry IV, protecting the Jews generally against physical attacks, was replaced by Article 11 of the decree of 1244; a detailed provision on a payment to be made by the offender to the Duke and to the attacked Jew. Both clauses (and the two other introductory clauses of the 1090 decrees) were omitted in the decree of 1238, which immediately preceded the decree of 1244.

The second article of the decree of 1238 was inserted towards the end of the decree of 1244, as Article 24. The third article appeared as Article 6. Articles 4-6 of the decree of 1238 were not included in the regulation of the Austrian Duke. Article 7, which prohibited exposing Jews to trial by ordeal, was replaced by Frederick Babenberg's Article 20, which provided that in certain cases the Duke would supply Jews "with a champion" (*nos iudeis contra suspectum pugilem volumus exhibere*). While the provisions were not identical, both rested on the principle that the Jews should not be compelled to engage in physical combat with their accusers at a trial. Article 8 of the decree of 1238 was replaced by Article 9 and Article 10 of the Babenberg decree. The fine of twelve pounds in gold for causing the death of a Jew appears in both decrees. Articles 9 and 10 of the privilege of 1238 were not repeated by Frederick the Warlike.

The reason that many provisions were added in the Babenberg privilege to protect the money-lending business of the Jews was obviously related to the change in the occupation of the Jews that occurred rapidly in Austria. Jews in Hungary, Bohemia, Poland, Moravia, and Silesia had become bankers at the time when the legislation concerning them was enacted.

With regard to the inner organization of the Jewish community, the privileges of 1238 and 1244 differed considerably. Emperor Frederick II recognized the right of the Jews to litigate their disputes before their own leaders (Article 9) and, in some instances, even recognized Jewish law as the grounds upon which cases between Jews and Christians might be decided (Article 6). Frederick Babenberg spoke of a "Jewish judge" (*iudex iudeorum*) (Article 22) who was a Gentile and who could take jurisdiction over disputes among Jews when he was authorized by them to do so "due to a complaint." The Austrian privilege also contained important provisions protecting Jewish cemeteries and synagogues against attacks by Christians. If a synagogue was attacked, the *iudex iudeorum* was the beneficiary of a two-talent fine (Article 15).[21] Other procedural provisions in the decree were aimed at improving the efficiency of the Jewish judges' court (Articles 16-19).

The Statute of Kalisz issued by Bolesław the Pious in 1264 repeated the privilege of Frederick Babenberg almost word for word. Four important additional articles dealt with the following situations:

(1) Consistent with Papal Decrees, no Jew was to be accused of use of Christian blood "because their law prohibits the use of any blood." Any Christian accused of such crimes, allegedly committed by Jews, was to suffer the same punishment as the the Jew would receive if the accusation were true.

(2) Jews might receive horses in pledge for loans only

during the day. This provision was intended to protect Jews against accusations that they had accepted stolen horses as pledges on the theory that transfers of stolen horses could not readily be concealed if done in daylight. A Jewish leader established his *bona fides* if he took an oath that the horse was brought to him during daylight hours.

(3) A Jew might be accused of forfeiting money only after the accusation was authorized by the Duke or by his local representative.

(4) A Christian who failed to help a Jew attacked at night was required to pay a fine to the judge or to the head of the district's authority (*capitaneus*).

In addition to these new provisions, other improvements were made in the Polish privilege of 1264. The maximum rate of interest stipulated in the decree of Frederick II Babenberg was omitted in the Polish privilege. This meant that the Jews were given unrestricted freedom in this aspect of their economic activities.

V

A close examination of all privileges, from the decree of Henry IV to Bolesław the Pious' Statute of Kalisz, compels a reassessment of the entire concept of *Kammerknechtschaft*.

It seems, first of all, that Jews occupied the same status when they were called *servi camerae nostrae* as when they were described as "belonging to our chamber." That appears clearly from a comparison of the documents of 1090 and those of 1238.

Second, the omission of the term *servi camerae* as well as of the description *ad cameram nostram attineant* in the documents of 1244 and the subsequent ones in Hungary, Bohemia, and Poland proves that the expression was more formal than practical. The status of the Jews under these documents was virtually identical to their status under other documents where the expression *servi camerae* or *ad cameram nostram attineant* was used.

Various documents which chronologically follow the statutes of Frederick II Babenberg, Bela IV, Premysł Ottakar II, and Bolesław the Pious reverted to the expression *servi camerae*. Rudolph I of Germany, in his decree of 1286, used this term.[22] So did Premysł Ottakar II in a decree for the Jews of Moravia of 1268, where he reverted to the original description *cum ad nostram cameram pertineant*. Duke Bolko I did the same in his privilege of 1295 (reaffirmed by Bolko II in 1328).

The original meaning of the term *servus camerae* as similar to "taxpayer" is also established by documents originating elsewhere than Germany and Poland. In 1176 it was said of the Jews of Aragon: "Jews are servants of the King and always subject to the royal treasury" ("*Iudei servi regis sunt et semper fisco regio deputati*").[23] In 1237, a Jewish physician, Busach of Palermo, was given a tax exemption. In a document signed by Emperor Frederick II as King of Sicily, he was described as *servus camerae*. When King Peter of Aragon conquered Sicily, the heirs of Busach, the physician David of Palermo and his brothers, received on January 24, 1283 a confirmation of this exemption. The document describes them as *servi camerae nostrae*.[24] Are these not indications that the words referred to taxpayers and their duties to pay the tax?

Documents of German origin tend to prove the same hypothesis. In 1266, the Jews of Augsburg were released from payment of taxes for a period of five years. It was clearly stated, on this occasion, that this particular grace was granted to those "who were related to the chamber of our Majesty" ("*Iudeis nostris spectantibus ad cameram majestates nostre nunc residentibus cum ipsis in Augusta hanc facimus gratiam specialem*").[25] The relation between the tax exemption and the expression "who were related to the chamber" is obvious from this context.

Even more convincing are documents from a later period.

Emperor Charles IV wrote, in 1359, to the aldermen of Zurich that "all *Kawerzin*, usurers, and Jews serve our and the Empire's chamber and belong to it" (*"alle Kawerzin, Wuocher und Juden unser und des Richs Camer dienen und gehoeren"*).[26] In the Law Book of Johannes Purgoldt (ca. 1503-1504), Christian usurers were described as follows: "There are some Christian usurers, called *Kawerzaner*, and they are under the protection of the princes.... They are the princes' *Kammerknechte* equally as the Jews, because they are money-lenders and with their lives not on their own."[27]

This last quotation illustrates how the *servi camerae* were transformed from taxpayers to "servants." Because of their occupation as money-lenders, Jews and *Kawerzin* alike became desirable financial assets for a King or Duke. It was important to the ruler to find a legal justification for inheriting the Jews. Rudolph I of Habsburg was probably the first whose counselors advised that he protect the Jews "who, under the prerogative of his special dignity, are distinguished to belong to the imperial chamber" (*"qui specialis dignitatis prerogativa ad imperialem cameram pertinere noscuntur"*); that statement was made by him in 1274. In 1286, when some Jews left the country, Rudolph confiscated their property under the following pretext:

> Since the Jews collectively and individually, in their capacity as *servi camerae nostrae*, specifically belong to us with their persons and all their property, just as some belong to princes to whom they have been transferred as a feudal benefice by us and the empire, it is right and proper...that if any such Jews become fugitives and, without our special license and consent as their master, render themselves beyond the seas and thus alienate themselves from their true lord, that we as the lord to whom they belong may freely enter into all their possessions, objects, and property, both movable and immovable, wherever they may be found and not undeservedly take them under our control.[28]

Rudolph plainly added his own elaboration to the concept of the "taxpayer" Jews. He deemed himself to be "the lord to whom they belong." Accordingly, the *servus camerae* became a real "serf." The "lord" could "enter freely into all possessions, objects, and property, both movable and immovable" of the Jewish "serfs."

In Poland, however, the new concept of a *servus camerae* was not adopted. Poland accepted only such content as a *servus camerae* had prior to 1244. The Statute of Kalisz began to regulate the status of the Jews in a manner that was substantially different from the German school of thought represented by Rudolph I of Habsburg and his successors

King Casimir the Great confirmed the Statute of Kalisz in 1334, 1364, and 1367, and once again on a date unknown to us.[29] All these reaffirmations avoided any misinterpretation along the line adopted by Rudolph I of Habsburg. King Casimir IV, in 1453, enlarged the privilege of Bolesław the Pious considerably and liberalized its provisions.[30] The privilege of 1453 gives evidence of real *noblesse* of spirit. It is probably the most humanitarian regulation of the status of Jews in any European country toward the end of the medieval period. From a noble beginning in 1264, Poland selected its own path and in a world of darkness proudly carried the torch of light.

Notes

[1]Printed by Jan Łaski, *Commune incliti regni Poloniae privilegium.* Cracow, 1506; later reprinted many times. The original does not exist; the text is known only frm later confirmations by Polish Kings, the first by Casimir the Great in 1334. Critical evaluations were made by many scholars. See Romuald Hube, "*Przywilej żydowski Bolesława i jego potwierdzenia*" [Bolesław's privilege for the Jews and its confirmations], in *Biblioteka Warszawska* (Warsaw Library), 1880, pp. 426ff. A recent article on the document is "*Bolesława Pobożnego Statut Kaliski w roku 1264 dla Żydow*" [The

Statute of Kalisz for the Jews of Bolesław the Pious in the year 1264] by Józef Sieradzki in the collective work *Osiemnaście wieków Kalisza, Studia i materiały do dziejów miasta Kalisza i regionu kaliskiego* [Eighteen centuries of Kalish, studies and materials for the history of the city of Kalisz and the region of Kalisz]. Kalisz, 1960, I, pp. 133ff.

[2]Printed by Jaromir Celakovsky, *Codex iuris municipalis regni Bohemiae*. Prague, 1886, Vol. I, pp. 5ff. (in the confirmation by Charles IV, dated September 30, 1356). The 1255 version, in German, printed by Johann Scherer, *Die Rechtsverhaeltnisse der Juden in den deutsch-oesterreichischen Laendern*. Leipzig, 1901, pp. 322ff.

[3]Printed by Endlicher, *Rerum hungaricarum Monumenta Arpadiana*. St. Gallen, 1849, pp. 473ff.

[4]Meiller, *Archiv fuer Kunde oesterreichischer Geschichtsquellen*, Vienna, 1853, X, pp. 146ff.; also Aronius, *Regesten zur Geschichte der Juden im fraenkischen und deutschen Reiche bis zum Jahre 1273*. Berlin, 1902, pp. 233ff.

[5]Václav I (1230-53) invited colonists from abroad to his country, among them could have been Jews from Germany. The suggestion that the unknown privilege of Václav I was possibly the prototype of the *Fredericianum* was made by B. Dudik, *Maehrens allgemeine Geschichte*, Bruenn, 1878, VIII, p. 223. He quoted Premysł Ottakar II's privilege for the Jews of Bruenn (Brno) in which he said that his act was made "in accordance with the form of the privilege granted to the Jews concerning their rights by our father." Scherer, *op. cit.*, pp. 177-8, opposed the view of Dudik because the Bohemian King's quotation refers to a special *privilegium fori*, granted by Venceslaus I to the Jews, and such *privilegium fori* was allegedly not included in the *Fredericianum*. However, the *privilegium fori* is unmistakably included in Article 8 of the Fredericianum (*si autem Vergebit in personam soli duci hic casus observabitur iudicandus*). Scherer's objection is, therefore, not valid.

[6]Boczek, *Codex diplomaticus et epictolaris Moraviae*. Olomuc, 1845, IV, pp. 17ss.

[7]Sommersberg, *Silesiorum rei historicae et genealogicae accessiones*. Leipzig, 1732, pp. 91ff.

[8]The expression *servi camerae* appears for the first time in Germany,

according to Guido Kisch, *The Jews in Medieval Germany* (Chicago, 1949, p. 133), in a privilege of Frederick II of 1236. This is however doubtful, because the expression *servi camerae nostrae* in the document of 1236 does not refer to the Jews but to the applicants. The Jews are mentioned differently: *omnibus Judeis ad cameram nostram immediate spectantibus.* See Aronius, *op. cit.*, p. 216.

[9]Publication by R. Hoeniger in *Zeitschrift fuer Geschichte der Juden in Deutschland*, Braunschweig, 1887, pp. 138ff; see also Aronius, *op. cit.*, pp. 74ff.

[10]*Ibid.*; Aronius, *ibid.*, p. 123.

[11]Aronius, *ibid.*, p. 133.

[12]*Proceedings of the American Academy for Jewish Research*, 1940, X, p. 69.

[13]*Monumenta Germaniae, Constitutiones.* I, 381, No. 277. See G. Kisch, *op. cit.*, p. 109.

[14]J. Scherer, *op. cit.*, p. 76; Altmann, *l.c.*; Kisch, *l.c.*, p. 123, 423.

[15]Aronius, *op. cit.*, p. 139. The same opinion was already expressed by Otto Stobbe, *Die Juden in Deutschland waehrend des Mittelalters*. Braunschweig, 1866, p. 13.

[16]*Mittellungen des Gesamtarchivs der deutschen Juden*, 4 Jahrgang, Leipzig, 1913, pp. 44ff.

[17]George Caro, *Social-und Wirtschaftsgeschichte der Juden*. Leipzig, 1908, I, p. 413.

[18]*Lehrbuch der deutschen Rechtsgeschichte*. Leipzig, 1902, p. 469.

[19]Printed in Scherer, *Die Rechtsverhaeltnisse*, pp. 135ff.

[20]On the differences between the two documents of 1090, see Aronius, *op. cit.*, p. 75; also see Sara Schiffmann, "Die Urkunden fuer die Juden von Speyer 1090 und Worms 1157" in *Zeitschrift fuer die Geschichte der Juden in Deutschland*. 2 Jahrgang, 1930, pp. 28ff.

[21] In the Latin text: *Si aliquis temerorie iactaverit supra scolas Iudeorum, iudici Iudeorum duo talenta volumus ut persolvat.* Aronius, *op. cit.*, p. 234, translates it erroneously in German: *Wenn einer ueber die Judenschulen "spottet," so soll er dem Judenrichter zwei Pfund zahlen. Iactaverit* means, however, not *spottet*, but *wirft*—in English "throws" (stones). Philip Bloch, in *Die General-Privilegien der polnischen Judenschaft*, Posen, 1892, pp. , quoted in this connection the original German wording of the decree of King Vaclav II: *Ist daz jemand freveleich auf der Juden Schul "werfe," der Schol czwai phunt gewen.*

[22] *Universi et singuli iudei, utpote camere nostre servi, cum personis et rebus suis omnibus specialiter nobis attineant vel illis principus* ...in *Monumenta Germaniae Constitutiones.* III, p. 368.

[23] F. Baer, *Studien zur Geschichte der Juden im Koenigreiche Aragonien waehrend des 13. und 14. Jahrhunderts.* Berlin, 1913, p. 12.

[24] George Caro, *op. cit.*, I, p. 413.

[25] Aronius, *op. cit.*, p. 297.

[26] Otto Stobbe, *op. cit.*, p. 204.

[27] Guido Kisch, *Jewry-Law in Medieval Germany.* New York, 1949, p. 100.

[28] English translation by S.W. Baron, *A Social and Religious History of the Jews.* New York and London, 1965, IX (2nd. ed.), pp. 153-4.

[29] See Moses Schorr, "Die Hauptprivilegien der polnischen Judenschaft," in *Festschrift Adolf Schwarz*, Berlin and Vienna, 1917, pp. 521ff.

[30] Philip Bloch, *op. cit.*, pp. 104ff. (in Latin) and pp. 46ff. (in German translation).

CHAPTER IV
A Jewish Lawyer in Poland
in the Fifteenth Century

The institution of lawyers began to appear in Poland in trials and lawsuits in the fourteenth century. The character of lawyers was regulated mostly by custom, until King Zygmunt II August issued a regulation in 1559 specifying their duties in Polish courts. Towards the end of Polish independence, in 1778, Andrzej Zamojski (in his volume containing laws on judicial procedures) devoted the thirteenth chapter to lawyers, whom he called "patrons of cases."

The bibliography of works dealing with the history of the Polish bar is quite poor. In 1882 Alexander Kraushar wrote a study "On the Ancient Polish Bar,"[1] which was followed by chapters or references in the works of scholars such as Anc,[2] Balzer,[3] Dunin,[4] Hube,[5] Dąbkowski,[6] and Kutrzeba.[7] In 1924 Józef Rafacz wrote a book on *Representatives of the Parties in the Old Polish Legal Procedure*.[8] In the same year Stanisław Car published a study called *The History of the Bar in Poland*.[9] My own book, *The Bar in Old Poland*, appeared in 1936 in the series *Pamiętnik Historyczno-Prawny*[10] under the editorship of Professor Przemysław Dąbkowski; it was based on the material contained in the Polish law collection *Volumina Legum* and on the minutes of Polish courts collected in the *Akta Grodzkie i Ziemskie*.[10A]

In one instance I found evidence of a Jew appearing as a lawyer in a Polish court, in the year 1456.[11]

In order to fully appreciate the importance and meaning of this discovery, we must take into consideration (1) the legal position of Jews in Poland in the fifteenth century and (2) the lawyer's status in Poland at that time.

Regarding the first point, we should recall the important decree of King Kazimierz IV of August 13, 1453. A Jew had been considered, according to earlier legislation, a *servus camerae* (servant of the chamber); he was under the special protection of the king, to whose treasury (chamber) he paid taxes. Did this status diminish his basic rights? While the statute of Kazimierz IV was only in effect for a short time (because the King yielded to the pressure of the nobility and the clergy and withdrew his signature[12]), its provisions were nevertheless important; King Zygmunt I and King Zygmunt II August later affixed their signatures to this important decree.[13]

Article 36 of this statute clearly exempted the Jews from military service (while granting them the right to own real estate through default of a mortgage on noblemen's properties), which would indicate that their status was inferior to noblemen. The same article even declared Jews free from contributing towards the cost of a war "because the Jews themselves belong to our treasury."[14]

However, the statute of 1453 includes a provision (in Article 43), which might almost place a Jew in the category of a nobleman. A Jew, when accused by a Christian of a crime which could cause loss of his life or property, could not be judged by anyone but the voievoda (the King's representative) or his deputy. Only such a royal representative could imprison him, and only he was empowered to release him upon the latter's offering a guarantee. The statute adds a very significant clause:

> In all punishments imposed on a Jew with regard to a Christian accuser or the *voievoda*, he has to pay as the natives (*terrigenae*) in accordance with the common law, because we have left our said Jews with the rights of our native nobility.[15]

Obviously, this could mean that in some respect the Jews had the rights of noblemen. This interpretation depends, however, on changing a letter in the Latin text ("iura *N*obilia" instead of "iura *M*obilia"[16]).

Concerning the second point: a lawyer was simply another man's helper. When any one had to appear in court but could not express himself freely, the lawyer appeared in his behalf. The oldest Polish provision in this respect (1347) stated clearly:

> Because no one should be denied his defense and care (that being a natural right), we have decided that in the courts of our Kingdom any man, no matter what his status or condition, may and should have his lawyer, procurator, or prolocutor.[17]

Obviously the lawyer was a "procurator" (representative) or a "prolocutor" (spokesman). He had to help the party in court to present its case. The two expressions, "procurator" and "prolocutor," were added to explain in detail the term "*advocatus*" in the original text.

The lawyer's status was even more clearly defined in a decree of 1454:

> If anyone stands in court and knows not how to present his

case properly, or has difficulty with his tongue and cannot present a friend willing to speak for him, the court sitting in the case will have the duty to appoint for the petitioner a proper procurator.[18]

The lawyer, appointed by the court, was simply a helper who spoke for a man unable to present his case himself.

However, abuses could occur in such representation. Were a lawyer to appear in court instead of the party, the court had to be convinced that he was really the representative of the party; otherwise a man supposed to be one party's lawyer might fraudulently help the other party to win the case. This was, of course, not the intention of the lawgiver (the King). In order to avoid such abuse (which probably occurred quite often), the court required the lawyer to present a written authorization to act on behalf of his party. Severe punishment was threatened against lawyers acting without such authorization or falsifying a document to this effect (1505).

With these two points in mind, we will understand the appearance of a Jewish lawyer before a court in Lwów in 1456.

A nobleman, Franciszek of Dziewiątniki, appeared in court and presented a claim against Aaron, a Jew. He demanded the return of a golden belt which Piotr Chinowski, a Polish nobleman, had deposited with Aaron as a pledge. Franciszek came to court with two witnesses—one a Jew, the other a Gentile.

In accordance with legal procedure, the defendant had to be present when the case was called. Aaron, however, did not appear. The judge waited some time and then sent an official to look for the defendant. Aaron was still absent. His wife, Judith, entered the room and said to the judge: "My husband is in jail, and he is therefore unable to appear." Several Jews accompanied Judith and pleaded with the judge not to condemn Aaron in his absence. This would be against the statute on Jews.

The plaintiff, Franciszek, was very outspoken. He stated

that he had no business with the Jews who appeared in court, and he moved to call the witnesses brought by him to prove the case. The judge agreed. The Jews who had raised their voices when speaking to the court were ordered to pay a fine for unauthorized intervention in court, and the witnesses were summoned.

Suddenly something unexpected happened. A Jew by the name of Dzathko asked to be recognized. The judge gave him the floor, whereupon he made a statement: "I am Aaron's lawyer." The judge agreed to let him act as lawyer for the absent defendant. Dzathko examined the witnesses and, in one instance, presented the argument that the witness brought by Franciszek was not a Jew but a Turk.

The law was that, in order to win a case in court against a Jew, Jewish witnesses must be presented by the plaintiff.[19] Franciszek did not have any Jewish witnesses, only Gentiles. As far as the critical witness was concerned, he stated several times that he was a Jew, but during Dzathko's interrogation he began to show confusion. Franciszek saw that he might lose the case. It occurred to him then that Dzathko's character as a lawyer could be questioned. If he were really properly appointed by the defendant, why had his wife not presented him right away? Why had he instead waited until the judge began to summon the witnesses? Franciszek stood up and asked the judge for permission to make a procedural statement: "Sir, I move that Dzathko be ordered to present his written *procuratorium* [document entitling him to appear in court] from Aaron."

The court agreed. Dzathko, however, did not have the document. The plaintiff then declared that he refused to discuss the case with Judith and the Jews present. Aaron should be sentenced to return the golden belt. The court issued a sentence against the accused. This took place in Lwów on May 14, 1456.

We do not know the final outcome of the case, whether Aaron returned the belt or not. What we do gain from this case, however, is clear evidence that a Jewish lawyer appeared in the court of Lwów some five hundred years ago. He lost the case because he was not equipped with a proper authorization from his party, but clearly his position as a lawyer had not been questioned because he was a Jew.[20]

Notes

[1]Alexander Kraushar, *O palestrze staropolskiej*. Warsaw, V, 1882.

[2]Dominik Anc, *Kilka słow o adwokaturze i aplikacji sądowej w dawnej Polsce, Gazeta Sądowa Warszawska*, 1899, pp. 193-6 and 210-13.

[3]Oswald Balzer, *Kancelarje i akta grodzkie w wieku XIII*, Warsaw 1882; *Geneza Trybunalu Koronnego*, Warsaw, 1886; *Przewód sądowy polski w zarysie*, Lwów 1935.

[4]Karol Dunin, *Dawne mazowieckie prawo*, Warsaw, 1880.

[5]Romuald Hube, *Prawo polskie w wieku trzynastym*, Warsaw 1875; *Ustawodawstwo Kazimierza Wielkiego*, Warsaw, 1881; *Sądy, ich praktyka i stosunki prawne społ. w Polsce, Warsaw*, 1886.

[6]Przemysław Dąbkowski, *Prawo prywatne polskie*, Tom II, Lwów 1911, p.547. *Kancelarje i księgi sądowe bełzkie za czasów polskich, Przegląd prawa i administracji*, Lwów, 1918, pp. 97-142; *Palestra i księgi sądowe trembo-welskie za czasów polskich*, Lwów, 1920; *Palestra i księgi sądowe sanockie w dawnej Polsce, Pamiętnik Historyczno-Prawny*, Vol. I (6), Lwów, 1925 (referring to the Bar in the towns of Bełz, Trembowla, and Sanok); *Urzędnicy kancelaryjni sądów ziemskich i grodzkich w dawnej Polsce*, Lwów, 1918; *Palestra i księgi sądowe ziemskie i grodzkie w dawnej Polsce, Pamiętnik Historyczno-Prawny*, Vol. III (2), Lwów, 1926.

[7]Stanisław Kutrzeba, *Dawne polskie prawo sądowe*, Lwów, Warsaw, Kraków, 1926.

[8]Józef Rafacz, *Zastępcy stron w dawnym procesie polskim (Rozprawy Akademji Umiejętnosci Wydział Historyczno—Filozoficzny, Serja II, Tom XXXVIII Nr., V 8, Kraków, 1924.*

[9]Stanisław Car, *Zarys historji adwokatury w Polsce*, *"Palestra"*, Vol. I, Warsaw, 1924, pp. 265-297, 380-405, 501-514; Vol.II (Warsaw, 1925) pp. 553-574, 1041-1063. Also his *Stan Adwokatury w Królestwie Polskiem*, Warsaw, 1915.

[10]I. Lewin, *Palestra w dawnej Polsce*, *Pamiętnik Historyczno-Prawny*, Vol. XII (1), Lwów, 1936.

[10]A Published in Lwów, 25 volumes, 1868-1935.

[11]*Akta grodzkie i ziemskie*, Vol. XIV, 3559. Józef Rafacz, *Zastępcy stron w dawnym procesie polskim*, p. 27, quotes from a source in Lublin in 1639 that two Jews were the plenipotentiaries of Samson Naftalowicz.

[12]See Philip Bloch, *Die General-Privilegien der polnischen Judenschaft*, Posen, 1892, p. 42 (quoting Bandtkie, *Jus Polonicum*, Statuta Casim. IV, Niessoviae, p. 289).

[13]Bloch, *ibid*. See also Moses Schorr, *Die Hauptprivilegien der polnischen Judenschaft* in *Festschrift Adolf Schwarz*, Berlin and Vienna, 1917, p. 532.

[14]Bloch, *ibid*., p. 57 (German translation) and p. 115 (Latin text): *quia ipsi judei nostri sunt thezauri*.

[15]Bloch, *ibid*., pp.59-60 (German text) and pp.117-118 (Latin Text).

[16]Bloch (*ibid*., p. 60, note 1) considers the version *iura mobilia* to be a mistake caused by misspelling. This spelling is included in the texts published by J. Perles, *Geschichte der Juden in Posen*, Breslau, 1865, and L. Gumplowicz, *Prawodawstwo polskie względem Żydów*, Kraków, 1867.

[17]*Volumina Legum*, Vol. I, p. 6 (reprinted in my *Palestra w dawnej Polsce*, p. 94).

[18]*Volumina Legum*, Vol. I, p. 252. (reprinted in *Palestra w dawnej, Polsce*, p. 94).

[19]Article 1 of the Kalisz Statute stipulated: *"Nullus Christianus contra Judeum nisi cum Judeo et Christiano in testinomium admittatur"* (Bloch, *Die General-Privilegion der der polnischen Judenschaft*, p. 12.

[20]The case is briefly mentioned in my *Palestra w dawnej Polsce*, p. 13.

CHAPTER V
How King Stefan Batory Determined that a Jew May Have Kosher Meat

In the 1560's, there lived in the Polish royal court a Jew named Salomon Calahora. Descended from the Spanish family Califari, he was a prominent physician and also traded in all sorts of goods, mainly in salt. In 1570 the last Jagellonian king, Zygmunt II August, appointed him court physician. Having the monarch under his care, Salomon Calahora also had the opportunity to make use of the King's friendship. As a merchant he was given a number of privileges: he paid no taxes, was free of any tolls, and was not subject to any court of law except the sovereign himself. Under such circumstances, of course, his business prospered.

When Zygmunt II August died and Stefan Batory took the throne, everyone was interested in the question of what would

happen to Doctor Calahora. The question was no less significant for the other salt merchants, because competing with a
tax-free and legally protected merchant was not easy. And the
Jews did not take too kindly to the idea that one man was
above the community and enjoyed special privileges. The well-
organized Jewish community in Poland reacted to such a
privileged status by refraining from any contact with Salomon
Calahora. If someone was to be a member of the Jewish
community, then he had to be treated the same as everyone
else. If he wanted to go his own way, then he could have no
relationship with the community. In such cases, the people
often used the dread weapon of *Herem*—anathema. The one
who had special privileges on the outside was also given "special privileges" on the inside. But the privilege on the inside was
a *privilegium odiosum*—excommunication.

One of the consequences of anathema was sometimes the
denial of the right to obtain kosher meat. In a letter which
Rabbi Moses Lima, author of *Helkat Mhokek*, once wrote to
the *Kehilla* in Zabłudowo, we find: "One who was excommunicated and refuses to leave the synagogue—you can consider
him a rebel or punish him so that no kosher-slaughtered meat
be sold to him."

It can readily be assumed that the commercial and personal
privileges of Dr. Calahora had a similar effect upon the Jews.
Perhaps they also threatened him with that terrible step whose
consequences would be banishment from the synagogue, ref-
usal to circumcise his children, or burial next to the fence in the
cemetery. In any event, Salomon Calahora was notified that no
kosher butcher would sell him meat.

When Stefan Batory was about to appoint Calahora as his
personal physician, he must already have had information that
the doctor's fellow Jews would not take this lightly. But not
only did he confirm all of Calahora's rights and privileges, he
also decided to make life easy for him. In his decree of July 31,
1578 he wrote:

The Jews must not try—by whatever royal or Jewish or public taxes or tolls, from which we hereby exempt him—to disturb him overtly or covertly, or to hinder him in the observance of the commandment of circumcision, or of entering a house of worship, or by refusing to bury him in the proper Jewish way, *or by refusing to sell him kosher meat*, or in the observance of all other customs and ceremonies prescribed for Jews, under penalty of a 2000 złoty fine, to be paid immediately, half of which goes to our treasury and half to the *voievode [*of the province*]*.

So it is written in black and white in the document of July 31, 1578, and signed by King Stefan Batory.[1].

All these penalties that were levied are understandable. The King did not want his personal physician to be subjected to anathema. Such cases are familiar enough to us in pre-partition Poland. What is unique, however, is the underscoring of the fact that the sale of kosher meat to the royal physician must *not* be prohibited. Salomon Calahora did not want to eat non-kosher food and fearing that the Jewish community would not permit him to buy kosher meat, he succeeded in having the King guarantee this for him.

Thus we have the interesting document in which Stefan Batory, the Polish sovereign himself, saw to it that his Jewish doctor not be deprived of kosher meat.

Note

[1]See M. Bersohn. *Dyplomataryusz*, No. 165. Also my book *Klątwa żydowska na Litwie w XVII i XVIII wieku*, Lwów, 1932, p. 99.

CHAPTER VI
The Jews' Role in the Sejm Elections
of Pre-Partition Poland

Parliamentary life in pre-partition Poland was characterized by many peculiarities. One of these, as we shall see, was that the Jewish community exerted considerable influence upon the election of deputies to the *Sejm*.

The *Sejm*, or Polish parliament, in reality represented only one class, the *szlachta* (nobility); on exception, it included representatives of the Cracow burghers. In the Saxon era, when dozens of *Sejms* were convened and barely five succeeded in showing any effectiveness, outside influences pushed ahead. Moreover, individuals who by law were unauthorized to do so directly took part in *Sejm* debates. Spectators obstructed deliberations at the *Sejm* with absolute impunity. On occasion these people would shove the deputies off their benches and occupy their places themselves. Sometimes they even attacked the deputies in a more aggressive manner, aiming, for example, an apple or a pear at the head of a deputy delivering a speech. This naturally resulted in the deputy's protesting to the Speaker of the *Sejm*: "I protest, Your Honor, the indignity shown to me as deputy by a spectator!" But this was ineffectual. "Find, Sir, the man who struck you," the Speaker would say,[1] "and you will see him duly punished." The *liberum veto* and the *sisto activitatem* no longer seem strange under such conditions. Therefore, in view of this procedure, was it difficult for a concerned individual to exert suitable influence? Obviously, it was not. It was equally possible to exert influence on the election of deputies.

Deputies were elected by local gatherings of the nobility (*sejmiki*). The *szlachta* did not pour all of their legislative powers into the deputies, but kept a good part of it for themselves. The *szlachta* considered the deputies to be plain plenipotentiaries, and retained the right to control them and instruct them during the polling of the views of the electorate. Consequently, at the sessions of the *Sejm*, it was not the deputies who were considered to be voting themselves, but the local assemblies of noblemen. From the time of King Zygmunt II August (1548-1572), written instruction had exerted an unequivocal influence on the deliberations of the *Sejm*. From this time also dates the origin of the need for a unanimous vote on the *Sejm*'s resolutions. There were an excessive number of instructions and details written into every elected deputy's mandate which the deputies were obliged to fulfill under oath.[2]

An even greater chaos prevailed at the local *Sejmiki* than at the *Sejm* itself. At the *Sejmiki*, according to an account by Andrzej Kitowicz,[3] everything revolved around pots of vodka, barrels of wine and beer, clusters of butter, and piles of bread and meat. The constantly intoxicated electors permitted their rowdy companions to lead the assembly. The participants most willingly voted for those who had slipped a gold coin into their hands. Obtaining influence was therefore easy, but a bit expensive.

Of course, the Polish Jews were well aware of the fact that the deputies' instructions weighed heavily on the *Sejm* debates. They knew that if some harmful action had been recommended in the instructions—i.e., an increase in the *per capita* tax (*pogłówne*) or something of the sort—it would prove very difficult and extremely expensive to prevent or undo the harm of such a recommendation at the *Sejm*. They were also aware that every deputy could play a pivotal role, and therefore they knew that they had to make every effort to assure that deputies favorably disposed towards the Jews be elected to the *Sejm*. Their activities towards this end commenced at the *Sejmiki*. In this way they played an active role in the *Sejm* election.

The ways in which these efforts were carried out are revealed to us in some interesting notes in old Hebrew record books (*Pinkas*) in Poland and Lithuania.

II

An accurate book of protocols from the sessions of the assemblies of representatives of the Jewish communities in Lithuania has been preserved,[4] permitting a close look at their activities. The book of protocols from the "Council of Four Lands" has unfortunately been lost. The traces preserved from this splendid institution of Jewish self-government in old Poland are faint, but they still give us an idea of the Council's sweeping scope, acquired over the course of time, and of the wide range of its activities. Therefore we must go back to the protocols of the individual communities in the Polish Kingdom.

In both of these sources (in the protocol book of the assemblies of the Lithuanian Jewish communities and in several of the record books of Polish communities—e.g., from Poznań and Opatów) a concern over the results of the election of deputies and over the content of the instructions is very clearly reflected. The Lithuanian protocol gives evidence that not only did individual communities pay careful attention to their local interests and attempt to cover them properly in the instructions, but also Jewry as a whole realized the great importance of the electoral process. Out of the assemblies, there emerged detailed recommendations on how the individual communities ought to proceed.

In the year 1623, delegates of Jewish communities from Brześć, Grodno, and Pińsk assembled for the first time in Brześć, and the following resolution was passed:

> In regard to all three main communities, the leaders are to be on guard during the gatherings of local *Sejmiki* before the *Sejm*, to investigate and carefully watch that, God forbid, nothing new be decided which would prove to be a painful thorn for us. As they arise expenses will be paid by each community together with its environs. Similarly, aside from three main communities, in every city where the *powiat* [district] gathers for the local *Sejmik*, it is the responsibility of the leaders of the respective community to stand on guard in the aforementioned way. As they accrue, expenses will be covered by the main community and its district. If a community does not stand guard and has not appointed its representatives [*Shtadlanim*] in the local *Sejmiki*, it will be punished with a fine of one hundred złoty, to be used for charitable purposes.[5]

The strength with which this resolution was enacted and the fact that this resolution was one of the first to be adopted by the session in Brześć indicate that the matter was considered extremely important. It explicitly stated that the Jews' concern should focus on the *Sejmiki* which took place before the *Sejm*. In the second part of the above cited resolution, *Sejmiki* in the "seat of the city" are mentioned, which could refer to the economic gatherings at which dozens of matters very important to the Jews regarding both treasury and administrative affairs were settled. Let us take a closer look at the activities of these local *Sejmiki*.

A great number of decisions of the local *Sejmiki* have hitherto remained unpublished. Among the exceptions are the materials pertaining to local *Sejmiki* in the "Red Ruthenian" sector, the so-called "Lauda decisions of Vishnia" published in the *Akta Grodzkie i Ziemskie* (in English: "The City and District Records" in Lwów, in 25 volumes, 1868-1935). We can immediately see that Jewish matters were being included in instructions and also in many other decisions (*Lauda*) which had enormous significance for the Jews. Let us take, for example, the *laudum* of the Vishnia *Sejmik* of July 4, 1640:

[Since] the Jews are now dealing with a collection instead of a double real estate tax, we wish that the Jews of all our cities and towns should pay one złoty from each and every house, which they will be obliged to pay within the fixed time to our tax collectors, besides the per capita tax prescribed in the *Sejm*'s resolution. We shall name a place [*forum*] in the cities where, under the same penalties and without the right of appeal, at the instigator's motion, payment should be made to the tax collectors who will also be empowered concerning the collection of other taxes.[6]

The following *laudum* of the *Sejmik* in Vishnia, January 8, 1643, is indicative of the positive results of Jewish efforts:

We, the senators, dignitaries, administrators, and the whole assembled nobility [knighthood] gathered at this *Sejmik* in Vishnia on the second day of January, make it known that the distinguished Piotr Ozga, secretary of the Lwów lands and administrator of the liquor tax, in a letter to us, has made a complaint and reported that the Jewish tenants of the liquor tax did not make the necessary payments and have not yet paid the full amount agreed upon...which caused a default. In view of this we have asked these noble gentlemen...to make, at a convenient time while in Lwów, a review of the present condition of the collection books in Lwów (if one of them is missing, that will not matter). Having reviewed the defaults in payment of the liquor tax, they will decide, as they deem justified, how the defaults should affect the Jews.... We have recommended this laudum to the most distinguished Chamberlain in Lwów, as the acting speaker of the *Sejmik* and surrounding districts, that he submit it with his signature and seal to the office of the city of Lwów.[7].

Naturally, in addition to such matters discussed in the *laudum*, the instructions included a great number of other matters as well. Of little import was whether the question concerned the Jewish community as a whole or only individual communities. Sometimes, several requests concerning Jewish matters can be found in one instruction. An example is the instruction of the Vishnia *Sejmik* dated December 9, 1636. Point 72 of this instruction states:

> The deputies should take care that the Jews not be forced to do more then they are obliged; also, that the laws concerning them be strictly observed.

Point 73 reads:

> In the future Jews have to pay the per capita tax (*pogłowne*) indiviudally, not in a lump-sum; also they have to pay other taxes, from which they were only exempt up until the last *Sejm*.

Point 83, on the other hand, relates only to the Jews of Przemyśl, and reads:

> The city of Przemyśl is very impoverished by permanent military posts and taxations; for this reason [the deputies] should ask His Majesty the King that, as is with other cities, it be exempt from military posts and that the Jews, of which there are no small number, should contribute to the armament.[8]

Great consistency was never shown by the *Sejmiki*. The

deputies were requested to take positions alternately in favor of and in opposition to the Jews' interests. For this reason too, the resolution quoted above at the assembly of Lithuanian communities in 1623, urging the undertaking of energetic action at the level of local *Sejmiki*, was to a great extent necessitated by actual needs. Soon, however, squabbles arose amongst the individual communities. Evidence of this is provided in the following resolution adopted by the Lithuanian assembly in 1627, barely four years after the previous one:

> It is explained that expenses for the local *Sejmiki* are to be covered by the communities together with surrounding districts; this means they are to give in proportion to their share in the tax quota, while the surrounding districts are to give also according to their share in the tax quota.[9]

We can infer from this that during the four-year period payments for intervention in local *Sejmiki* were made; they acquired the name *"Sejmik* expenses" (*hotsaot Sejmiks*). Furthermore, we can infer that these *hotsaot Sejmiks* were not small, since a dispute arose over the sources to be used to cover them. Neighboring *Kehillot* in the jurisdiction of the three main communities evidently shirked payment. The delay in payment of their share necessitated the issuing of an authoritative statement by the Assembly that the main communities were by no means obliged to carry the whole burden.

III

Why was the burden so great that the leading communities found it difficult to carry it alone, and why within their jurisdiction the did *Kehillot* engage in disputes over the distribution of these payments? An answer to these questions is given in the assembly's resolution of 1628, which contains more detailed instructions relating to the steps which the *shtadlanim* were to take at the *Sejmik*. There, we read:

Three or four weeks before the local *Sejmik* convenes, the leaders of the Assembly in each of the greater communities should send out written requests to the men living in the vicinity of the *Sejmik* and alert them that, God forbid, nothing new be passed and that they prevent any harm that can still be prevented. They must give presents to the deputies who will be elected to the *Sejm* and request that they be favorable towards us at the *Sejm*.[10]

Hence the most important item in the "election fund" of the Jews of pre-partition Poland: "presents." This was in fact the only way in which anything was achieved. If what was essentially wanted was to favorably dispose the deputies or other dignitaries in old Poland toward a particular matter, then the simplest and most reliable way of bringing this about was through presents. This argument was persuasive and therefore in permanent use in Poland, with a tendency to increase in weight and volume.

In 1633, a settlement concerning financial matters was reached between the *Vaad Arba Aratzot* and the Assembly of Lithuanian Communities. The verdict rendered[11] referred to the *Vaad*'s claim for partial reimbursement of the costs connected with "presents for the deputies." The Council of Four Lands lost this claim for a very simple reason, "...for they also [referring to the Assembly of Lithuanian Communities] give to the Lithuanian deputies." Apparently this was also the justification given for dismissing the claim that the Lithuanian *Vaad* should partake in buying presents for the Speaker. The *Vaad Arba Aratzot* obviously would not have made a claim if only a small amount of money were involved.

Apart from presents to the deputies, huge sums of money were needed for gifts to the participants in local *Sejmiki*. As already mentioned, the stipulations in the instructions drawn up prior to the elections in old Poland played a very significant role. Therefore, the creation of a favorable mood in the *Sejmik* was imperative. This was neither easy nor cheap.

Record books of the Jewish communities from various parts of Poland explicitly attest to the dimensions of the "local *Sejmik* expenses." We cannot supply the exact amounts. But E.N. Frenk, in his book *Ha-ironim v'ha-Yehudim b'Polin* (Urban Dwellers and Jews in Poland),[12] has reprinted excerpts from the *Pinkas* of Opatów. Among them are several items such as: "For the Speaker," "for the Deputy Speaker," "for the secretary and two deputies," "for the Speaker's servants," "for the defender in the commission." In each case a sum is specified. Several items further on in the list provide an ample quantity of names of people generously rewarded, all partici-pants of the local assembly.[13] This is how the mood before the election was formed.

Materials from the Poznań *Kehilla* supply several character-istic figures. Recorded in one protocol book under the date 1646 is an expense for the "*Sejm* and *Sejmik*" which amounted to the considerable sum of 1500 Polish złoty.[14] This refers to the *Sejmik* in Środa, which in the year 1646 obviously required such a sizable sum. The *Sejm*'s share of this amount probably consisted of the value of the presents that the deputies elected to the *Sejm* had received.

The expenses of 1646, however, were far exceeded by the "*Sejmik* costs" of 1688. This was spent mostly on pushing a decision of great importance through the *Sejmik* in Środa: abandoning the per capita tax, which had been increased by the constitution of the *Sejm* by 50,000 złoty, in exchange for the Jews' exemption from payment of the *podymne* (real estate) tax. The note in the *Pinkas* of Poznań states:

> All of the representatives (*shtadlanim*) both from our commun-ity and the surrounding districts have carried out heroic efforts in order that the matter of an increase in the per capita tax be dismissed. God has helped them, their efforts have been rewarded by a favorable result, and the increase in the per capita tax has been abandoned. However, the good deed by the *Sejmik* was not complete; they have decided to levy forty-five

quotas of the *podymne* tax—and no amount of treasures could induce them to abandon this tax...."[15]

And so it cost "treasures" at that time to avert one danger, even as they were falling into another. The note of 1688 does not reveal what kind of treasures these were. We learn of the amount only accidentally from a later note of 1715.[16] At this time a dispute had arisen between the community of Poznań and the nearby community of Swarzędz, which had been obliged to raise ten percent of all costs of this kind but had not contributed in any way to the expenses for the memorable *Sejmik* of 1688 in Środa. We learn from the complaint that the claim came to 800 Polish złoty; thus the entire expense reached the amount of 8000 Polish złoty.

At the *Sejmiks*, huge sums of money were thrown about. This is clearly expressed in the resolution of the Assembly of Lithuanian Communities, held in Sielec, in the year 1670:

> Insofar as the expenses for the *Sejmiki* of the leading communities are concerned, taking into consideration that there are large [Jewish] concentrations there and that the nobility is greedy for Jewish money, this decision was passed: [the expense] up to 150 Polish złoty will be paid by the Assembly (*Vaad*) verifiable under the threat of anathema, whereas in the [small] settlements up to 30 Lithuanian sixty-grosh-coins, also under the threat of anathema. Every community and settlement, however, is obliged to meet the expense and endeavor in the interest of the country [that is, the Jewish community as a whole], in order that nothing suspicious and dangerous be recommended in the instructions.[17]

Precisely this point, "the nobility is greedy for Jewish money," caused the "election fund" of Polish Jews to be indeed formidable. It resulted in a saying which was popular throughout Poland: "He who speaks well of the Jews has already been bribed; he who speaks ill of them only wishes to be bribed."[18]

As is apparent, there was an ample number of both. The result was a constant increase in the expenditure and in the *Hotzaot Sejmiks.*

IV

It is interesting to note that during a relatively short period of time, less then fifty years, the Assembly of Lithuanian Jewish Communities altered its position several times regarding the source from which the *Sejmiki* expenses had to be covered.

In the resolution quoted above, adopted at the first organizational meeting in Brześć in 1623, the entire financial burden connected with the search for influences at the *Sejmiki* was placed on the larger communities. Concerning the funding of presents for the elected deputies as opposed to gifts for other dignitaries and the King, the principle was reiterated in the year 1628:

> The presents which the three main communities give to the dignitaries who travel when a general *Sejm* is announced and who are in the vicinity of the King, through whom it is possible to reach a favorable result for the good of the Jewish community, will be paid by the whole country, that is, the Assembly or the *Vaad*; whereas presents for the deputies to the general *Sejm* and dignitaries elected deputies in the respective districts will be covered by the community itself and its affiliated environs.[19]

The communities were to be aided by their "affiliated environs." The whole of Jewry, represented by the Assembly of the communities, did not want to participate in "election costs." Naturally, in the interests of the community as a whole, it was necessary to recommend that in spite of this the *Sejmiki* always be covered. It is not surprising, that due to a lack of greater means, apathy developed among the local activists. Such a recommendation on the part of the Assembly, as we have already seen, was in fact issued. However, this position of the Assembly of Communities was impossible to maintain. The burden was too heavy for the communities to cope with alone, and the smaller ones could not be forced to share in these expenses. Evidently, the strongly worded recommendation of 1623 was not sufficient. Even the new supplementary decision of 1627, which we have quoted above, did not work. The decision reminded the smaller communities, to no avail, that they were obliged to come to the aid of their "central" authorities. And so, activity concerning the *Sejmiki* elections slowed down.

Similar conditions also prevailed in the Kingdom, where the "Council of Four Lands" refused to bear the expenses of the *Sejmiki* costs. A note dating from 1627 relates:

> The communities and surrounding districts wanted to include the recent cost of the *Sejmik* in the account made at the fair but the Elders of the Council from Wołyn did not want to accept this in the account. Because of this, we have postponed the matter until the next fair in February, when the lands [The Council of Four Lands] will settle the matter between the leaders of the three lands and the leaders of Wołyn. Similarly, the Elders of Poznań wanted to add the expense of two previous *Sejmiki* to this account in the amount of 130 Polish złoty, which already includes the *Sejmik* held recently, and this too we have postponed until the February fair of 1628...[20]

Thus, despite the fact that a majority of Elders in the "Council of Four Lands" wished to release the individual main communities from bearing the entire burden, the question remained open until 1628. The sources do not reveal whether it was decided at this time. We have more precise information from Lithuania. In 1634, it was decided to open the treasury of the *Vaad* in order to revive activity at the *Sejmiki*.

This was the first reversal of policy. Full powers were then granted to the head of the community of Wilno to lay out the Assembly's funds for *Sejmiki* expenses in urgent cases without consulting the neighboring communities (should the expenses not exceed the sum of fifty Lithuanian sixty-grosh-coins), but otherwise with the prior consent of the nearby *Kehillot* (Nieś-wież, Słonim, and Nowogródek). Later the following was added:

> The *Sejmiki* expenses, which will arise in those places where they are held, will be included in the *Vaad*'s account of expenses.[21]

In this way, the principle adopted in 1627, that the main communities together with their surrounding areas were to bear the burden of payments to the *Sejmiki*, collapsed.

The principle was completely abandoned after another five years. In 1639 the following decision was taken:

> Expenses for the *Sejmiki* will be paid by the whole country [i.e., the treasury of the Assembly of Communities]. The surrounding areas are to accept the orders of the main communities.[22]

No clauses were added to this resolution, and the point was not even stressed that the individual communities would have the obligation to work on the *Sejmiki*. Such an addition would frankly have been altogether superfluous: when money was supplied by the *Vaad*, one could be sure that the work would be done. The final sentence concerning the responsibility of the surrounding communities "to accept the orders of the main communities" was added to strengthen the prestige of these main communities. One thing was certain: the local activists would always willingly follow orders if those orders did not involve additional expenses.

However, some financial disorders did seem to arise. The communities began to spend (or at least record on a debit account) huge sums on *Sejmiki* expenses. They intervened frequently, and their expenses formed a considerable item in the budget of the Assembly of Communities, the *Vaad Medinat Lita*. At a meeting in Chomsk in 1667, a statute containing regulations for all the "unforeseeable expenses" (*noladot*)[23] was adopted. The head of each main community was ordered to keep a separate book in which the respective intervenor or sexton would record all such expenses once a week, or at least once a month. Following this, he would have to take an oath to prove the veracity and honesty of all expenses. Specific registers from the outer cities located in the district of the main community were required to be sent every three months. The local rabbi's notation, stating that the proper oath had been administered, was required in the registers of expenses. The oath could not be vague, since it had to encompass all of the individual items. The register had to be entered into the main book "to know the exact nature of the business and the way in which it was carried out." When the statute was issued it was explicitly stipulated that "expenses for the *Sejmiki* should also be entered immediately into the main book."

Despite these controls and restrictions in making expenditures which were introduced by this decision of Chomsk, a limitation of credit for the work at the *Sejmiki* occurred shortly thereafter. This may have been caused by abuses. Perhaps the burden of expenses proved to be too heavy for the Assembly's treasury. In any case, in 1670, the Assembly of Lithuanian Communities in Sielec was forced to pass a resolution limiting the expenses for the *Sejmiki* to 150 Polish złoty and 30 Lithuanian sixty-grosh coins for the larger and smaller communities respectively. We have already quoted this resolution. If we take note of the reference to the "greediness" of Polish nobles, we would be inclined to accept the second interpretation (that the burden of the expenses was too great). At this meeting in Sielec a second resolution relating to this question had also been passed.[24] The statute of 1667 was reaffirmed in a stronger form, and every Elder was granted the right to veto expenses not registered in accordance with the statute and in the manner defined by the statute. In addition, it was announced that each Elder who departed from one of these conditions and accepted such expenses would be considered to be seizing public property and would be himself subject to punishment by the rabbis. What conclusion can we draw from this? We can probably infer that, because of past misappropriations, confidence in local intervenors had considerably declined.

It turns out that not only did considerable sums flow to the *Sejmiki* in the large communities, but even in the smallest localities activists shaped opinions in the *Sejmiki* at the expense of the Assembly's treasury. In order to put a stop to the squandering of public money the Assembly of Communities in Sielec made this decision in the year 1673:

> From the localities in which there is no permanent Jewish house of prayer, the Assembly will not accept expenses larger than twenty Polish złoty for the *Sejmiki*, even if the real expenses exceed this sum, and this is to be verified using the threat of a *Herem*.[25]

We see that even in tiny localities, in which there were practically no Jews, large amounts were spent on the *Sejmiki* or on their individual participants. It was necessary to slow down the flow of this river. The Assembly of Lithuanian Communities closed the lid to its cashbox slightly, and that step proved sufficient.

V

Apart from the question of who took money from the Jews during the elections to the *Sejm* in pre-partition Poland, another matter is also relevant to our discussion. Who gave this money? That is, who delivered it into the proper hands? This was the task of the *shtadlan*, the official Jewish representative to the authorities.

It is impossible to discuss Polish-Jewish relations in pre-partition Poland without mentioning the *shtadlan*. On the one hand, he was the channel through which the needs of Jews were made known to the outside world; on the other hand, he communicated to the Jews what the government stewards had in store for them. He was the individual who, in the name of the Jews, established contact with Polish officials and acted on the outside for Jewish causes. He protected Jewish interests at the *Sejmiki*. He served the local community, but there was of course a chief *shtadlan* who was in charge of matters on a higher level.

Already there is mention of a *shtadlan* in the Brześć resolution of 1623. A fine of 100 złoty was placed on the communities which did not appoint *shtadlanim* (plural form of *shtadlan*) at the *Sejmiki*. Their task, roughly defined, was to investigate and make sure that nothing would arise which could be a "painful thorn" for the Jews. Hence they were to work against imminent danger and to find the means to get the votes of the assembled *szlachta*.

In a majority of cases, the *shtadlan* was very professional. Intervention in Poland required firstrate cunning and endurance. For this reason, the only persons able to undertake this effectively were men who consistently maintained contact with the officials and dignitaries. Here it is necessary to differentiate between the two categories of *shtadlanim*: those of the lower level, who simultaneously performed the functions of provincial sextons, and those of the higher level, who represented the Jews at the *Sejm*.

Shtadlanim delegated by the community to work at the *Sejm* played a prominent role in Jewish life. There were usually several from the *Korona* (Poland proper) and several from Lithuania. At the Assembly of Lithuanian Communities in Prużany in 1628, three *shtadlanim* were elected to work on the

Sejm: Shaya of Wilno, Beyrach of Brześć, and Mordecai of Łomża. Each chief community had to delegate one additional *shtadlan*. Together, the Lithuanian delegation at the *Sejm* consisted of six people. It was decided that two of the *shtadlanim* had to appear at the session of the *Sejm* on the first day, while the third could appear slightly later, but without great delay.[26] We encounter Mordecai of Łomża four years later, in 1633, as a Jewish representative at the *Sejm*, when a new King had to be elected after the death of Zygmunt III. At that time the Assembly of Lithuanian Communities, at its session in Sielec, had also decided that all three main communities send ⸺⸺⸺ the cost of the Assembly. These would be men "who possess the power and weight to stand in the King's palace." This was to be in addition to the *shtadlanim*, Zelman and Mordecai of Łomża. The community in Mińsk was also to send a personal delegate and be reimbursed for half the cost. Unclear in this decision is the figure of Zelman the *shtadlan*, who is apparently identical with Zelman the sexton, and who had participated on many occasions in earlier sessions of the Assembly of Lithuanian Communities.[28]

Upon the election of a general *shtadlan*, a document was drawn up in which his rights and duties were specified. In a document, signed in Słuck on the 24th of *Tamuz* 5521 (1761) by all the rabbis and elders of the five main communities, we read:

> We have found the one whom our souls have been longing for, a wise and reasonable man, from whose mouth flows myrrh...who has the power and authority to stand in the palace of the King and his dignitaries, in order to express ideas in a beautiful and eloquent language, whose mouth and heart are equally sincere....
>
> And we have reached an absolute accord, to have this outstanding fellow-believer, Hayim, son of Joseph, elected *shtadlan*, in order that he be God's delegate and our delegate, intercessor and defender for all the lands of Lithuania. Let his eyes

be open to all the needs of our country, that he may raise its defense before His Majesty the King and the dignitaries of Poland.

And we have appointed him, to great fortune, from the date given below for a period of three years under the following conditions: his salary will constitute one-half grosz from every złoty of the per capita tax, according to the tariffs.... His permanent place of residence is to be solely in the city of Wilno. At the commencement of the tribunals, the aforementioned Mr. Hayim, is to remain in Wilno for at least six weeks without interruption. He is not permitted to stray from there during this period of time to any other locality....

It is explicitly stipulated that, during the three-year period when Mr. Hayim will be living in Wilno, he will be exempt from all taxes collected and levied in Wilno, even from the meat *krupka* [tax]. Similarly, the Elders of Wilno will give to Mr. Hayim a home deserving of his dignity....[29]

In this document, the relationship of the *shtadlan* to his electors—i.e., to the five main communities as well as to other Jewish communities—is exactly stipulated. His responsibility was to represent their interests at the *Sejm* and before the Tribunal, as well as to protect their interests before the noblemen and clergy. From the descriptions and titles in the introduction it is clear that a great deal of weight was attached to his function and personality. This was also implicit in the decision of the Assembly of Lithuanian Communities adopted in Chomsk in 1691 regarding the personal qualifications of the *shtadlanim*. It was then decided that among the delegates to the *Sejm* "there should be at least two *shtadlanim* able to stand in the palace of the King and his dignitaries, and the rest should be wise, reasonable, and men of intellect."[30]

The placing of so great a demand upon the *shtadlanim* was the result of great concern for the good of the community, which a poorly chosen spokesman could easily jeopardize. This same motive also brought about a decision to exclude all outside persons from establishing contact with deputies or other dignitaries. A "monopoly" was created in this respect for the *shtadlanim* and communal delegates—a monopoly upon intervening or even appearing at the *Sejm*. This decision of the Lithuanian *Vaad* was taken in 1623 and 1662.

According to the first decision,[31] it would be necessary to punish "physically and financially" anyone present at the *Sejm* without the written authorization of his respective parent community. All possible obstacles had to be created so as to prevent him from appearing at the *Sejm*. If in spite of this an unauthorized intervenor should appear at the *Sejm* and suffer some misfortune there, he would be left to his own destiny. The *shtadlanim* in the *Sejm* had, in fact, the duty to warn him on the spot and later to inform the respective community, so that he may be excommunicated (put into *Herem*).

According to the second decision,[32] which alluded to a growing number of illegal and very detrimental interventions, the communities' delegates at the *Sejm* were to immediately punish and persecute uninvited guests. This duty was passed on later to the Elders of the main communities, who would be liable to the same punishment if they did not act properly. In every parent community it was required that announcements be made at least two or three times in the synagogue thirty days before the convening of the *Sejm* stating that no one was to arrive at the *Sejm* without the written permission of the main community's Elders.

VI

An additional concern of the Assembly of the Lithuanian Communities was the question of traveling costs and allowances for the *shtadlanim* and delegates attending *Sejm* sessions.

What we have observed with regard to the *shtadlanim* at the *Sejmiki* (based on regulations of 1667, 1670, and 1673) was repeated with regard to the *shtadlanim* to the *Sejm*. Aside from compensation which the *shtadlanim* received as professional functionaries—either as a certain percentage of the per capita tax in a lump sum, or in the form of an annual salary[33]—they received reimbursement for their travel costs. Delegates of the communities did not receive a permanent salary, and because of this they were all the more entitled to a travel allowance. The Assembly of Communities certainly concerned itself with the financial aspects of the interventions at the *Sejm*. In addition to the strict directives which it repeatedly issued to all communities and settlements concerning the collection of specified amounts[34] before each session of the *Sejm*, the Assembly also showed interest in the maintenance of the *shtadlanim*. For example, at its (last) session in Słuck in 1761, the *Vaad* decided that a permanent salary must be provided for the *shtadlanim* so that they need not collect anything for themselves.[35] But the question of allowances created greater difficulties for the *Vaad*.

In 1670 a decision was made at the *Vaad* meeting in Sielec that "at every *Sejm* session two delegates of the communities are to attend, and the head of the *Kehilla* of Brześć should be present at least at the opening of the *Sejm*."[36] Three years later, in 1673, the following compensation was provided for these delegates, the number of whom had increased in the meantime:

> To the *Sejm* in Warsaw, one senior from each of the four main communities is to attend. For his expenses the senior of Wilno will be given 150 Polish złoty as compensation for his costs and work. Each of the remaining three is to receive only 30 Lithuanian sixty-grosh coins for his work, not more. This quota will be accepted in the accounting at the next session as "unforeseeable expenses" (*noladoth*). If the respective community gives him more for his work, this excess amount will be covered by the community. Twenty Lithuanian sixty-grosh coins are to be given to the country's *shtadlan*.[37]

In this way, a lump-sum compensation was granted to the delegates, with the stipulation that one of them (from Wilno) should receive much more than the others as leader. For all the delegates, this compensation had the character of reimbursement for costs as well as payment for work. The *shtadlan* was to receive the least, barely twenty Lithuanian sixty-grosh coins. Striking here is the unusually rapid growth of the influence exerted by the *Kehilla* of Wilno, which had been authorized to pay the highest compensation for its delegate and to charge this expense to the Assembly. In 1652, only twenty-one years earlier, the *Kehilla* of Wilno had just obtained the right to send its *shtadlan* to Warsaw for the *Sejm*'s session, and at its own expense.[38] Could Wilno have already developed a dominating position in such a short period of time?[?] It seems that the privilege for Wilno was rather the result of a temporary situation—perhaps a concession for other services Wilno had offered to the remaining communities. This is best evidenced by further developments in this matter.

In 1679, the Assembly of Communities in Chomsk again regulated the problem of travel allowances for the delegates attending the *Sejm*. Two decisions were made and entered one after the other in the book of protocols. The first reads:

> For the Warsaw expenses, and for every *Sejm* and commission, each senior shall be paid only twenty Polish złoty per week for his travels both to Warsaw in Poland and to the Lithuanian *Sejm*. It is not necessary to give him more than the above amount, counting from the day he sets off on his journey until his return; and it is not permitted to accept the expenses of the cook and servants, as well as of the aides. Also, for his work he is to be given nothing in any way except reimbursement of expenses for the transportation there and back, and nothing more.[39]

The second decision states:

> One Elder from each of the main communities should go to the *Sejm* session in Warsaw, to the session held in Grodno, and

to the commission. No more than fifty Polish złoty should be given to the Elder of this community for work and food supplies, i.e., to the senior Elder of the community at the commission. But at the general *Sejm*, the Elder should be given thirty Lithuanian sixty-grosh coins, wherever the *Sejm* is being held.[40]

These two decisions are, of course, in contradiction with one another. Furthermore, they are recorded in broken Hebrew, making it difficult to decipher their contents. How then can they be reconciled? Let us assume that the first decision pertains to the allowance paid to the senior Elders for their journeys to Warsaw—not for visits to the *Sejm* (in Warsaw), but rather for coincidental interventions, therefore the first decision refers not to the *Sejm*, but to the Jewish *Vaad*, and to the joint meetings of Jewish delegates from Poland and Lithuania (which were sometimes held). Supporting this is the insertion in this decision (between the words "Warsaw expenses" and "for every *Sejm*") of the conjunction "*and*," delimiting the Warsaw expenses from expenses concerning the *Sejm*. For this reason, the number of delegates was also not fixed, since it was not possible to determine the number in advance, not knowing for what purpose they would set off on their journey and how many would be necessary. For a similar reason, the compensation was not defined in a lump sum, for it was impossible to predict how long the journey would last. Thus, the allowance was granted per week. A further conclusion is that it was not permitted to pay compensation for the work because these trips were considered the responsibility of the Elders and only their actual expenses had to be reimbursed.[41]

The second decision refers very clearly to the general *Sejm*, which, in accordance with one line in the decision (from the year 1673), was convened occasionally (every third *Sejm*) in Grodno.[42] Here the delegates received compensation in a lump sum in which payment for work was also included. The allowances of the representatives of Brześć, Grodno, and Pińsk had not been reduced; only the valuable privilege of the Wilno delegate was lost, and he was suddenly put on equal footing with his remaining colleagues. Why? Evidently because the other communities no longer depended on Wilno, and this also affected the question of travel allowances.

The community of Wilno did not, however, agree to such a reduction. The sources do not reveal in what way its dissatisfaction manifested itself—whether a dispute broke out with the Assembly or whether it simply did not recognize the decision of 1679. But from 1691 we have a note stating:

During the Assembly it is not necessary to accept the expenses of the delegates to the general *Sejm* in an amount larger than 150 Polish złoty, which has to be stated under the threat of anathema (*Herem*); this applies only to delegates from the main communities and not from the settlements.[42A]

What conclusion can we draw from all this? That the delegate of Wilno kept his travel allowance in the full amount fixed in 1670. The effect of the reduction decided upon in 1679 was solely to increase the travel allowance of the delegates of the remaining communities.

It is possible that this entire episode had a slightly different background. The delegates from Brześć, Grodno, and Pińsk felt wronged in receiving only 30 Lithuanian sixty-grosh coins and wanted to exert pressure on the community of Wilno in order that their allowance be raised to 150 Polish złoty. They did not succeed immediately. They therefore seized the last remaining effective option: they lowered the travel allowance of the Wilno delegate to 30 Lithuanian sixty-grosh coins as well. The effect was instantaneous. Without any opposition, and by quiet understanding, *all* the allowances were raised to the level demanded by the other communities.

VII

Against the background of *Sejm* expenses and travel allowances of the *shtadlanim*, conflicts broke out between the Jews of Poland and those of Lithuania. Because of the inflated expenses, the Lithuanian *Vaad* delayed sending its *shtadlanim* to the general Sejm. The whole burden and costs of the work then fell on the shoulders of the delegates sent by the *Vaad Arba Aratzot* (Council of Four Lands). All expenses were scrupulously recorded and a bill was presented to the Lithuanian *Vaad* several times thereafter with a request that it pay its share. The Lithuanians continually refused. As time progressed, the claims of the Jews from Poland concerning the Lithuanian Assembly's participation in the expenses for the *Sejm* work grew to larger proportions. Reconciliation became impossible and the conflict had to be settled by a court of rabbis.

In 1633, a rabbinic court had settled the claim of the *Vaad Arba Aratzot* against the Lithuanian Assembly, in which a claim for participation in the costs of presents given to the deputies and the Speaker was also included. We have already noted above that the *Vaad Arba Aratzot*'s claim was dismissed. This did not, however, deter the Polish leaders from submitting a similar claim to the rabbinic court sitting in session in Łęczna in 1681. It called for "participation in the payment of a salary for the *shtadlan* of the Council of Four Lands in Warsaw and for the expenses at the Warsaw *Sejm*, as well as for presents for His Majesty the King and his dignitaries at the *Sejm*, and for the prevention of calamities in Warsaw both at and outside the *Sejm*."[43] In addition, the *Vaad Arba Aratzot* lodged a number of other claims. The Lithuanian representatives denied any obligation on their part to share in these and other expenses; on the contrary they brought a counterclaim against the Council of Four Lands concerning its duty to participate in expenses incurred in repelling the dangers which threatened the whole community in Lithuanian territory.

The court of rabbis settled all the claims of the Polish *Vaad* together, giving it the choice of asking from the Lithuanian Assembly either one-fourteenth of the total sum of costs or a lump sum of 9,000 Polish złoty. Several possibilities for paying in installments were noted. It was clearly stipulated that the claim concerning sharing the salary of the *shtadlan* was already covered, while nothing had been stipulated with regard to expenses for the *Sejm*, "since they too [the Lithuanian Jews] have a *Sejm* in Grodno."[44]

As a result, the partnership between the Jews of Poland and the Lithuanian Jews was completely broken. The verdict reads:[45]

At all the *Sejm* sessions in Warsaw or in any other locality in Poland or Lithuania, the senior Elders of Poland will from now on give separately from their treasury gifts to His Majesty the King and to the State dignitaries on behalf of the Four Polish Lands; also to the King's servants, dignitaries, and servants of the dignitaries, called *renerlech*,[46] from Poland, the Polish Elders will give from their treasury; and to His Majesty and State dignitaries as well as their servants and *renerlech* as above, in Lithuania, the Lithuanian senior Elders will give from their treasury, for themselves; each is to give from his own treasury to his dignitaries.

The principle of complete separation of the interventions in Poland and Lithuania was maintained in this verdict of 1681, even when Jews of Poland and Lithuania were trying to avert the most terrible calamities—for example, an expulsion of the entire Jewish community from the country. If this threat were made, for instance, on the Jews of Poland, they were to cover by themselves the cost of the necessary intervention, and the same would hold true for Lithuanian Jews if such a calamity were to threaten them. They were to help each other only in the following way: if the catastrophe concerned the Jews of Poland, the Lithuanian Jews had the duty to intervene on their behalf with respective Lithuanian authorities and this at their own cost; Jews of Poland were obliged to reciprocate in cases in which dignitaries of Poland might be favorably disposed toward the Lithuanian Jews. Both groups of Elders had the right to maintain control with regard to the interventions. This duty was, however, limited to events which threatened expulsion of all the Jews from the respective country.

Nevertheless, the cost of both the intervention and the maintenance of the *shtadlanim* was enormous. The question therefore arises: was it worth the price? Were the interventions at least effective? Notes in the book of protocols of the Lithuanian Assemblies indicate that the *shtadlanim*'s activity was intensive and spread the costs over many affairs. They were primarily active in the settlement of the *pogłówne* (per capita tax) and other taxes[47] and were usually quite absorbed by this topic. They also had the task, however, of bringing certain matters to the *Sejm*, which matters directly involved legislation.

The Assembly of Lithuanian Communities in Sielec decided therefore in 1655:

> The *shtadlanim* who attend the Warsaw *Sejm* are to make efforts that it should be written in the constitution [the law] that every dignitary and functionary be obliged to help in the collection from every community and settlement of all payments ordered by the Elders of their main communities, and also of arrears in payments.[48]

This was obviously an instruction commanding the *shtadlanim* to put legislation through the *Sejm* which would be applied only to the internal life of the Jewish communities. If this lay within their power and if they could bring about the passing of such laws, then they were richly deserving of their allowances.

And so the money of the *Vaad* did not go for naught.

Notes

[1] A. Mościcki and W. Dzwonkowski, *Parlament Rzeczypospolitej Polskiej* [Parliament of the Polish Republic], Warsaw, 1928, p. 15; see also Stanisław Kutrzeba, *Sejm Walny Dawnej Rzeczypospolitej Polskiej* [General Sejm of the Old Polish Republic], Warsaw (undated), p. 144.

[2] See also Stanisław Kutrzeba, *Sejm Walny Rzeczypospolitej Polskiej* [General Sejm of the Old Polish Republic], p. 110ff.

[3] *Opis obyczajów i zwyczajów za panowania Augusta III* [Description of customs and habits under the rule of August III], chapter X, 2: "O częstowa-niu i i initial va ai ii seinininwei ii [i ili iiie piiiiie iipais andi ai iini iiij hniiiv ai the Sejm]; quoted by Mościcki and Dzwonkowski, p. 13.

[4] Simon Dubnow, ed., *Pinkas Ha-Medina o Pinkas Vaad Ha-Kehilot Ha-Rashiyoth Bi-Mdinath Lita*, Berlin, 1925. We shall quote it later using the acronymic PML (Pinkas Mdinat Lita) with the Arabic numerals denoting the current number of the resolution.

[5] PML 10.

[6] *Akta Grodzkie i Ziemskie*, vol. XX, Nr. 210-4.

[7] *Ibid.*, vol. XX, Nr. 216.

[8] *Ibid.*, vol. XX, Nr. 200.

[9] PML 111.

[10] PML 147.

[11] Published in the PML Appendix, p. 278.

[12] Warsaw, 1921.

[13] E.N. Frenk, *Ha-ironim v'ha-Yehudim b'Polin*, Warsaw, 1921, p. 48.

[14] Louis Lewin, *Die Landessynode der grosspolnischen Judenschaft*, Frankfurt a.M., 1926, Nr. LII, p. 89.

[15]Louis Lewin, *Neue Materialien zur Geschichte der Vierlaendersynode*, Part II, Frankfurt a.M., 1906, Nr. LII, p. 30.

[16]*Ibid.*, p. 41, Nr. LXXV.

[17]PML 654.

[18]See Frenk, *Ha-ironim v'ha-Yehudim b'Polin*, Warsaw, 1921, p. 44.

[19]PML 162.

[20]Louis Lewin, *Neue Materialien zur Geschichte der Vierlaendersynode*, Part II, Nr. XVI, p. 14.

[21]PML 296.

[22]PML 369.

[23]PML 616.

[24]PML 652.

[25]PML 691.

[26]PML 206.

[27]PML 269.

[28]In PML 91 Zelman "*shames*" is mentioned; in 98, 126, 158, this same Zelman is called "Zelman the '*shtadlan*'."

[29]PML Appendix, pp. 301-302.

[30]PML 855.

[31]PML 39.

[32]PML 534.

[33]Zelman the *shtadlan* collected twenty-four Lithuanian sixty-grosh coins as an annual salary; PML 91.

[34] PML 441, 455, 486, 543.

[35] PML 1014.

[36] PML 636.

[37] PML 688.

[38] The verdict of the Rabbinic Tribunal in the matter of the conflict between Wilno and the Assembly of Lithuanian Communities, issued in Chomsk in 1652, is published in the PML Appendix, pp. 291-292.

[39] PML 760.

[40] PML 761.

[41] S. Dubnow believes this resolution to be in reference to the general *Sejm*; and therefore its entry in the index at the end of the book (PML p. 345) is *sub verbo Vaad Malchuth*. This index is however imprecise and cannot be relied upon.

[42] Stanisław Kutrzeba, *Sejm Walny dawnej Rzeczypospolitej Polskiej*, p. 70.

[43] PML Appendix, pp. 284-289.

[44] *Ibid.* p. 288.

[45] *Ibid.* p. 287.

[46] The origin of this word as well as its meaning is unclear. Harkavy believes that it means messengers carrying out the orders of the dignitaries; then it would originate from the German *Renner* (see Dubnow in the PML Appendix, p. 287, note 1). Also in the *Pinkas* of Opatów one can find in the registry of expenses the item "to the *renerlech* at the *Sejmiki* (Frenk, *Ha-ironim*, p. 48); what, however, did they do at the *Sejmiki*? Another item in the *Pinkas* of Opatów reads: "to the official for his expenses to Sandomierz to raise a protest against the robbery, that the *renerlech* had attacked houses" (Frenk, *ibid.*). As a result, these *renerlech* present a rather enigmatic picture. It should also be noted that in the rabbinic verdict of Łęczna it is possible to read the word *renerlech* also as *rendlech* or *rendelech* (Daleth instead of

Reish). This version, however, does not elucidate anything either.

[47]PML 2, 123, 1000.

[48]PML 518.

CHAPTER VII
History of an Old Controversy
in the Jewish Community of Lwów

In the 1750s, Lwów was rocked by a serious dispute. Jews fought in the streets and quarreled and insulted one another. Tempers flared, emotions were ignited, and finally it all ended up in a lengthy trial before the Lwów regional court. On one side were Yerakhmiel Moniszowicz and Zalman Pinhas Rabinowicz, representatives of the Lwów *Kehilla*, and on the opposite side none other than Hayim Cohen Rappaport, the chief rabbi of that city. Here is how it happened.[1]

I

One of the distinguished Jews in Lwów in the first half of the eighteenth century was Hirsh Koziner—a wealthy man and a leader of the Jewish community. His high reputation is confirmed by the inscription on his tombstone—that whenever Jews needed someone to mediate for them with the nobility, he was ready to go and do so, especially if it had to do with helping a scholar. Men who were learned in the Torah were particularly dear to his heart. He brought up his own sons to be Torah scholars. Being one of the outstanding men in the city, he, together with the other *pernassim*, led the Lwów Jewish community with a firm hand.

In 1737 Hirsh Koziner died. The estate left for the children was not too large. The good friends of the deceased, the leaders of the Lwów Jewish community, began to look around for a means of livelihood for the sons who, as previously mentioned, were Jewish scholars. For one son they found an honorable post: Leibush Koziner (also called Leibush Mieses) became a member of the Lwów *Bet Din*.

Hayim Cohen Rappaport had just been appointed rabbi; he had come from Słuck to take over the post which, twenty-two years earlier, had been assigned to his father, the Lublin rabbi, Simcha Rappaport. In 1717, on his way from Lublin to Lwów, he had suddenly taken ill and died.

Hirsh Koziner left another son, Moses, who also called himself Mieses and was no less learned than his brother. In addition, he was a cabalist. Though he was greatly respected in Lwów, no suitable position could be found for him, and since his brother was a member of the *Bet Din*, it was impossible for him to serve on that body. This state of affairs continued until 1753, when Moses was almost forty years old. And it was on account of him that the great controversy erupted.

II

The dispute arose over the position of *Rosh Yeshiva* (head of a yeshiva). Several distinguished scholars had held that post. Rabbi Joshua Falk (c. 1550-1614), the renowned author of *Sepher Meirat Enayim*, began the line of the Lwów heads of yeshiva, and following him came a long line of great scholars. Sometimes the chief rabbi himself was also the official head of the yeshiva, but usually the positions were kept separate. That was the case in the days of Rabbi Hayim Cohen Rappaport. He was not the head of the yeshiva; because of his full schedule of duties he could not have handled the additional responsibility.[2]

The leadership of the *Kehilla* contemplated, in 1753, offering Rabbi Moses Mieses the position of *Rosh Yeshiva*.[3] Whether the position was unfilled at that time or whether a new yeshiva was established for Rabbi Moses is not clear. Suffice it to say that those who had the power and the decision-making function in the community, remembering the old *parnas* Hirsh Kozhner, wanted his son to take over the post. Perhaps no one would have opposed this, because Moses Mieses was well qualified to be the head of a yeshiva. It so happened, however, that Rabbi Hayim Cohen Rappaport, the Lwów chief rabbi, launched a strong campaign in opposition to that decision.

He did it for the simple reason that he himself had a son whom he wanted to see in that post. Aryeh Leib Rappaport was the name of the rabbi's oldest son, and he was a Talmudic scholar who had worked at his father's side in the *Bet Din* for more than ten years.[4] In the Council of the Four Lands he had been active since 1742. His own son, still a very young man, was already rabbi in Kałusz.[5]

The struggle flared up immediately. Supporters were not lacking on either side, nor were opponents in short supply. Very soon two strong parties developed—a "Mieses party" and a "Rappaport party." Each one entered the fray with its own pack of arguments. The Rappaport party argued: "It is unheard-of insolence to oppose the will of the community's religious leader, whose son is a learned scholar himself." Along with that they described the virtues of Rabbi Leibush: "He has a good reputation, he feels at home with the Lwów rabbinate, many people have turned to him already for approval of their books, he stems from an old and honored family." The opposition, for their part, enthusiastically sang the praises of Moses Mieses and enumerated the many services his father had performed for the city.

The matter did not end there, however. Each side not only praised its own candidate but insulted the opposing one. They hurled fire and brimstone, and slung mud at each other. The whole city went topsy-turvy. The struggle grew more and more personal and became an open war between the rabbi and the obdurate leaders of the community.

III

Rabbi Hayim Cohen Rappaport, who was now drawn into this bitter conflict, was not a rabbi to keep his distance from the internal life of the community. It was no surprise that in 1753 he took up the cudgels for his son; on the contrary, he always intervened in such matters. Soon after he had assumed the post of rabbi, elections were held in Lwów, and he had taken an active part in them, helping to elect his candidates. In general he made his voice heard in all communal matters, and this may be the reason he had many enemies.

Due to these enemies, the prosecutor Ulanowski, in 1743, drew up an indictment in the regional court charging that the rabbi of the Lwów region was an out-and-out revolutionary; that in the elections he put into office community leaders who themselves paid no taxes; that he issued verdicts and permitted no appeals to the regional court; that he violated the long-standing *Kehilla* constitution; that he sought bribes, bought up high officials, etc.

Ulanowski's indictment of 1743 never reached trial, however, probably because Rabbi Rappaport had many friends and protectors among the Polish nobility, especially among the government officials. Virtual autocrats (in that period of Poland's decline), they did whatever they pleased, and they were able to prevent his actual prosecution on these charges.

Nevertheless, he had plenty of trouble. In 1747 a Lwów Jew named Israel Peysis accused him of issuing an incorrect ruling in a *Din Torah*. The relevant document is harsh testimony to the low moral standing of some Lwów Jews of that time. The plaintiff suspected the rabbi of having been "bought" by the other side and therefore of having ruled unjustly. Further, the rabbi was charged with excommunicating the accuser's father, David Peysis, because the latter dared to criticize the rabbi after he rendered his false decision.

A similar episode took place in the critical year 1753, and this too had a bearing on the great dispute over the post of a *Rosh Yeshiva* in Lwów. This story is not found in any official documents; it is told by an objective observer, with no ulterior motive. But perhaps that gives it even more credibility. Ber Birkenthal tells the story in his memoirs (p. 33).

Around 1753 a wealthy Jew named Aaron died in Komarno, leaving his estate to his sons. Their brother-in-law, Samuel of Kałusz, claimed half the inheritance of one of the sons,[6] with the value of 40,000 złoty. The heirs argued that the note was false, that the entire estate would not cover that sum. This matter was brought to a *Din Torah* before Rabbi Hayim Cohen Rappaport and his *Bet Din*. After lengthy negotiations they ruled that Samuel must swear in a synagogue that his claim was a true one, and that he must do so in the presence of his wife, the sister of the heirs, and that she must say amen. Only then would the 40,000 złoty be paid to him. Both sides were given written copies of this decision.

The wife, however, refused to come to the synagogue and say "amen" to her husband's oath, because she did not wish to act against her brothers. So there was no alternative but to reach a compromise, selecting arbiters and going to the rabbi of Lwów for a new decision—which is what they did. This time the ruling was that Samuel was to receive 10,000 złoty without taking an oath. The rabbi took the arbitration fees and wrote down the new decision.

Samuel deeply resented the loss of 30,000 złoty, however. Even more resentful was his father, a leading Kałusz citizen named Yacov, who, as he thought about the matter, was struck by an idea. Taking with him copies of both decisions, he went to see the influential Commissar Cieszkowski, who happened to be in Kałusz at the time. Cieszkowski was the right-hand man of the Lwów *voievode* Czartoryski and the manager of his estates.

Yacov said to him: "Here are two decisions of Rabbi Hayim of Lwów. One is exactly the opposite of the other. For the first one, my son gave him forty złoty. For the second, the other side paid him. Absolutely for no other reason my son lost the amount of 30,000 złoty." And he concluded with horrendous accusations against Rabbi Hayim Cohen Rappaport.

Yacov's story made Cieszkowski very angry. He immediately summoned the young rabbi of Kałusz, Hayim Cohen's grandson and a son of Leibush Rappaport, who had been the center of the Lwów controversy, and he told him:

"Do you see what your grandfather did? First he took a bribe of forty złoty from one side and rendered a decision. Then he took more money from the other side and rendered the opposite decision! You'd better let him know that, just as I have been a good friend of his up until now and have spoken well of him to the *voievode*, so will I now be after him for all his wrongdoing. Before I come to Lwów he'd better move as far away as possible from there, otherwise he'll never get out of this mess without severe punishment. Tell him also that he'd better not wait until I come to Lwów, because if I ever get my hands on him he'll suffer the punishment that a corrupt judge deserves!"

The young Kałusz rabbi left, filled with dismay, and sent a messenger to his grandfather at once. The messenger arrived in Lwów just at the time the controversy over the post of *Rosh Yeshiva* was in full swing.

IV

One can imagine what effect this news must have had on Rabbi Hayim Cohen Rappaport. He did not have much time. The issue had to be explained to the Commissar as soon as possible, so that he would not intervene. The rabbi called upon Ber of Bolechów to compose a detailed report in Polish concerning the inheritance trial at Komarno. A special messenger was hired to find Cieszkowski and deliver the report into his hand. The messenger did find him somewhere in Brzezany and eventually the matter was explained to his satisfaction.

In the meantime, however, Rabbi Hayim Cohen Rappaport lived in terror. The community leaders were ruthless. As soon as they learned that something was amiss with the rabbi, they grew eager for battle and more zealous than ever in their desire to demonstrate their power. The relationships were already strained. Relationships between the *Kehilla* and the rabbi in Lwów were never very good in those days.

In November 1751 (around Kislev 5512), a special commission of the *voievode* issued a number of regulations intended to prevent the continuing conflicts between the rabbi and *Kehilla*, but these only resulted in utter confusion in all community affairs.

These regulations were confirmed by Prince Czartoryski in a special ordinance dated January 1, 1752, with the warning that they must be strictly enforced. Perhaps they would have been the basis of some agreement between the *Kehilla* and Rabbi Rappaport. But the controversy over the yeshiva directorship was so inflamed that it did not permit any improvement.

One fine morning, the bomb exploded. The community leaders met in the *Kehilla* office and elected Rabbi Moses Mieses to be the head of the yeshiva in the city. Despite the ensuing uproar he was immediately installed in the position. The *Kehilla* people rubbed their hands in glee—they had won!

But their joy lasted only one week. The affair had a tragic ending, one that nobody could have foreseen.

The "Rappaport party" did not sit by with folded arms. It went to work with all of its forces to annul the decision of the *Kehilla*, but it seemed that all such efforts, at least for the time being, would be to no avail. They went to great lengths, however, in their agitation against Rabbi Mieses. What gall he had, what insolence, to cause so much pain to the Rabbi, that great man and religious leader! All week long the campaign went on, until *Shabbat*. Rabbi Mieses was to deliver his first sermon. Friend and foe came to the synagogue. A crowd of curious people streamed in from every street. The synagogue was packed. Rabbi Moses Mieses stepped up on the *bimah* and...

What happened exactly is not known, because it is not written in the records, but we can imagine that the atmosphere in the synagogue was not very calm. Whether Rabbi Mieses in his sermon agitated the congregation still further or whether the propaganda of the Rappaport party had already excited them enough makes no difference. But certainly Rabbi Mieses himself derived no spiritual pleasure from that sermon. He went home in a state of dejection. The hostility of the congregation had left a deep wound in his heart. As he entered the house he suddenly felt ill and lost consciousness. He never regained it. Apparently his heart could not stand the anguish—and perhaps the disgrace—and simply broke.

Lwów was disconsolate.

V

Moses Mieses was only forty years old when the terrible misfortune happened. Both sides in the controversy felt guilt over his death, and everyone began wrestling with his own conscience. The Rappaports reproached themselves for having waged such a bitter fight. Perhaps they had gone too far. They recalled the piety of the deceased; they memorialized his virtues. Especially distressed was Rabbi Hayim Cohen Rappaport himself. But the *Kehilla* also reflected that perhaps this was a sign from on high that none other than Rabbi Leibush Rappaport should fill the post of *Rosh Yeshiva* in Lwów. For a short time this feeling of mutual regret was predominant. Rabbi Leibush took over the post, and for a while the controversy abated.

It was not a total peace, however; it was only a "ceasefire." The accumulated antagonisms were too deep to be overcome in a moment. The dispute between rabbi and community was soon renewed. The controversy flared up again. And this time it was not over something "trivial" —the position of head of the yeshiva—but over the rabbinate of the entire Lwów (then known as the "Ruthenian") region, and not over any son or relative of Hayim Cohen Rappaport, but over the rabbi himself. This is how it came about.

When Hayim Cohen Rappaport was accepted as rabbi of Lwów in 1741, he was granted a jurisdiction only over that city's local rabbinate; his authority did not extend over the entire region (with the possible exception of several small communities near Lwów). It seems that the entire region, was under the competence of another Lwów rabbi, the president of the *Bet Din* of the Lwów region, at that time Isaac Landau of Żółkiew, later rabbi of Cracow.[7]

For twelve years Rabbi Hayim Cohen Rappaport himself tried in vain to acquire the position of "General Rabbi." Perhaps he did not succeed because it could not be taken away from Isaac Landau, or perhaps the leaders of the community would simply not agree to it. Suffice it to say that, without their agreement, the *voievode*, Prince Czartoryski, had no wish to give him the jurisdiction of General Rabbi. And the "general rabbinate" was an extremely significant position: aside from status—all the rabbis in the region were subordinate to the chief rabbi—there were apparently some substantial revenues connected with the post.

In 1754, soon after the great controversy, Isaac Landau became rabbi of Cracow. The last obstacle to acquiring the general rabbinate thus disappeared. Now the time had come for Rabbi Hayim Cohen Rappaport to redouble his efforts with the regional *Kehilla* and with the *voievode*. This he accomplished with the aid of his protectors, of which he had quite a number. From the local Lwów *Kehilla*, however, he could not obtain any specific agreement. The old enmity was revived. The community leaders did not want the authority of the rabbi to be extended. Behind the scenes they campaigned against it. Nevertheless, this time Rabbi Rappaport turned out to be stronger than they—he was given the jurisdiction and officially recognized by the *voievode* as General Rabbi of the Region.[8]

Then, suddenly, the *Kehilla* leadership stopped paying him his salary.

VI

The result of this unprecedented event was a long trial before the Lwów regional court, in which Rabbi Hayim Cohen Rappaport sued the community for payment of his pension. This trial took place on December 24, 1754. According to the official transcript, the following appeared:

Plaintiff: Rabbi Hayim Cohen Rappaport, Chief Rabbi of the Lwów region.

Defendants: Yerakhmiel Moniszowitz, the Mayor of the "suburban" Jewish community, and Zalman Pinhas Rabinowicz, Mayor of the "town" community, in their own names and in the name of their respective communities. Also: the prosecutor of the regional court and a certain Israel Józefowicz, tenant of the community taxes.

The court first heard the arguments of the plaintiff, who offered in evidence the official authorization which he had received from the *voievode* that same year. He explained that, since the community and its treasurer were not paying him the salary due him under the authorization, he therefore requested the court to grant him his salary plus the interest on the amount due.

The community representatives offered in evidence a document written in Yiddish, which was translated into Polish. It had been signed by Rabbi Rappaport and dated January 23, 1753. The document read:

> I, the undersigned rabbi, do hereby swear under oath that
> ⟨illegible⟩
> will not deviate from them one iota, as though they had been handed down at Mount Sinai.

Then came the following ten points:

1. That he must obey the ruling of the prince, commissars issued in November 1751, and must not permit any weddings to be held unless the couple pay the *Kehilla* tax. (The document actually says 1752, but this must be an error, because the relevant regulation was issued November 2, 1751.)

2. That if he is appointed General Rabbi by the *voievode*, he will not accept any salary from the Lwów community.

3. That he must not sit on the *Bet Din* with a relative. (Perhaps this war directed at Leibush Rappaport, who had been active—probably unofficially—in the *Bet Din* for approximately ten years.)

4. That he must immediately turn over the to *Kehilla* all papers which have anything to do with him, even before the *voievode* signs the authorization.

5. That he must return all documents which belong to the city of Lwów as well as all books which belong to the Lwów Jewish community.

6. That he must make available all the documents in any important community matters which were deposited with him.

7. That if he receives the authorization from the *voievode*, he

must not accept it for a period longer than the community agrees to, and that thereafter it is null and void.

8. That he must not include in the new Lwów authorization any privileges other than those that were in the previous one, and that he swears to this unequivocally.

9. That he will henceforth not have any claims against the community, because he has already received everything owed to him as rabbi.

10. That if other documents or papers appear which can be useful to the *Kehilla*, he will turn them over.

Both of the mayors thought that by producing for the court a document which stated all this clearly they would certainly win the case. They relied particularly on Point 2, which stated specifically, "If I become General Rabbi and receive authorization from *Kehilla* that I alone shall be the rabbi over all of the Ruthenian region and I will receive the other half of the pension in the Lwów region, then I shall not receive any salary from the Lwów *Kehilla*."

And then came the decision. The Lwów Jewish community must pay the rabbi, without interest, the entire sum withheld, retroactively and in the future.

Thus the conflict ended with a total victory for Rabbi Hayim Cohen Rappaport.

VII

Whether this was really the end of the controversy, we do not know. It does not seem likely that the community leaders would have admitted defeat immediately. In all probability they still kept trying to get the decision reversed. But with what success and by what means—on that the sources are silent.

But there is an interesting epilogue. In 1759 Leibush Rappaport, the head of the yeshiva, died. His father remained inconsolable. Was this a punishment for the terrible episode with Rabbi Moses Mieses, who had died prematurely because of the bitter controversy? In order to obtain forgiveness for the soul of his son in the next world and to reconcile the two deceased *tsadikim*, a highly original match was arranged: Rabbi Mieses' son Elijah—"a righteous man on whom the world rests," as his contemporaries called him—was married to Hayim Cohen's granddaughter, and the weddng was celebrated with great pomp.[9]

This was the real final act of the momentous controversy which so severely shook the Jewish community of Lwów in the fifth decade of the eighteenth century.

Notes

[1]This account is based on the following main sources: (1) three documents published in Zbigniew Pazdro's *Organizacya i Praktyka Żydowskich Sądów* Podwojewodzińskich, (Lwów, 1903), Nos. 25, 30, 35; (2) a note in the supplements to *Tsemakh David*, published in C.N. Dembitzer's *Klilat Yofi*, Vol. I, Cracow, 1888, p. 138, along with the biography of Rabbi Hayim Cohen Rappaport, p. 137; (3) various articles by Salomon Buber in his *Anshei Shem*, Cracow, 1895, particularly Nos. 96, 168, 195, 427, 489; (4) the report in Ber Birkenthal's (of Bolechów) *Zikhronot* (Berlin, 1922), p. 23. When I compared all these sources, the background of this great dispute became clear. In 1932 Professor M. Bałaban published his book *Z zagadnień ustrojowych żydostwa polskiego*, in which he printed from the archives some important facts concerning the history of the Lwów rabbinate (pp. 12-20).

[2]The extent of Rabbi Rappaport's assiduousness is vividly expressed in his Responsa. In many of them he signs himself "*Ha-tarud*" (The Busy One). See Responsa of Rabbi Hayim Cohen, Part *Even Ha-eser*, Nos. 57, 61; in No. 62 he signs himself "The Very Busy One." In one Responsum (part *Even Ha-eser* No. 17) he writes: "It is well-known how busy I am." Interesting is the beginning of the Responsum 15 in Part *Yore Deah*: "I received your letter and could not make myself free to answer you because of my being busy with community affairs, and especially because of the judge." This responsum bears no date and we do not know when Rabbi Rappaport had anything to do with the "judge." Perhaps this was during the dispute of 1753-54.

[3]I accept the date 1753 according to S. Buber (*Anshei Shem*, No. 96, p. 41), although in *Tsemakh David* it is not clear. But one can not rely on the data in the supplement to *Tsemakh David*, as has been demonstrated by C.N. Dembitzer in *Klilat Yofi*, Vol. I, p. 139.

[4]In the Lwów community records, which Buber had before him, there is confirmation of a bill of sale for the year 1743 (5503) with the signature "Arych Leib Cohen Rappaport, residing (*honeh*) in Lwów." In the same document there is the signature of Leibush Koziner (*Anshei Shem, p. 42*).

[5]Ber Birkenthal, *Memoirs*, p. 25. There his name is not listed, and the publisher of the *Memoirs*, P. Wischnitzer, theorizes that Dov Berish Rappaport was meant, who, according to Buber, was rabbi in Międzybór.

[6]On the basis of a document called "Shtar Hatzi Zachar" signed by Aaron (in favor of his daughter).

[7]The jurisdiction of the *Bet Din* president of the Lwów region is not entirely clear. In the 18th century two rabbis bore that title—Isaac Landau and Meyer Margulies. Apparently the latter became president of the *Bet Din* after Rabbi Landau went to Cracow in 1754. But in 1745 he still signed himself "*ha-honeh*" (who resides) in the Lwów region, just as Rabbi Landau did in the same year. (Buber, *Anshei Shem*, No. 353.) Concerning the relationship of the *Bet Din* president to the general rabbinate, it should be noted that the two positions are not identical, because we have a document of appointment for Rabbi Hayim Cohen Rappaport as General Rabbi in 1763 (apparently he already had it in 1754 and perhaps even earlier); and at that time Rabbi Meyer Margulies was undoubtedly the official president of the *Bet Din* of the Lwów region. Furthermore, he bore that title during Rabbi Rappaport's entire lifetime and only several years after Rappaport's death did he leave Lwów to become rabbi in Ostróg. It is interesting that in 1776, Hayim Cohen Rappaport's successor, Rabbi Salomon, author of *Markevet Ha'mishna*, signed "*honeh* (residing as a rabbi) in the community of Lwów and the *entire* region," from which fact Dembitzer deduces that he encompassed both rabbinates, although in that same year Rabbi Margulies was still in Lwów. According to the findings of Prof. Bałaban the rabbinate was divided into two parts and thus there could have been two rabbis at the same time with the title "President of the *Bet Din* of the Lwów Region."

[8]Salomon Buber, in his *Anshei Shem*, writes that Hayim Cohen Rappaport did not become General Rabbi until 1763; as evidence he cites a copy of

the official authorization which was found in the Lwów Bernardine archives, But, in the document which reports the 1757 trial, one can clearly see that at that time Rabbi Rappaport already had the authorization. The fact that in 1763 he received a fresh authorization does not prove that he could not have gotten it earlier. On the contrary, the official appointment (which was for three years) was evidently renewed at that time, perhaps for the second or even the third time, judging from the year listed—1754, 1757, 1760, 1763.

Upon further study, my surmise, that Hayim Cohen Rappaport was General Rabbi even earlier than Buber assumed, was confirmed incontrovertibly by the note in the Lwów regulation of 1752 which Bałaban cites in his book, pp. 17 and 25. It thus becomes evident that on October 6, 1752 a council of the *Kehillot* took place in Przemyślany, where, for the first time, they signed the official authorization for Rabbi Hayim Cohen Rappaport as General Rabbi for the Ruthenian region

---

[9]See supplement to Section 3 of *Tsemakh David*, cited in *Kelilat Yofi*, Vol. I, p. 139. For the date of Leibush Rappaport's death, see *Kelilat Yofi*, ibid., and Buber, *Anshei Shem*, p. 42.

CHAPTER VIII
How A Wealthy Gentile
Once Became A Dealer in Etrogim*

In the second half of the seventeenth century the Jewish communities in Poland had one major common concern: where would they get the money to pay their debts? The tremendous expenses incurred in helping the tragic victims of Chmielnicki's bands, who began the massacres of Jews in 1648, virtually exhausted the budgets of the individual *Kehillot* and of their central body, the *Vaad Arba Aratzot*. Without an adequate income, there was nothing else for them to do but borrow the money somewhere. They could not afford to think about it too long; the need was too pressing. They borrowed wherever they could—from priests, from nobles, from Gentile merchants in the marketplaces. Nor did they bargain too hard

Etrogim are citrons (paradise apples) used by Jews to recite a special blessing during the holiday of *Sukkot* (in accordance with the Bible, Leviticus 23:40). They had to be imported to Poland from abroad.

about the rate of interest. Often, when the time came to pay a note, they made a new loan in order to be able at least to pay the interest on the old one. In this way they put patches upon patches, and the nightmare of paying off the debts became more difficult and more oppressive with each passing year.

I

In 1676 the *Vaad Arba Aratzot* borrowed a considerable sum of money in Wrocław, the capital city of Silesia. It is possible that this was not a new debt but the settlement of an old one. Whatever the case may be, there is a document which reports that in 1676 the leaders of the *Vaad* advised the municipal authorities of Wrocław that they owed the merchant Christopher Bresler a total of 12,120 reichsthaler and that they were obligating themselves to pay off that debt over the next twelve years.

But that was easier said than done. The *Vaad* was unable to pay. In 1677 Christopher Bresler received not money but a new promise to pay—the following year. In 1678 the same story was repeated. In 1679 the man lost patience and ordered the arrest of *Vaad* representatives who were in Wrocław on business. They were not imprisoned, but were forbidden to leave the city.

They then hit on the following idea: they assessed every Jewish merchant who came to Wrocław a certain sum. Since trade through Silesia was very active, they hoped to raise enough money quickly for an installment payment to Bresler. Whoever did not pay voluntarily would be stigmatized. But here a new complication arose. The royal tax collector in Wrocław was afraid that the assessment would force merchants to bypass Wrocław, and this would hurt local business. The president of the Imperial Chamber therefore sent a letter to the City Council of Wrocław strongly protesting the action, urging instead that the Jewish representatives be compelled to pay back the loan to Bresler themselves.

At that time Poland was ruled by King Jan III Sobieski, who was friendly to the Jews. It was not difficult for them to approach the King and tell him what the Jews in Wrocław were suffering because of that burdensome debt. On October 20, 1679 he sent a letter to the Wrocław City Council asking them to influence Christopher Bresler to be lenient with the Polish Jews.

Apparently Bresler wasn't too impressed by the King's intervention, because very soon afterward the Chamber president (most likely at Bresler's request) issued a new charge against the *Vaad* representatives demanding that they be fined 10,000 thaler and incarcerated until the fine was paid. This charge was based on the fact that they had acted criminally against the *jus superioritatis* of His Majesty the Holy Roman Emperor (that was the official title of the German ruler) by attempting to defraud him of tax revenue.

At the trial, the Jews were acquitted by the City Council (probably because of King Sobieski's letter). However, this did not bring in a single penny in payment of the debt, which kept increasing from year to year. The interest was not paid either, and several years later the documents speak of 15,000 thaler owed to Christopher Bresler by the *Vaad Arba Aratzot*.

II

On April 13, 1685 King Sobieski agreed that "his Jews" could be arrested in Wrocław for nonpayment of the debt. This aroused a furor. It became urgent that some arrangement be made with Christopher Bresler, because that threat of imprisonment was now quite real. The *Vaad* authorized Aaron Yitzhak, *parnas* of Lissa, and two other emissaries to settle the matter. But with authorization alone, Aaron Yitzhak could accomplish nothing. Along with that, he needed something else—money—which he didn't have. He therefore did not even go to Wrocław. In his place came the *parnas* of Poznań, Shmuel Leybl, and another *parnas* from Lissa, Leybl Yonah. They, of course, explained that they did not have full authorization from the *Vaad*. On December 22, 1685, when they could not prolong the negotiations any further, they signed a formal document stating that in three weeks Aaron Yitzhak would appear in Wrocław, and if he did not, then they themselves would pay the debt.

Early in 1686 they were again negotiating with Bresler. Aaron Yitzhak asked for a reduction in the interest, but the German would not hear of it. They protracted the matter as long as they could. Meanwhile, others went to Sobieski for help. On May 28, 1686 the Polish King wrote another letter to the City Council of Wrocław asking for leniency for the Jews and reminding them that the implacable creditor should take into consideration that he had given the Jews not cash but merchandise, and "at a very high price"—a cryptic allusion which Bresler himself must have understood very well.

By 1691, 412 thaler had been paid on the debt. Bresler then arrested four *parnassim* who happened to be in Wrocław— Leybl Mordecai of Krotoszyn, Yaakov Zelick of Kalisz, Moshe Leybl of Poznań, and Shimon Yaakov of Wojdysław. With his consent they were released on September 29, 1691, but not until they signed an assurance that in seven weeks the debt would be handled by the *Vaad*. Otherwise Bresler would have the right to imprison not only them, but any Jews who came to Wrocław and to confiscate their goods.

But even with the knife at their throats the *Vaad* could not pay. On December 10, 1691 the Jewish representatives in Wrocław again promised to do everything possible to satisfy Bresler. The relevant document does not say how they intended to do this, but apparently they again planned to put a tax on all goods brought into Wrocław. The Jews then began to bypass the city, taking their goods to Danzig (Gdańsk). On January 7, 1692 the Imperial Chamber in Wrocław protested vehemently to the City Council against the harm that this could bring to His Majesty.

The situation grew more and more desperate. On July 5,

1692, Jewish emissaries in Wrocław again signed a document in which they assured Bresler that in two months' time the *Vaad*, at the fair in Jarosław, would liquidate its debt. King Jan Sobieski thereupon ordered his ambassador to the German Emperor to take up the question of the protest which the Chamber in Wrocław had sent to the City Council. At the same time the King wrote to the City Council himself informing them of his intervention with the Emperor and asking them to hold in abeyance any steps against the Jews.

All of this would have been to no avail, however, since the treasury of the *Vaad* was empty (and no one has ever managed to pay a debt with empty hands), had the heads of the *Vaad* not hit upon a brilliant idea which saved the situation.

III

Thinking of ways to pay the debt, they decided in 1692 to look for a new source of income in Wrocław itself, a way which would not meet with the opposition of the German Imperial Chamber. The new source that they found was—the business of *etrogim!*

For due compensation, they leased to Heshel Benjamin of Beuthen in Upper Silesia a twenty-year monopoly to import *etrogim* into Poland. They drew up an agreement which was entered into the official Wrocław "Signature Book" on January 3, 1693 and which contained the following points:

(1) The representatives of the *Vaad*—Chaim David of Lwów, Feivish Joseph of Poznań, Hellman Shmuel of Krotoszyn, and Yaakov Lazarowicz of Pinczów—granted to Heshel Benjamin of Beüthen the right, for twenty years, to import *etrogim* (in German, Paradise Apples) for the Jews of Poland exclusively through Wrocław.

(2) If any other individual should get the same right to import *etrogim* into Poland—either by His Majesty the King or from a nobleman—then the leaders of the *Vaad* would be

responsible for persuading that individual to decline that right. Should they fail to do so, then they must pay a fine of 4,000 reichsthaler, each thaler worthy thirty silver grosz, which sum must be distributed as follows: for His Majesty, 1,000 thaler (through the Chamber in Wrocław); for His Majesty in Poland, 1,000 thaler; and for Heshel Benjamin, the remaining 2,000 thaler.

(3) If the aforementioned Heshel Benjamin did not abide by the agreement, that is, if he did not pay as much for the *etrogim* monopoly as he obligated himself for, then he must also pay the same fine of 4,000 thaler. In that case, the shares of both kings were not to be reduced, but rather the *Vaad* must get the 2,000 thaler from Heshel.

What benefit would Christopher Bresler derive from this agreement? Apparently he became a partner in the *etrogim* monopoly in two ways: (1) he immediately received, at the begining of 1693, an installment of 1,000 thaler (because the *Vaad* received payment from Heshel), and (2) the Jew from Beuthen (or Będzin, as it was called in another document) was only a fifty percent monopolist. He was supposed to transport the *etrogim* from Wrocław to Poland. But who was supposed to bring them to Wrocław? None other than Christopher Bresler.

The wealthy German began dealing in *etrogim* in the same year, 1693, and bought a large shipment from Genoa, Italy. Heshel Benjamin convinced him that they would make a fortune in the *etrogim* business. So Christopher Bresler invested hard cash in this "gold mine."

Whether some misfortune occurred en route is not known, but under the date of October 7, 1693 there is a new document in this matter: Heshel Benjamin, "the Jew from Beuthen" promised to pay 334 reichsthaler that he still owed to Herr Christopher Bresler for the "Paradise Apples" that he had ordered from Genoa. Since the German had little faith in such promises, Heshel had to provide a substantial pledge—four necklaces containing 1400 pearls. In addition, there was a note for 194 thaler signed by Heshel and two *parnassim*, Chaim David and Michał Abraham, plus a promise to pay 250 reichsthaler, signed by the *parnassim* from *Matopolska*.

This is followed by a note: "The Rabbi of Krotoszyn who was present, promised to turn over to Bresler the money he received from the sale of the *etrogim* which he took to sell." The German, it seems, got a garnishment on the income of his new business from the customer!

Once in the *etrogim* business, however, Christopher Bresler could not get out of the quagmire for a long time. Beginning in 1693 he had to keep importing "Paradise Apples, myrtles and palms"—*etrogim*, *hadasim* and *lulavim*—from Italy, because on those items depended the payment of the installment which the *Vaad* had promised to pay. Evidently he had no end of trouble with the venture. Whatever money he received in payment of the debt he had to put back into the business. And thus it went for several years until the *etrogim* monopoly became a matter for the official decrees of the Polish monarchs.

IV

A number of competitors began importing Italian *etrogim* into Poland through avenues other than Wrocław and thus placed the whole agreement in jeopardy. There was no other way out but to ask King Sobieski to sanction the *etrogim* monopoly. In the Wrocław archives there is a copy of Sobieski's decree, issued in 1698, which reads as follows:

> Inasmuch as the Jews of the Polish kingdom have found a way to pay their debt to Herr Christopher Bresler, and [in connection with that] Heshel Benjamin and two other Jews—Matityahu Vedlinus and Hertz Abraham—now have the exclusive right to deal in *etrogim* [the Latin text of the decree uses the phrase *poma paradisiaca*], which no one but the aforementi-

oned Christopher Bresler must import from Italy, it is hereby decreed that no other Jews shall import *etrogim* from Italy. Should anyone dare to do that secretly he will be punished.

The King's decree was addressed to the *starosta* (chief captain) of Silesia and it was couched in terms strong enough to satisfy the German *etrogim* dealer. Evidently he appointed the two other Jews, in addition to Heshel, as his agents to represent him, because he himself was not an expert in *etrogim*.

However, soon after Sobieski issued this decree, he died, and again the monopoly was in danger.

Herr Bresler's plenipotentiary in Poland—this time Hertz Abraham—did not procrastinate in bringing the matter to the attention of Sobieski's successor, King August II. And on May 28, 1698, August II signed a new decree affirming Sobieski's first *etrogim* monopoly. His decree is brief, but includes even more than the previous royal decree stipulated. It encompasses not only Poland and Lithuania but also Saxony, the country where August had ruled before he was chosen to be the Polish King.

Did this settle the *etrogim* affair? That's difficult to say, because Bresler still continued to have problems with his *etrogim* business. To be sure, the original debt was becoming smaller—in 1702 the Polish Jews owed him only 8,000 thaler. But the hearings and trials resulting from the *etrogim* debts still went on for a good many years.

Note

The sources for this chapter are to be found in the documents that were printed in *Pinkas Vaad Arba Aratzot* (Jerusalem, 1945) pp. xxvii, xxix, xxx, xxxi, xxxii, xxxviii, as well as in various notes in this *Pinkas* which have to do with Christopher Bresler (pp. 152, 160, 161, 162, 167, 203, etc.)

CHAPTER IX
ELECTIONS IN THE KEHILLA
OF OLD LWÓW

I

In the 1760's the Jewish district of Lwów was a bustling community.[1] Pan Starosta Skrzetuski and Pan Podstoli Orlewski, both stewards in the court of the Under-*Voievode* of Lwów, were no longer able to cope with the endlessly mounting number of complaints. Every few weeks they had to bring various important dignitaries to court: the mayors of the *Kehilla* (the Jewish community), the elders, the caretakers of the welfare funds, the tax collectors—and even the rabbi of Lwów, Hayim Cohen Rappaport, was forced to defend himself against severe accusations. The public prosecutor, Ulanowski, spared no one. As soon as he was convinced that a certain party had committed some infraction of the law or that a dignitary had intentionally allowed a transgression, he immediately reached for his legal arsenal and wrote out a terrifying summons. Incidentally, it was not difficult to convince the prosecutor, since the *Kehilla* at that time was rife with discord and quarrels. Besides, the prosecutor was a man with whom one could come to an understanding, and to whom certain arguments spoke directly to his heart and even more to his reason.

It was not always necessary, for that matter, that Ulanowski should take the initiative. Since the opposing side may have already managed to inform the presecutor sufficiently, individual citizens frequently brought their complaints personally to the Under-*Voievode's* Court when they sensed that a wrong had been committed. This occurred especially when some powerful notable was to act in the role of the plaintiff. If, for example, the mayor of the *Kehilla*, aware of his power and, perhaps, taking into account the mournful state of the community treasury, did not deem it practical to outbid his adversaries in appealing to the public prosecutor's sense of justice— he simply went to the office himself and presented his complaint.

One morning in the year 1762, there appeared, in the office where the Under-*Voievode* was holding court, Marko Wrocławski and Moshko Itzkowicz Menkis, the "city" and the "suburban" mayors of the Lwów *Kehilla*, respectively. (At that time two separate *Kehillot* existed; the city *Kehilla* was secondary in power and importance to the suburban.) They delivered their protest against several "rebel Jews of the community" who had dared to affront the honor of the two mayors in a threatening manner.

But just who was this Moshko Itzkowicz, mayor of the surburan *Kehilla* of Lwów at that time? He was a typical old Polish "Senior." A man of great wealth, the lessor of the Under-*Voievode's* pension, a despot who acknowledged nothing save his own will, an individual of extraordinary ambition, who interfered in everyone's affairs, a man without a trace of a heart and without a modicum of pity. For many long years the

Jews of Lwów trembled before this man, who was not himself a native-born citizen of Lwów, but a stranger from the city of Brody.

By trade he was a brewer. A whole gang of attendants, side-kicks, and good-for-nothings swarmed around him constantly and helped him to wield his power. Each of these lackeys brought him news "from the city", all kinds of rumors, and they participated readily in the Mayor's intrigues and conspiratorial plots. Moshko Menkis was in the best of graces with the local authorities. There he was affectionately called "Mosieczko," and he enjoyed favor and support; for as a brewer he had at his disposal invigorating drinks and a storage house of bottles of liquor, which, at the appropriate moment, willingly wandered into the cellars of the powerful dignitaries. Because of this Mosieczko Menkis was so powerful that no one dared to challenge his position.

The situation in the Lwów community was very critical at this time. Wielding power in the *Kehilla* was not an enviable job at all. The debts incurred by the *Kehilla* were so enormous that when the time came to pay the interest on the so-called *wyderkaf* loans and it was necessary to find fresh money, the Elders began to sweat. Often the only alternative was to put a patch on a patch and take out a new loan in order to pay the interest on the old. Whenever one of the wiser Elders reflected on the significance of this, shudders would run through his body.

For how could the thousand Jewish families in Lwów ever hope to pay off the 400,000 Polish złoty which haunted the community budget like a terrible nightmare? How in fact could the mayors obtain so much money? The mayors also suffered severe headaches when the promissory notes were presented for payment. It once even reached the point where they ceased to pay the rabbi's salary. They demanded that he sign a document stating that he had voluntarily relinquished his *salarium* and would take payment only from the provincial communities (*ziemstwa*) belonging to Lwów but "not a penny from the Lwów *Kehilla*." The energetic rabbi Hayim Symchowicz Rappaport did not succumb to this. He brought legal proceedings against the *Kehilla* mayors and won.[2] But even if he had lost, it would not have helped the *Kehilla* treasury very much. The deficit was simply too large.

Somehow in the year 1761 the money needed to pay the debt and the interest on loans was unavailable. No longer was anyone willing to risk a private loan to the Lwów *Kehilla*. No one was willing to put money into a sack full of holes. But money was needed desperately, and the only alternative was to mortgage the synagogues. With the synagogues as collateral the *Kehilla* borrowed an additional 25,000 Polish złoty, and for a moment it was possible to breathe more easily.

Mosieczko Menkis, who took the haunting specter of the community's bankruptcy most deeply to heart, was again able to raise his head.

However, this new loan provoked much commotion in the community. Public opinion began to revolt. Discontent prevailed everywhere. The mortgaging of the most valuable pieces of communal property was sharply criticized, and signs pointed to the fact that this had been only a marginal solution. Moreover, it did not end only in criticism.

At first there were only whispers. Then it gradually grew into loud discussions of terrible things. Evil tongues began to spread rumors throughout the city that a part of this loan had found its way into the pockets of the Elders!

Soon it was openly stated that there had been a misappropriation of community funds. Of course no one was able to specify how and when this had occurred. But these undefined rumors (and because they were undefined, they lent themselves even more to exaggeration) were enough to bring the mayors of both the Lwów *Kehillot* to life. A clear revolt was in the making, and it was necessary to curtail it in time.

The mayors met to consult. After long debates they decided

to make the following public announcement in the two main synagogues during the holiday of *Shevuot*:

> We the Elders of the city and suburban *Kehillot*, hearing that there are rebel Jews here in Lwów acting against us, the Elders of the city and suburban *Kehillot*, Jews who speak dishonorably about our community and who murmur behind our backs only to slander us—as if we, the *Kehilla* leaders of last year as well as of this year, had brought harm, i.e., misappropriated funds of several tens of thousands of złoty belonging to the community and the whole city of Lwów. Therefore, we the Elders of the *Kehilla*, weighing and hearing such ignoble and unworthy talk before various kinds of people (behind our backs only, not to our faces), and hearing the undeserved prattle and murmurs against our community leaders, have ordered both the city and suburban sextons to announce in the synagogues during the *Shevuot* Holidays that these rebels should stand before the rabbis and the entire population of the city and suburbs and tell us face to face what they have spoken and whispered behind our backs and prove and demonstrate this to us. And if face to face in the presence of the rabbis and the entire community they will stand and prove that we have misappropriated a formidable sum of the *Kehilla*'s money, we shall acknowledge ourselves worthy of punishment and judgment. But if they do not give evidence of what they accused us by this vile prattle and murmuring, then they will be liable to exemplary punishment.[3]

II

The plan was splendidly thought out. Menkis knew that no one would have enough courage to openly come out with an accusation. No one at that time could venture to do so in the face of the community's power. The mayors' announcement was therefore meant as a proud refutation of all the slander, a rebuttal to all the rumors. "After this announcement it will be possible to boldly bring all of this prattle to order," Menkis told himself.

But no one sat with folded arms in the camp of his adversaries. They were led by Menkis's professional rival, another brewer from Lwów, David Soboliszyn.[4]

He too was not a native-born Lwów citizen; he came from Tyśmienica and was a man of unusual *hutzpa*. He was a blusterer, a shouter, willingly taking to his fists, shoving his elbows forward, and seeing the seat of the *Kehilla* Mayor in Lwów as the pinnacle of his dreams, he had but one obstacle to surmount: Menkis. Nevertheless, he was well aware that, despite his zeal, exposing Mosieczko as an embezzler was an impossible task. For very rarely could a community embezzlement be proven before the authorities. There was always some answer, always some loophole. But it was possible to undermine the prestige of Menkis in another manner, Soboliszyn proposed a plan which was accepted by his group, namely that of not allowing the community edict to be read at all. Soboliszyn reasoned that if a tumult should arise in the synagogue in the mayor's presence and the announcement should remain unread, this would be the best sign that he is no longer a favorite of the crowds, as the authorities had presented him. At the same time this would prove that the Jews of Lwów believed the hearsay evidence that community funds had been stolen.

On the first day of the *Shevuot* Holiday in 1762, in the great synagogue of Lwów, the sexton, upon completion of the morning prayer, struck the table and called on those who were praying to observe silence for the reading of a *Kehilla* edict. Soboliszyn gave the awaited signal and a storm broke loose. "We do not want such a *Kehilla!*" The scream came from somewhere in the back, some inconspicuous follower of Soboliszyn, a man hired for this purpose, a halfwit with a stentorian voice.

The notables, seated on the first bench on the east side of the synagogue, rose from their places and began to implore that the profanation of the synagogue cease. The venerable and hoary rabbi grew irritated. But by this time no one would listen to anyone else.

Some raised a tumult by screaming loudly; others mitigated them by screaming still louder. Soboliszyn himself behaved irreproachably, and Menkis sat pale as a corpse in the honorable seat of the Mayor (he purchased his own seat only later[5]) and began to bite his lips in anger. He immediately recognized whose trick this was and swore in his soul a horrible vengeance on Soboliszyn. But in the meantime he was forced to give up. The rabbi, seeing that the tumult would not cease, gave the sign to begin the next prayer. The Torah rolls were taken from the ark. The resonant voice of the cantor filled the room and peace finally prevailed.

Immediately after the holiday, Menkis and Marek Wrocławski made their way to the office of the Under-*Voievode* and there presented a complaint in person against the "rebellious people" of the community, including in their documentation a copy of the unposted community announcement.

At this moment the five-year war for control of the Lwów *Kehilla* commenced.

It consumed an enormous amount of energy on both sides. It was a war which inscribed itself deeply in the annals of Jewish Lwów and about which horrifying stories were told many years later.

Soboliszyn was the man primarily involved. It was no trifle at that time to have the *Kehilla*'s mayor as an enemy. David Soboliszyn and his followers immediately felt this when it came time to assess the *sympla* tax. If there were only some vague suspicion that somebody had participated in the revolt during the *Shevuot* Holiday in the great synagogue, the suspect was the object of special attention for the commissars appointed to assess the *sympla* tax. As a result of this, the rebel learned well what it meant to be involved in a plot against the *Kehilla*'s mayor.

However, the action taken in court by Mosieczko Menkis and his colleague-mayor of the other *Kehilla*, Marek Wrocławski, had no significant effects, for it did not include the names of the rebels. It was only a warning addressed to the opponents of the *Kehilla* leadership, that from then on nothing would come to them easily.

Soboliszyn and his persecuted followers had no remaining alternative but to await the next *Kehilla* elections, which were to be held during the intermediary Easter Holidays in the year 1763. Only then could there be a general reckoning.

III

David Soboliszyn prepared himself for the elections with

reached an understanding with all those who harbored even slight resentment toward the Menkis clique. He gained the favor of the influential Mizes family and won over two *Kehilla* Elders to his side: Jacob Lewkowicz Byk and Israel Rays. A common hatred for Mayor Mosieczko united them all. All strove to achieve one objective: his removal from office. The winter of 1762-63 passed quickly in these preparations.

The Under-*Voievode* of Lwów, who had a decisive voice in all Jewish affairs, knew what was going on. He supported Mosieczko, but he did not welcome a war among the Jews, since it demanded both his concentration and effort in the arbitration of these incessant squabbles. Therefore, to insure peace and order during the elections, he issued a decree just before they were to start. It included various regulations relating to the election of the *Kehilla* Elders.

The elections were not direct. In some Polish communities lots were first drawn from receptacles containing the names of the various categories of citizens. From this lottery five or six electors were chosen. There were three boxes. The first contained the names of the outgoing *Kehilla* Elders, and from this box two electors were drawn. Subsequently the remaining cards which had not been selected were deposited into the second box, in which were the names of the welfare administrators (*szpitalni*) and other social workers—and again two cards were drawn to select the next two electors. All remaining cards were then thrown into the third box where the names of all taxpayers had been placed, and from here the remaining two electors were drawn. A sexton drew the lots. The chosen electors were called *borrim*; they nominated the entire *Kehilla* leadership at will.

Mosieczko Menkis naturally concentrated all his attention on the drawing of the electors. Fortunately for him, it was much easier to manipulate and create a "favorable opinion" in the boxes among the cards than it was among living people in the community. With the numerous drawings and deposits of cards into various boxes, "miracles" were easily brought about. It was not at all necessary to enjoy great popularity within the community in order to be elected. It was enough to know the "psychology" of the electoral urns or the secret passageways through which the cards had to travel between one box and another. Mosieczko Menkis was well aware of this. He was also certain of his own victory and rubbed his hands with joy, thinking about the excellent order that these cards would be in at the upcoming elections.

He had slightly overestimated his power, however. Either someone from his trusted circle of men had disturbed his arrangement, or perhaps the wrong cards had been stuck to the fingers of the sexton, so that Mosieczko did win the elections of 1763, but not completely. David Soboliszyn was defeated, but two Elders were re-elected from the opposition group of the previous *Kehilla*, and a third may have been added. They, of course, raised a protest against these elections, for their leader had suffered a defeat, but Mosieczko, at whom the new *Kehilla* began to brandish its horns, was still more displeased by the results.

The first function of the newly elected Elders was to choose the functionaries who would make the tax estimates for individual members of the community. These officials were extremely important, since it was easy to document who was with the mayor's party and who was against it in assessing the *sympla* tax. Mosieczko naturally lent his support to the appointees of the previous year, Shmelke and Moshek Manelowicz. But the *Kehilla* Elders did not choose them. This led to a fight. For the next several months, until August, there was no legal way to get Shmelke and Moshek into office.

When the tax revenues did not come in, and big delays were caused in the payment of debts, the creditors began to take legal action. Menkis resorted to other methods: he let himself (through the public prosecutor) be accused of negligence in the administration of the Kehilla, which supposedly caused the delay in interest payments. When the Under-*Voievode* officially learned of the cause of the disorder, he immediately appointed the two candidates of Mosieczko, Shmelke and Moshek Manelowicz, tax assessors. But even then success was not fully achieved. The Under-*Voievode* realized that the opposition was strong, and so he added two controllers to the two assessors "to be in attendance." They were Azriel Złoczowski and Marko Boruchowicz from the city, and Lewko Malowany Mizes and Israel Rays from the suburbs, all members of the opposition.[6] Thus, Mosieczko's opponents had penetrated even here, and they began to sharpen their claws instead of thinking about peace for the community, which was as vital as air to breathe.

But who cared for the good of the community? Everybody was eager to cast aspersions, accusations, and bring legal actions against the other. Each party wanted to destroy and eliminate the other. The accusations were drastic. The most horrible crimes were named: stealing of public funds, embezzlement of the *Kehilla*'s money, misappropriation of the community's property.

As a result of one such allegation a trial ensued between the party of Soboliszyn and one of the former mayors of the *Kehilla*, Zelman Pinkas Rabinowicz, who "during his time as mayor had harmed the community, involving it in financial intrigues and not rendering the financial report due from his office." Zelman Pinkas accused Soboliszyn and his comrades of defamation. At the trial the Under-*Voievode* ordered the verification of the entire *Kehilla* economy not only during the term of office of Rabinowicz, but for the last three years as well. What was the reason for this? The Under-*Voievode* justified it in the following manner:

> The public good of the *Kehilla* as a whole, the entirety of its income and its order in times to come, demands that not only the named Zelman Pinkas, but also the mayors, administrators, and Elders who are involved in financial transactions, should make calculations, summations and justifications of all of it.[7]

There was also a more profound reason: the repercussion of the previous year's affair with the *Kehilla*'s loan. The communities themselves had, after all, agreed to a revision of the books and accounts. Mosieczko also wanted to have these testimonials to show that everything was and is in order. As usual, an administrative revision of the *Kehilla* did not and could not yield negative results.

IV

In both Lwów *Kehillot* the year 1763 passed in an atmosphere of extreme tension. The patience of the community members had been exhausted. By late autumn Menkis felt that the ground was tottering beneath him. The treasury was empty, the debts were pressing, and the specter of a major catastrophe was growing ever more threatening and more visible. Money was desperately needed, and without it there was nothing the *Kehilla* could do. In this mood of the community's threatened bankruptcy, if Mosieczko had offered his hand to the opposition, if he had wanted to forget the animosity and bitterness he harbored, then perhaps his opponents might have agreed to a truce. But he had lost control of himself. He would never consent to exchange a word with such men as David Soboliszyn, Israel Rays, or Salomon Malowany. He well remembered the shame they had brought upon him on that day during the *Shevuot* Holiday, when they did not allow the Mayor's proclamation to be read aloud. Shivers came over his whole body when he recalled the accusations and aspersions they had directed at him, accusations of theft and misappropriation of the *Kehilla's* money. He therefore instinctively denied any notion of a reconcilliation with the enemies. He sought instead to find a remedy for himself in the tragic situation, but this was to no avail. Slowly he tumbled into the abyss.

The elections of 1764 were not at all certain. Still worse, Mosieczko's defeat was altogether possible. The *Kehilla's* leadership was consumed by internal quarrels and rarely was it able to reach a resolution of any kind.

The Passover Holiday of 1764 drew near, and the defeat of Menkis was becoming more and more probable. Black clouds hung low on the *Kehilla's* horizon and had taken away Menkis's peace of mind. He was haunted by invisible handcuffs which the opposition had so surreptitiously slipped on him. He felt like an eel in a trap. The awakening spring enlivened only the spirits of his adversaries, who knew that this time the boxes containing the names of the *Kehilla's* electors would be carefully watched by members of the opposition. Alas, Mosieczko himself had lost confidence in his victory. Shortly before the election he relinquished the direction of the suburban *Kehilla* to Liber Rabinowicz. Menkis did not want to be a witness to his own defeat.

The final days before the elections of 1764 passed in a frenzy. A black despair had seized the Menkis clique. The boxes containing the cards were suddenly inaccessible. All persuasions met with indifferent silence. The lots rested in their urns with stoic composure. The news from the battle fronts in the synagogues, *Batei-midrash* and the *mikva*, where the opposition had taken the leading bench, was desperate.

The result of the elections proved horrifying: Mosieczko Menkis was completely defeated. All the rebels were elected: David Soboliszyn, Salomon and Levko Mizes, Byk, Rays, and their allies.

Mosieczko Menkis suffered a double defeat in the year 1764: he had lost, and his enemies were elected. Hence David Soboliszyn also had a double victory: he and his party took control of the *Kehilla*, and the despised Mayor had been overthrown at last.

But not entirely.

Mosieczko Menkis alone, in this difficult and cumbersome situation, had not lost his head. Unnoticed by all, he suddenly set off for the Kampianowska building to His Excellency the Under-*Voievode* and there poured out his aching soul in full. He beseeched that he not be allowed to fall, or at least that his enemies not enter the leadership. The Under-*Voievode* felt terribly sorry for Mosieczko. Without delay irregularities were discovered in the elections, and it was decided that "while the elections would not be declared invalid on account of the irregularities the Under-*Voievode* would *ad interim* order the previous *Kehilla* Elders to govern, forbidding the newly elected to take over the government.[8]

Before the first spark of joy had faded in the camp of Soboliszyn, before the victors were able to calm down from their triumph, a veritable bomb exploded. News spread that old Joseph Cymelis had been appointed mayor in the city *Kehilla*, while the entire former leadership had been temporarily reinstated in the suburban community, with Liber Rabinowicz as its head.

Then a terrible storm broke out.

Never before had the will of the electorate been so trampled. The population could not understand how someone would dare to prevent the newly elected Elders from taking office.

The authority of the *Kehilla* was so strong at that time that, as soon as the results of the elections were posted, all quarrels and differences ceased. Woe to the man who would venture to oppose the will of the people! And so, when the second half of the Passover Holidays arrived in 1764, the Jewish population of Lwów was extremely agitated. The Elders were afraid to show their faces on the street. The population declared that it would not condone this intrigue. Liber Rabinowicz was particularly frightened. He appeared in the synagogue, but when the sexton, David Gershonowicz, called him to the Torah, at the place where the mayor was usually called, Rabinowicz refused to accept, exclaiming: "Leave me in peace, for I am afraid of confusion, give this honor to whom you wish!"[9]

The Mayor's *Aliya* (the honor of being called to the Torah) was put up for auction and was purchased by one of the citizens, Kisiel. However, this was not enough. The people's wrath had mounted and was blazing in a consuming fire.

Horrible things began to happen in Lwów.

V

It reached a point that the people forcibly prevented the old non-elected *Kehilla* Elders from fulfilling their duties. Chaos arose. "The dead are lying, and their bodies have not been buried," states a contemporary record.[10] For there was no caretaker at the cemetery. The previous year's leaders of the *Kehilla* did not go there out of consideration for their personal security, and the newly elected leaders did not have the right to allocate the graves. It would have appeared at the time that an end to the noble Lwów community had arrived. There seemed to be no exit from the situation. To make matters worse, the Under-*Voievode* had left for a few days, and there was no one who could say a powerful word and allay the passions.

The despairing rabbi intervened. He convinced the victorious opposition to agree to Cymelis. The fire was extinguished in the city *Kehilla*. But this was of small consequence. There were burning issues that could not wait in the suburban community. So the rabbi together with the rebels sent a communication to Rabinowicz stating that they would allow him to rule for the next few days until the return of the Under-*Voievode*.[11]

Despite this a revolution still loomed in the air. Any spark could ignite it with force. Before long such an occasion arose. Shortly after Passover, the Catholic Easter Holidays arrived. There was an old custom that the Elders of the *Kehilla* were to deliver their Holiday greetings to the city chief (*Burgrabia*). Liber Rabinowicz considered it natural that his administration carry out this responsibility. But the newly elected Elders, for lack of anything better to demonstrate their self-esteem and dignity, also decided to set off with a similar delegation to see the *Burgrabia*. At its head was David Soboliszyn. The two groups met at the castle. This ignited the fuse to the dynamite, and a terrible commotion erupted.

Barely had the two delegations left the castle and come outside the gates when David Soboliszyn began to yell at Rabinowicz: "Why do you walk behind us; you are not the Mayor!"[12] Everyone was still. But Soboliszyn took yet another step; he tightened his fist and cried out at the top of his voice: "I'll punch you in your stupid face!"[13] He was seconded in this by Salomon Mizes, who was equally enraged and reiterated: "Certainly you should not walk with us!"[14]

Who knows what this would have led to if Mosieczko Menkis had not actively entered into this struggle. The stalwart brewer with broad shoulders broke up the fight by separating the opponents. He himself had nothing to fear. No one would dare strike him, for the power of a *Kehilla* despot was so great that it would not suddenly disappear.

When Rabinowicz returned to the castle and found the *Burgrabia*, he recounted the whole incident to him. The *Burgrabia* calmed him down and gave heart to his spirit. But, disturbed by the affront he had suffered, the mayor fell ill. It was then that fate took its turn.

David Soboliszyn, Salomon Mizes, and their comrades in victory were accused by the public prosecutor of a series of crimes and transgressions. All the sins which they had committed against the mayor appointed by the Under-*Voievode* were enumerated at the trial. To accelerate a trial was no problem. Everything sped like lightning. By May 17, 1764 investigations had been closed and the verdict rendered. The sentence was: Salomon Mizes, since he had transgressed not only against the "present disposition," but had also, in earlier times, opposed the jurisdiction of the Under-*Voievode*,[15] was ostracized from the community of Elders for two years. David Soboliszyn was deprived of his administrative position for one year. Jacob Byk was fined the sum of three ducats. The others were acquitted.

In this manner the opposition was "driven out" of the *Kehilla*, and Mosieczko Menkis again took the reins of government into his mighty hands.

For two years there was peace. No one dared to criticize; no one even uttered a word. The elections of 1765 were conducted without emotion. Mosieczko's slate was accepted by the electors. Naturally, neither the names of the Mizeses nor of David Soboliszyn appeared on it. The *Kehilla* Elders Rays and Byk were barely able to persuade the others to let them remain in the administration.

But Soboliszyn did not surrender so easily. As soon as he had recovered from the blow dealt to him, he set to work once again. An ambition not easily visible further supported him toward his goal. Ingenious as he indeed was, he immediately recognized another road opening up to him, and he seized upon altogether new methods.

He had decided to win the favor of Mosieczko. He began to praise him to the heavens. As soon as he sensed that one of the mayor's attendants was nearby, he began to sing veritable hymns of praise, which the eager servants related immediately to Menkis. This went on for the entire year of 1765, near the end of which Soboliszyn had become a frequent visitor at Mosieczko's. Finally, when the second half of the Passover

Holidays and the second anniversary of Soboliszyn's triumph and defeat arrived in 1766, the constellations had changed. The mayor's party was no longer battling with Soboliszyn, and because of this he entered the *Kehilla*'s leadership.

The first step had been taken. It was still a long way to the Mayor's office, but certainly closer than it had been one or two years ago. At this time it was easier to breathe in the *Kehilla*, for in precisely this year Menkis could not be formally re-elected. This was in accordance with the old law, which stated that whoever "has been an Elder for three years, must vacate the office for one year."[16] As luck would have it, the year 1765 was Menkis's third consecutive year as an Elder, and he was therefore forced to withdraw in the coming year. Lewko Bałaban assumed the office of mayor, and he was the sole obstacle which kept Soboliszyn from attaining the honor he desired.

Soboliszyn's luck began to increase. Six months after the elections Lewko Bałaban had a quarrel with one of the Elders, Eli Ablowicz, and he became entangled in a grand trial with a disastrous verdict; for his guilt he was to serve time in the school belfry for two days and one night. Thus the authority of the unfortunate mayor had been completely shattered. David Soboliszyn decided to take advantage of this, and in Mosieczko's absence he once again stepped into his old shoes.

As the *Kehilla* elections of 1767 drew nearer, Soboliszyn rapidly came to an understanding with the Mizes'es and other enemies of Menkis. The shaping of opinion had already begun in the election urns, but in a different direction. The cards were easy to convince, and the *borrim* were drawn from the boxes with Rachmil Mizes at the head. A warring *Kehilla* leadership was thus formed, Soboliszyn-Mizes, still worse than the raging *Kehilla* of three years before. There was a terrible outcry of treason among the Menkis clique.

How indeed was Menkis to cope with this? An old lion awakened inside him and leaped into action. Moreover, he had come to an understanding with the Under-*Voievode*, who continued to have sympathy for Mosieczko. But he no longer desired to repeat the order of three years ago and not allow the new *Kehilla* leadership to take office. First of all, the Under-*Voievode* did not wish to overexert his authority (he had, after all, not forgotten the lesson of three years ago). Secondly, Soboliszyn was also a member of the previous *Kehilla* leadership, and so it would have no effect. The only course remaining to Menkis was to file a "manifesto" protesting the elections.

On April 13, 1767 Moshko Landys and Mendel Michlewicz, two *Kehilla* leaders from the Menkis party, appeared in the office of the Under-*Voievode*, and the protest was raised. They accused the electors of four deviations of the law. 1) The law existed that no one from the suburbs may be elected to the posts of city elder or city elector until they have lived in the city for ten years, but as in the past, not taking the law into account, they elected Rachmil Mizes to the Elders and electors of the city, though he had lived in the city for only one year. 2) In spite of the Under-*Voievode's* decree, the lots of those who owed arrears in their taxes were recognized. 3) The law concerning the necessary vacancy of Elders who have held office for three years in a row had been bypasssed (this was directed at Lewko Bałaban, who was indirectly the cause of the entire upheaval and had entered the new *Kehilla*). 4) The essential point: David Soboliszyn had no passive electoral rights "as he himself had been ostracized from the Elders without the knowledge of the *Kehilla*, so that, if it were to be against the law, the *Kehilla* would not [have to] answer for him."[17]

The protesters intended simply to remove Rachmil Mizes from the body of electors and Soboliszyn from the body of Elders. Here the sequence of events was altogether different from that of three years ago. The new *Kehilla* was assembled immediately, and David Soboliszyn was elected mayor. Having achieved his aim and standing finally at the top, the new mayor was able to deliberate on the ways to ward off the attack.

Soon a retaliating protest initiated by the electors sailed into the office of the Under-*Voievode*. "We are electors too," they claimed, "and have acted according to the decree granted to us by the Under-*Voievode*." Namely, 1) Rachmil Mizes had justly entered the city and not the suburban body of electors, since he came out first in the lots and was married in a city, not a suburban school. His mandate was therefore valid. 2) Lots had been acknowledged only to those to whom the cashiers Moshko and Shaya have agreed, supplying evidence that they were not in arrears with their taxes, and this should be enough. 3) With regard to the laws and anathema in the written book, at the end of three successive years each Elder of the *Kehilla* must vacate his office, this referred to Lewko Bałaban, who had not yet come to the end of his three year term. 4) David Soboliszyn had been justly elected according to the old custom, whereby, as before, the lessors of the pensions and sub-pensions of the Under-*Voievode* as well as of the Elders, had always been Elders of the *Kehilla*.[18] On the contrary, argued the electors, they now regretted that, on orders from the Under-*Voievode*, two protesters, Landys and Michlewicz, had been elected Elders.

The phlegmatic and at times cynical tone of this retaliatory protest brought Mosieczko to life. He could hold out no longer. Every day that passed with Soboliszyn in the Mayor's Office seemed like a century to him. His former anger was revitalized and his envy reawakened. But he was unable to do anything and had to wait for the trial, which had been scheduled for June 1, 1767.

When this day arrived both sides were filled with hope. The trial was properly prepared. The law required that an appeal not be made before the actual trial, but the judges' reason had been addressed earlier. Each side presented their supporting arguments, which had a strange persuasive power, and undoubtedly each had received the assurance of victory. For this reason the Under-*Voievode* found himself in grave trouble on

June 1. An exit had to be found which would satisfy both zealous opponents. But where could such reason and shrewdness of a high dignitary in the administration of the Under-*Voievode* be found? On June 1, 1767 he pronounced the following sentence:

> Although the elections have yielded results which violate the law, nevertheless they are affirmed. However, in Soboliszyn's place as mayor is appointed the non-party *Kehilla* member Joseph Nechles, and in his place another has been appointed.

Joseph Nechles was thus the first "government commissar" of the Lwów *Kahilla*, ruling together with the entire elected *Kehilla* council. And only this nomination quieted the numerous outbreaks of passion and silenced the war which had for five years held the Lwów Jewry in tension.

Notes

[1] This essay is based on judicial records of the Under-*Voievode's* court in Lwów, published by Z. Pazdro in *Organizacya i praktyka żydowskich sadów podwojewodzińskich* (Organization and practice of the Jewish Under-*Voievode* Courts), Lwów 1903, as well as on the manuscript of the "Pinkas," of the Lwów *Kehilla*, which, until the outbreak of World War II, was found in the Library of the Jewish Community in Lwów.

[2] Cf. Chapter VII in the present collection, pp. 122-3.

[3] *Acta Vcpl.* V. III. A. p. 17-18 (Pazdro, appendix Nr. 41).

[4] The origin of David Soboliszyn came to light by the comparison of several documents in the Under-*Voievode's* records with the manuscript of the *Kehilla*'s "Pinkas". We can in this way solve many problems. Beyond any doubt the identification of Soboliszyn seems to be with David Lejzerowicz, *suburban* mayor in 1771 (Pazdro, appendix Nr. 78). We discovered this "David son of Lejzor of Tyśmienica" in the *Kehilla* Pinkas folio 145 (note

dated from 1774 where it is mentioned that in the synagogue he was the neighbor of Aron Drohobycki, who appears also many times in the Under-*Voievode's* records).

[5]According to the handwritten *Kehilla* Pinkas, folio 84, the purchase of his own seat came about in 1767.

[6]*Acta Vcpl.* V. II. A. p. 151 (Pazdro, appendix Nr. 44).

[7]*Acta Vcpl.* V. II. A. p. 175 (Pazdro, appendix Nr. 17).

[8]*Acta Vcpl.* V. II. A. p. 186 (Pazdro, appendix Nr. 50).

[9]*Ibid.*

[10]*Ibid.*

[11]*Ibid.*

[12]*Ibid.*

[13]*Ibid.*

[14]*Ibid.*

[15]*Ibid.*

[16]*Acta Vcpl.* V. III. B. p. 42 (Pazdro, appendix Nr. 63).

[17]*Ibid.*

[18]*Ibid.* (appendix Nr. 64).

CHAPTER X
A Desecration of Yom Kippur in Pre-Partition Poland

The years 1771-1772 were a period of severe strain for the Jews of Lwów. On the 13th day of Tamuz 5531 (1771), the revered old Rabbi Hayim Cohen Rappaport passed away. For thirty years he had led the Jews of Lwów and enjoyed a well-deserved reputation not only in his own city but in the entire region under his jurisdiction as General Regional Rabbi.

Difficult struggles and conflicts began soon after that day in Tamuz when Rabbi Rappaport passed away. First of all, a struggle erupted among the Jews of Lwów over who should take the departed rabbi's place. At the same time, there was a bitter fight between the two local Lwów communities, on the one hand, and the Jews of Żółkiew, Brody, and Tyśmienica on the other hand, who had grown rebellious and refused to participate in the elections for the new General Regional Rabbi. Their intention was probably to separate themselves

141

completely from the Lwów central *Kehilla*. A defiant spirit was in the air, intensified by the revolutionary atmosphere in the last year of Polish independence prior to the first partition. In the Jewish world of Lwów, things also heated up.

As is usual in such periods, the first sounds of the *shofar* failed to arouse any particular stirrings toward repentance among the conflicting parties. The *Elul* days went by amidst a ceaseless uproar. The shouts of the opposing sides at times rose all the way to heaven. *Rosh Hashana* 5532 (1771) was approaching and the mood was still painfully inflamed. Naturally, under such circumstances, religious life regressed. Spiritual authority was lacking. Lawlessness increased. No one paid any attention to the sad state of religion.

But that such things could happen as happened on that *Yom Kippur* of 1771, no one could ever have imagined. Such lawlessness had never been seen in Lwów before.

That morning the Jews of Lwów were on their way to synagogue, each to his own place of worship. Passing the home of a certain Isaac Jakubowicz, they heard unusual sounds coming from behind the house. A few people stopped, wondering what could be going on in Jakubowicz's home on such a holy day. Others thought nothing of it and proceeded on their way. Still others became curious enough to forget for a moment that the cantor would not wait for them. They opened the gate, entered the yard, and stopped in their tracks before an incredible scene. A group of Christian workmen was busily engaged in various jobs—digging a well, chopping wood, and similar activities.

The first thought that entered the heads of the Jews was that there must be some mistake—Jakubowicz had forgotten to tell his workers that it was a Jewish holy day and that they must not come to work that morning. But the workmen maintained that such was not the case. They had been expressly instructed to come to work on that particular day.

Someone ran off to find Isaac Jakubowicz. Everybody

talked to him at once. But Isaac made no reply. He had no intention whatsoever of sending the workmen away.

It did not take long before people came running from all the places of worship. Isaac was publicly desecrating the holiest day of the year! And since there was no chief rabbi in town, Rabbi Berish (the *dayan* and head of the yeshiva) sent him a warning in his own name and in the name of the entire Jewish community. But Isaac replied:

"I can do whatever I please, because the *Kehilla* once allowed work to be done for it on the Sabbath." When and where this had happened he did not say. His reply was pure insolence and nothing else. He continued his activity, and all the Jews in Lwów looked on and grieved over this awful blasphemy.

But Isaac's lawlessness was too flagrant to be overlooked. Immediately after *Yom Kippur* the leaders of both Lwów communities, with Rabbi Berish at their head, met to consider what should be done. Several of them were not particularly good friends of Isaac Jakubowicz, but even without that consideration, he would have fared very badly. Various opinions were expressed on how to uproot this wicked man, but the final decision was to sentence him to a whole year in prison, plus a substantial fine. "Let the scoundrel remember that you can not simply do whatever you please in this world!"

Hearing the verdict, Isaac began to change his tune. The money? Well, that was one thing. But the other part was intolerable. He offered to give contributions to the hospital and to the synagogue in conciliation. But no one was in a mood to listen to him. No! The complete punishment must be carried out!

Having no other alternative, Isaac ran to the highest authority over the Jews of Lwów, the Vice-*Voievode* Orlewski, and accused the *Kehilla* and the rabbi's representative of personal animosity in meting out such severe punishment for a minor offense. The Vice-*Voievode* allowed himself to be persuaded.

In those days the rulers over the Jews were distinguished for their remarkable sense of sight and touch: they often saw and heard more than was present in reality.

So Isaac Jakubowicz worked it out that Pan Orlewski himself, on September 18, 1771, signed an order to the prosecutor, Andrzej Pohoricki, instructing him to summon the entire community leadership immediately (except for Rabbi Berish) and to demand justification for the crime they had committed. How serious the conversation between the Vice-*Voievode* and Jakubowicz was can be seen from the fact that in the order of September 28th it was decided: (1) to demand that the community carry out the decision, (2) to demand exoneration, (3) to interrogate the plaintiff, the defendant, and the witnesses on both sides—in no longer than three days, by October 2nd! That was the tempo ordered by the Vice-*Voievode*. He probably sensed that the whole matter could evaporate into thin air if it stood around too long.

So on October 2nd, 1771, there appeared before Judge Chrząstowski all the sides in the dispute: the prosecutor, the plaintiff Jakubowicz, and all the defendants—Yosl Nechlish, head of the suburban community; Mordecai Feyglish, head of the city community; and the *parnassim* (Elders) David Sobels, Zalman Pinchas, Joseph Heshlis, Anshel Jakubowicz, Israel Rays, and Hayim Tarnigroder.

The indictment of the Vice-*Voievode* was read, and both sides were interrogated. The testimony of the witnesses was postponed until the next day. Then everything was written down meticulously; all the documents were signed, sealed, and sent to the Vice-*Voievode* so that he himself might make the final decision in such an important matter.

One would expect that, if the Vice-*Voievode* had insisted on such haste, without a moment to spare, he would have made his decision known without the slightest delay. But no, in those days a ruler loved to wait as long as possible and give the opposing side time to think about the matter and maybe come in for a chat. "If he is a clever man, then he will know what to do; he will be able to take a hint. If not, it's not the end of the world either...."

For a whole week the record of the trial and the interrogation, and all the various papers, documents, and charges, lay on the desk of the Vice-*Voievode*. And the *Kehilla* did not consist of fools. The leaders of the suburban community took the hint; they probably had a meeting with the official in charge and enlightened him on the matter at hand. How eager he was to understand!

The result was that the Vice-*Voievode* understood both sides of the dispute and issued the following verdict:

It is true that Issac Jakubowicz desecrated *Yom Kippur* (the Vice-*Voievode* knew this because he appreciated the community's feelings) and therefore he merits punishment. It is also true, however, that the community went too far and acted prejudicially (which the Vice-*Voievode* knew because he "understood" Jakubowicz) and therefore the community too deserves to be penalized.

What punishment does Jakubowicz deserve? He is obliged (the Vice-*Voievode* ruled) to stand before the Ark of the Torah on the Sabbath following the decision and say the following: "I confess before all present here that I violated Jewish law and the law of the land when I ordered the men to work on *Yom Kippur*. I desecrated the holy day. Therefore I beg you to forgive me and not to follow my example." In addition, he must pay a fine of one hundred złoty immediately to be given to the hospital.

And the community? First they received a sharp reprimand and a warning that from that day on they must judge everything strictly according to law and justice, without any deviations or distortions, and if such a situation were ever repeated they would be punished to the full extent of the law. The city leaders particularly (because the court decided they were more guilty) received a light fine in addition—fourteen grzywna—to be paid to Isaac, and the same amount to the high court, without delay, under penalty of dire consequences.

Naturally, the leaders of the "suburban" community learned their lesson, and between October 3 and 11 did not sit with idle hands. They talked to the high official and reached full "understanding" with him.

These were the results of the desecration of *Yom Kippur* in pre-partition Poland.

Note

This chapter is based on the *Lwów Acta Vicepalatinalia*, Vol. IV & V, printed by Zbigniew Pazdro, *Organizacya i praktyka żydowskich sądów pod-wojewodzińskich*, Lwów 1903, supplement, Nos. 83-84.

CHAPTER XI
The Rabbinical Literature
of Polish Jews in the
Post-Partition Period

By the end of the eighteenth century Polish Jewry, once a unified organism, had become split asunder into several distinct ideological-spiritual groups.

These groups began to develop independently and to acquire individual characteristics. The formerly cohesive, unified mass of Polish Jews became divided into three parts. The uniting force, which until the end of the eighteenth century had held the Jews together from the eastern and western parts of the Polish Commonwealth, was forcibly broken. With the partitioning of Poland, Jews from the Prussian and Austrian sectors were pushed to the west, while Jews from the Russian sector gravitated to the east. Members of the first and second sectors were influenced by German culture, whereas members of the third were drawn to the Russian environment. To be sure, under German and Austrian occupation the Jews maintained most of the features and attributes of Polish Jews, but they also developed significant deviations.

Can we suggest that the different way of penetrating and understanding Talmudic and Rabbinical sources, observed over the course of time in the three sections of Polish lands, was also an outgrowth of this physical breakup? It is difficult to decide this matter categorically. In fact, Jews from the eastern parts of the former Polish Kingdom consistently strove to memorize Talmudic texts (*bkiuth*), whereas Jews of central Poland chose to construct intricate logical structures aided by subtle interpretations of the texts (*harifuth*). The former group exercized their minds in a "horizontal" direction, to encompass a great multitude of sources and "separate them out" in practical application; the second group worked in a "vertical" direction, to study, as it were, a smaller quantity of sources, but to formulate and comprehend them in a more fundamental and exhaustive manner. Still another difference: Polish Jews from the northern regions, who in time became known rather incorrectly as "Lithuanian," put their emphasis first on the study of the Talmud, and then on the earliest sources of Rabbinical literature; the Jews of the central lands of the former Kingdom devoted themselves to the study and interpretation of the Caro-Isserles code, *Shulhan Aruch*, and they produced in this field a series of immortal works which have fundamental importance for Jewish law and ritual. The third group of Polish Jews, under Prussian rule, kept pace at first with the Jews of the Russian and Austrian sectors; however, this did not last long. The study of the Talmud in the Prussian sector was considerably weakened as a result of the assimilation process which occurred in this region during the nineteenth century.

These lines of demarcation are, of course, variable. Between one method and the other there existed some leeway in forming an interpretation of rabbinical teachings both in the Russian and Austrian sectors. There were, for example, outstanding authorities in the Austrian sector who gravitated towards the Lithuanian mode, and vice versa. There were even luminaries who combined a broad knowledge of the Talmud with the ability to supply a penetrating interpretation of all the sources. But, indeed, in the world of the spirit there never exist permanent boundaries, and the field of Talmudic study is no exception in this respect.

Maintaining chronological order, we will attempt to give a survey of rabbinical literature written on Polish lands during the period of partitions. For methodological reasons, we will limit the study to the realm of the *halakha*, and thus to Rabbinical studies in the true sense of the term. We will consider the most important legal commentaries to the ancient sources of Jewish law, the attempts at independent codification, the authoritative collections of responsa, and so on.

To facilitate clarity, we will divide the 130-year epoch of the partitions into three periods. In the first, we will discuss the works of authors who lived until 1850, in the second those who lived until 1900, and in the third those who lived till the end of World War I.

1795-1850

In the second half of the eighteenth century, rabbinical literature blossomed splendidly in Poland. The fame of Polish rabbis echoed throughout Western European Jewry; its great luminaries of the time shone from Poland: Samuel Shmelka Hurwitz from Nikolsburg, Arye Leib of Metz (the *Shaagat Aryeh*), Meshulem Igra of Pressburg, Saul Levin of Amsterdam, Joseph Teomim of Frankfurt-on-the-Oder (the *Pri Megodim*), Ezekiel Landau of Prague (the *Noda bi-Yehuda*), Raphael Hacohen of Hamburg, and Pinhas Horowitz of Frankfurt-on-the-Main (the *Haflaah*). All were sons of Poland, who were called from tiny Polish cities to accept the greatest spiritual positions of leadership in Western European Jewry at that time, owing to their remarkable writings or their yet unpublished works which passed from hand to hand with great alacrity.

To these names, one can deservedly attach a series of rabbinical authorities who at the turn of the nineteenth century were living in Poland.

A. The Austrian Sector. Commentaries of extraordinary value to specific parts of the *Shulhan Aruch* were written by: Aryeh Leib Hacohen, Jacob Lorberbaum, and Jacob Meshulem Ornstein.

1) Aryeh Leib Hacohen, rabbi in Rożniatów and Stryj (d. 1813), wrote a commentary to the civil code *Hoshen Hamishpat* entitled *Ktzot Hahoshen*, which, owing to its unusually penetrating insights, soon became famous. It was reprinted several times during his lifetime, and in the second half of the nineteenth century it entered the published editions of this code as a marginal commentary.

Apart from this, he wrote a work entitled *Avney Miluim* (a commentary to the code *Even-Haezer*), published by his student Enzel Tzosmir and his son-in-law, Salomon Leib Rappaport (later rabbi in Prague, Bohemia).

2) Jacob Lorberbaum, rabbi in Kałusz, later in Lissa, and finally in Stryj (d. 1832), wrote a commentary entitled *Havot Daat* to the ritual code *Yore Deah*, and a commentary to the code *Hoshen Hamishpat* entitled *Nethivot Hamishpat* in which he refuted many times the comments of the aforementioned Rabbi Aryeh Leib (who responded in a book entitled *Meshovev Netivot*). Both of Lorberbaum's major works received great recognition in his lifetime and were printed several times, as were his other works: *Mekor Hayim*, *Torat Gittin*, *Kehilat Jacob*, and *Bet Jacob*. His decisions on questions of Jewish liturgy, compiled in a book entitled *Dereh Hahayim*, were almost unequivocally accepted.

3) Jacob Meshulem Ornstein, rabbi in Żółkiew and Lwów (d. 1839), is the author of a work entitled *Yeshuot Jacob*; the first three parts are a commentary to the code *Even-Haezer*; the next four apply to the code *Orah Hayim*; the remaining three pertain to the code *Yore-Deah*. His works also include remarks and responsa of his son Mordecai Zeev Ornstein (d. 1836), and his grandson, the rabbi of Brest-Litovsk, Rzeszów, and later Lwów, Hirsh Ornstein (1816-1888).

Not a rabbi himself, Zalman Margulies was one of the most renowned Talmudists of the nineteenth century (d. 1828). As an ordinary but very wealthy citizen, he lived in Brody and from there sent his responsa. He authored works which to this day are held in high esteem and attest both to his masterly knowledge of the Talmudic sources and to his systematic way of thinking. His collection of responsa is called *Bet Ephraim*. Other works: *Rosh Ephraim*, *Yad Ephraim*, *Shaarey Ephraim*, *Mate Ephraim*. Published for the first time in 1823 in Żółkiew, his work *Tiv Gittin* is accepted by most rabbinates concerning the question of the spelling of names of husbands and wives in divorce papers.

A master of methodology was Jacob Hirsh Yolles, rabbi in Dynów and Głogów (d. 1825). His work entitled *Melo Haroim* (three parts) contains an outline in alphabetical order of the most important Talmudic questions, specific derivations of hermeneutic rules, and indications on how to resolve halakhic questions in cases of differing opinions by competent authorities.

Abraham David Wahrman, rabbi in Buczacz (d. 1841), was the author of the work *Daat Kedoshim*, which is very important for rabbinical decisions in questions of ritual, which are dealt with in the first part of the code *Yore Deah*.

B. The Russian Sector. The school of Rabbi Elijah, the "Gaon of Wilno," and his pupils, the brothers Hayim and Zelman of Wołózyn, produced scores of first-rate scholars; however, this group published very few Talmudic works. This is not the only school sparse in literary output. At the turn of the nineteenth century we encounter many rabbis in the Russian sector who were widely renowned in the Talmudic world but who left behind no printed literary works. Ezriel of Lublin (popularly called "Der Eiserne Kopf," d. 1819), Abe Posvoler of Wilno (d. 1836), and Leib Katzenelenbogen of Brest-Litovsk (d. 1837) are three examples.

Rabbi Shneur Zalman of Liady (1747-1813) was an extremely interesting figure: he was the creator of a new current in Hasidism known by the name *Habad*. As one of the great thinkers of religious Jewry, he undertook in his early years to complete the code *Shulhan Aruch* with the inclusion of over 200 years of research from the time of the code's first printing. Scattered about in numerous works by different rabbis, the halakhic decisions during those 200 years were frequently at variance with one another, requiring ordering and classification. He carried out this work with great precision. He reformulated the actual text of the code and added a commentary known as the *Kuntres Ahron*. This work, encompassing the section *Orah Hayim* and parts of *Yore Deah* and *Hoshen-Hamishpat,* was published many times and achieved enormous authority.

Almost at the same time, a member of the Wilno rabbinate, Abraham Dantzig (1748-1820), was working on a compendium which contained the rules of the code as applied to the changed conditions of life. His work *Haye Adam* (a compendium to *Orah Hayim*) and *Hokhmat Adam* (a compendium to *Yore Deah*) achieved great popularity.

An author of scores of writings which entered the most distant realms of Rabbinical knowledge was Arye Leib Zunz, rabbi in Płock and Praga near Warsaw (d. 1833). His works *Ayelet Ahavim*, *Pne Arye*, *Hiddushey Maharal*, *Get Mkushar*, *Mshivat Nephesh* were published after his death from an entire original collection of manuscripts, because of the promise that he who printed one of Rabbi Zunz's works at his own expense would be assured by the rabbi of deliverance from worries and troubles. Publishers were therefore not hard to find.

A contemporary of Zunz enjoyed great acclaim: Rabbi Salomon Zalman Lipshitz (first in Nasielsk and Praga, and from 1819 in Warsaw; d. 1839), the author of a collection of responsa called *Hemdat Shlomo*. His glosses to the five Talmudic treatises *Yevamot*, *Ketubot*, *Kiddushin*, *Gittin*, and *Bava Bathra* were posthumously published under the same title.

Important works in the field of Talmudic discipline were written by these rabbis: Hayim Mordecai Margulies of Dubno, brother of the renowned Zalman Margulies of Brody (*Shaarey Tshuva*, the quintessence of 200 collections of responsa arranged as a commentary to the code *Orah Hayim*), Tuvia Hochgelernter of Zamość (*Mishnat Hakhamim*, a collection of halakhic debates based on Maimonides' writings); Abraham Zvi Hirsh of Piotrków (a collection of responsa *Brit-Abraham*); Moses Zeev Volf of Białystok (*Marot Hatzovot*, questions concerning marital law and glosses to *Shulhan Aruch*); Aron of Pinsk (*Tosaphot Aharon* in which he elucidated problems which had remained unresolved by previous glosses on the Talmud of the Tosaphists); and Yehuda Bacrak of Seyny, famed for his breadth of knowledge of the Talmud (and author of glosses entitled *Nimukey Ha-griv*).

C. The Prussian Sector. Excellence in rabbinical studies was reached by the scholars who resided in Poznań. Most notable among them were the brothers Joseph and Samuel Falkenfeld. The former (d. 1800) was the son-in-law of the famed Rabbi Ezekiel Landau of Prague (Bohemia). As a result of his unusual piety, he acquired the cognomen "Reb Joseph Hatzaddik." In addition to Poznań, he served as a rabbi in Witków, Sokal, and Jaworów. He left no Talmudic works (other than a small booklet published in 1881 entitled "Sheerit Joseph"). His brother Samuel Falkenfeld (d. 1808), formerly a rabbi in Przeworsk-Kańczuga and Tarnopol, succeeded him. He was the author of a collection of responsa, *Bet Shmuel Ahron*.

Another rabbi of Poznań, Akiva Eiger (1761-1837), stood out among his predecessors as the author of diversified responsa and glosses to most of the sources of Jewish law. His works, most of which were published posthumously, bore the author's surname in the titles: *Tshuvot Rabbi Akiva Eiger*, *Tossafot Rabbi Akiva Eiger*, *Hiddushey Rabbi Akiva Eiger*, *Hagahot Rabbi Akiva Eiger*, etc. His short but extremely accurate remarks on the Talmud entitled *Gilyon Ha-Shas* were also enormously popular.

In addition, we would like to mention the following authors: Israel Yonas Landau, rabbi in Kępno (*Meon Habraknot*, a commentary to the tractate *Berakhot*); Yehuda Leib Kalisher, initially a business man and then a member of the rabbinate of Lissa (*Hayad Hahazaka*, a collection of subtle Talmudic dissertations); and Hayim Auerbach, first in Lissa and then in Łęczyca (*Divrey Mishpat*, glosses and remarks to the code *Hoshen-Hamishpat*).

1850-1900

A. *The Austrian Sector*. Salomon Kluger, known as the "*Maggid* (Preacher) of Brody" (1783-1869), was a rabbi in Rawa, Kulików, Józefów, and Brzeżany and spent fifty years of his life in Brody as a member of the rabbinate and as a religious preacher. The quantity of his works is almost immeasurable; he wrote in 1854 that he had already composed 136 Talmudic manuscripts each over 200 pages long. Legends which formed around this remarkable rabbi of the nineteenth century maintain that he wrote 375 works, corresponding to the numerical value of the four consonants in his Hebrew name (*ShLoMoH*= 375). All of his works enjoyed enormous authority. Some of the most important: *Sefer Hahayim* (remarks to *Orah Hayim*), *Mey Nidda* (commentary to the tractate *Nidda*), *Nidrei Zrizin* (commentary to the tractate *Nedarim*), *Shnot Hahayim* (collection of responsa to *Yore Deah*), *Hiddushey Anshey Sheim* (collection of responsa to *Even Haezer*).

Hirsh Hayes (1806-1855) was a rabbi in Żółkiew and Kalisz.

His rather brief but profound works are highly valued, among them: *Torat Neviim*, a study of the essence of Jewish law; *Ateret Tzvi*; *Darkei Hahoraah* (on legal custom and methods of final formulation of legal norms); *Mevo Hatalmud* (an introduction to the Talmud explaining its structure and origin, translated into German by I.M. Jost in 1854); and a collection of responsa, *Rtzah* (the initials of *R*abbi *Tz*vi *H*ayes). His glosses to the Talmud are also well known.

A famous partnership of writing existed between the two brothers-in-law Mordecai Zeev Ettinger and Joseph Saul Natansohn. Together they are known by the name *Meforshey Hayam*, which is taken from the title of their first joint work (remarks to the Talmudic commentary *Yam Hatalmud* written by Rabbi Joshua Heshel of Tarnogród, at the end of which they added a series of responsa to contemporary rabbinical scholars. This appeared in Lwów in 1827. They also jointly published *Magen Giborim*, 2 volumes: commentary to the code *Orah Hayim*; *Meirat Einayim*.) The paths of these two distinguished Talmudists eventually parted, when Natansohn was called to become the Rabbi of Lwów in the year 1857. Ettinger (d. 1863) published separately a collection of responsa, *Maamar Mordecai*. Natansohn (d. 1875) published a series of valuable works whose fame spread throughout the rabbinical world: *Yad Yoseif Ve-Yad Shaul* (a commentary to the code *Yore-Deah*), *Avodat Haleviim*, *Divrei Shaul we-Yosseif Daat* (a collection of responsa), and most importantly, a collection of responsa in fourteen parts and five volumes entitled *Shoel Umeshiv*.

Two extremely prominent Talmudic authors of this period are Rabbis Hayim Halberstam of Nowy Sącz (Sanz) (d. 1876) and Joseph Babad of Tarnopol (d. 1876). The former, a founder of a new Hasidic dynasty of thousands of followers, attained unusual authority with his two-volume collection of responsa, *Divrei Hayim*, and a series of other works. The latter wrote a commentary of the thirteenth century work *Sefer*

Ha-Hinukh by Aron Barceloni entitled *Minhat Hinukh* and containing many subtle Talmudic dissertations which were highly regarded in learned circles.

In addition to the above, the following also deserve mention: Enzel Tzosmir, rabbi in Stryj, and Przemyśl (author of a valuable collection of responsa); Abraham Thumim, rabbi in Buczacz (*Hesed le*-Avraham); Meyer Wittmayer of Sambor (*Rematz*); Meyer Horowitz of Dzików-Tarnobrzeg (*Imrei Noam*); Moses Thumim of Horodenka (*Dvar Moshe*); Salomon Drymer of Skala (*Bet Shlomo* and the Talmudic commentaries *Yashreysh Yakov*); Meshulem Horowitz of Stanisławów (*Bar Livai*); Hirsh Ornstein of Lwów (*Birchat Rtzei*); and Isaac Ettinger of Lwów (*Maharya Halevi*). (All of these books are collections of responsa unless otherwise indicated).

B. The Russian Sector. Foremost among Talmudic authorities of this period was Rabbi Itzhak Meyer Alter (1799-1866), the founder of a great Hasidic dynasty from Góra Kalwaria ("Ger"). A student of Rabbi Leib Zunz of Płock, he acquired fame while still a young man under the name "*Der Poylisher Iluy*" (The Polish Genius). At the age of seventeen, he wrote his first work, *Hiddushey Harim*, a commentary to the tractate *Gittin*. He published all his later works pertaining to other tractates under the same name (as well as two volumes on the code *Hoshen Hamishpat*). A collection of his responsa, together with short glosses to the tractate *Hullin*, was published in Józefów in 1867 under the title *Tshuvoth Harim*. (The word *Rim* is an abbreviation of his name Rabbi Itzhak Meyer.) All of Alter's works are characterized by an unusual depth of thought.

Abraham Hirsz Eizenstadt (1813-1868), originally from Białystok, created a work of enormous importance entitled *Pithey Tshuva*. This book summarizes briefly and concisely the essence of many previous collections of responsa, and in the form of annotations to the *Shulhan Aruch* it assembles the various opinions of competent authorities, simultaneously indicating (under the name *Nahlat Tzvi*) which opinion should be accepted. In 1837 his first volume on the code *Yore Deah* was published; subsequently later works appeared, which were published together with the code itself and appeared as marginal commentaries.

The Lithuanian trend in the early years of the period under discussion was represented by, among others, R. Eisig Chaver (d. 1852), a rabbi of Wółkowysk, Tykocin, and finally in Suwałki (works: *Bet Itzhak*, *Binyan Olam*, *Seder Zmanim*), and by Isaac-ben-Aron, a rabbi in Karlin (also d. 1852), author of a several-volume work, *Keren Orah*, containing discourses on several Talmudic tractates, Jacob Meyer Padua (d. 1855) was a rabbi in Brest-Litovsk and the author of a two-volume work, *Mekor Mayim Hayim* (short addition to *Yore-Deah*); *Ketonet Pasim* (super-commentary to Alfasi).

Remarks on the sources quoted in the Talmud were written by Rabbi David Luria of Bychawa (*Hagahot Rdal*). Rabbi Shaya Mushkat, author of the work *Rashey Bsamim*, was from the Warsaw suburb of Praga and enjoyed great respect. Warsaw rabbis prominent at the time were: Hayim Davidson (d. 1854); Ber Meizels (deputy to Parliament in Kremsier, Austria, and a rabbi in Cracow in his youth; he was famous for his participation in the Polish Uprising of 1863 and was author of a commentary to Maimonides' *Sefer Hamitzvot* entitled *Biure Maharidav*, [d. 1870]); and Jacob Gesundheit (author of numerous works under the title *Tiferet Jacob*, d. 1878).

Joshua Eisig Spira, known by the name "*Reb Eisel Harif*" (d. 1873), was a fruitful and original scholar. A rabbi in Kalwaria, Kutno, Tykocin, and finally in Słonim, he published collections of responsa, *Eymek Yehoshua* and *Nahlat Yehoshua*, as well as a four-volume commentary to the Jerusalem Talmud entitled *Noam Jerushalmi*. This book gave incentive to more intensified study of the heretofore neglected Jerusalem Talmud. In addition, he created a new current in rabbinic homiletics with his works *Avi Hanahal* and *Sfat Hanahal*.

Samuel Strashun (1794-1872) lived in Wilno as a business-man. He recorded his glosses to the Babylonian Talmud assid-uously, and their publication assured him renown. He also wrote a commentary to the Midrash and glosses to Maimo-nides' work *Mekorei Harambam*. Betzalel Hacohen (1820-1878), a member of the Wilno rabbinate, was a recognized authority due to his works *Reshit Bikkurim* (responsa), *Tosafet Bikkurim*, and glosses to the Talmud *Mare Cohen*.

The rabbi of Kalisz, Meyer Auerbach (1815-1878), pub-lished a multi-volume commentary to the *Shulhan-Aruch* as well as a collection of responsa entitled *Imrey Bina*. He emi-grated to Jerusalem. Hayim Eleazer Waks, rabbi of Kalisz (d. 1889), was famous for his work *Nefesh Haya*. His father-in-law, a rabbi in Kutno, R. Israel Jehoshua Trunk (d. 1893), was the author of a remarkable commentary to *Hoshen Hamish-pat*, entitled *Yeshuot Israel*, and a number of other works, most of them published posthumously.

A very original rabbinical author was Gershon Henokh Leiner of Radzyn (1839-1891). His work *Sidrey Taharot* is most interesting as an imitation of a portion of the Talmud, which he accomplished in the following way. The Talmud, as is well known, is comprised of two parts: the *Mishna* and the *Gemara*. The *Gemara* consists of investigation of the text of the *Mishna* by scholars during the period between 200 and 500 C.E. Several parts of the *Mishna* section "*Taharot*" do not have *Gemara*. R. Leiner attempted in his early years to com-plete this missing section on his own by compiling all the notes (pertaining first to tractate Kelim, then to tractate Ohaloth) from Talmudic and Midrashic sources and skillfully grouping them so that they imitate the Babylonian Talmud. In addition he wrote two marginal commentaries to this "Talmud" which he constructed imitating the works of Rashi and the Tossafists. After its publication this work invoked great opposition on the part of some authoritative rabbis. Rabbi Betzalel Hacohen of Wilno came out against Leiner's book stating that it is not permissible that a contemporary rabbi should continue the work of the Talmud. However, because of its refined form and learned content, the book won widespread recognition. The same author also published other works of great renown, e.g., *Sfunei Tmunei Hol* (a discourse on the Biblical *Tchelet*, the blue thread prescribed in Numbers 15:38 for the fringes [*Tzitzit*] of a man's garments). Leiner discovered the mollusk called *Halazon* in Hebrew and recommended that from its blood the blue thread be manufactured. His numerous followers accepted his opinion.

In addition, the following renowned rabbinical authors should be mentioned: Israel (Lipkin) Salantor (1810-1883), author of the works *Tvuna, Imrey Bina,* and *Even Israel,* who lived for some time in Wilno; Naftali Tzvi Yehuda Berlin, rector of the Talmudic academy in Wołozyn (1817-1893), known by the abbreviation of "Ntziv," author of a collection of responsa, *Meshiv Davar,* and a three-volume commentary to the work *Sheeltot* of Rabbi Ahai Gaon; Joseph Ber Soloveitchik, rabbi of Brest-Litovsk (d. 1892), author of *Bet Halevi;* and Itzhak Elhahan Spector (1817-1896), rabbi of Kowno (who before assuming this post was a rabbi in Nieswież and Nowogródek), the author of a collection of responsa, *Beer Yitzhak,* and the works *Nahal Yitzhak* and *Ayin Yitzhak.*

C. The Prussian Sector: In the forefront of the dwindling number of rabbinical authorities in this region there appeared the rabbi of Poznań, an important Talmudist, Salomon Eiger (1783-1852), author of the glosses entitled *Gilyon Rsha.* Tzvi Hirsh Kalisher (1795-1874), a rabbi from Toruń and a well-known pioneer of the movement to colonize Palestine, was the author of the outstanding Talmudic work *Even Boheh* and *Moznayim Lemishpat* (2 volumes, pertaining to Hoshen Hamishpat). Eliahu Gutmacher, rabbi of Grodzisko, who associated with Kalisher in his pro-Palestine work, was the author of several important rabbinical works as well as glosses to the Talmud. The rabbi of Kępno, Jacob Simha Rehfish, was the author of the works *Shaarei Simha* and *Mishkan Haëiduth* (d. 1877).

Known as the "*Maggid* of Kępno," Meyer Leibish Malbim (1809-1879), a man whose biography is an interesting tapestry of wanderings through various countries, combined excellent Talmudic knowledge, philology, poetry, and social activism in one person. He spent fifteen years of his tempestuous life in Kępno, from whence came his cognomen. Among his numerous works are his well-known commentary to 24 books of the Bible, and the work *Artzot Hahayim* (a commentary of *Orah Hayim*).

1900-1918

A. The Austrian Sector. The greatest authority at the turn of the twentieth century was the rabbi of Lwów, Isaac Shmelkes (1827-1905), formerly rabbi in Żurawno, Brzeżany and Przemyśl. Insight, extraordinary logic, and acumen mark his responsa, collected in a six-volume work *Bet Yitzhak* (arranged according to all the parts of the *Shulhan Aruch*. They reached the most distant Jewish communities, were acknowledged everywhere, and evoked the awe of all communities with their thoroughness. The value attained by this collection of responsa was monumental.

Rabbi Shalom Mordecai Shwadron of Brzeżany (d. 1911) was famous for his erudition; he mastered the most distant realms of rabbinical knowledge. Among his works which enjoyed great influence are the multi-volume collection of responsa, *Maharsham*, and the treatises *Mishpat Shalom* and *Giluy Daath*.

Outstanding authors of the pre-war period were (taking into consideration only those who did not live to see the new Polish state in 1918): R. Leib Horowitz, rabbi of Stanisławów, author of a two-volume collection of responsa *Harey Bsamim*; R. Osias Horowitz, rabbi of Tarnobrzeg (Dzików), author of the works *Emek Halakha* and *Ateret Yeshua*; and R. Joseph Engel, member of the Cracow rabbinate, author of numerous and valuable Talmudic works.

B. The Russian Sector. The rabbi of Góra-Kalwaria Leib Alter (d. 1905), created a multi-volume, widely acclaimed work *Sfat Emet*, of which specific parts relate either to Talmudic tractates or to the Five Books of the Torah. The rabbi of Lublin, Hillel Lipshitz, wrote the work *Bet Hillel*, a commentary to Hoshen Hamishpat (d. 1908). Yehiel Michel Epstein, rabbi of Nowogródek (d. 1908), authored the most recent adaptation of the *Shulhan Aruch* code, called *Aruch Hashul-han*. He was unable to complete his work on the entire code, but the parts which were published became popular and widely accepted.

A rabbinical sage on a monumental scale was Rabbi Abraham Bornstein of Sochaczew (earlier in Parczew, Krośniewitz, and Nasielsk—d. 1910), author of a collection of responsa, *Avnei Nezer*, as well as the highly valued work *Eglei Tal*, dealing with rules of the Sabbath.

A rabbi of Pińsk, R. David Friedman, became famous for his extensive commentary to the code of Maimonides, entitled *Piskei Halakhot* (or *Yad David*). Another great authority was Rabbi Hayim Soloveitchik of Brest-Litovsk. Rabbi Moses Nachum Jerozolimski of Kielce attained recognition through his two-volume collection of responsa, *Minhath Moshe* and *Beer Moshe*.

C. The Prussian Sector. In the twentieth century the study of the Torah had already been extinguished in these lands, which could earlier point with pride to their great stars on the horizon of Talmudic knowledge.

Note

This essay was originally published in Polish in the collective work *Żydzi w Polsce Odrodzonej* [Jews in reborn Poland], edited by Ignacy Schiper, Arieh Tartakower, and Aleksander Hafftka, Vol. II, Warsaw, 1933, pp. 103-113.

CHAPTER XII
The Jews in Galicia

I

Only rarely is it possible to determine, for purposes of a historical survey, the precise beginning and end of a country's history. Galicia is one of the few exceptions.

Before 1772 Galicia did not exist. Before 1772 no one knew what "Galicia" really meant. The kings of Hungary had, for some time, been using the title "King of Galicia," actually a fictitious name. Its origin could be traced to Bela III, King of Hungary (1173-1196), who, in 1190, occupied the town of Halicz and then called himself "King of Galicia." He held the territory of Halicz for exactly *one* year, lost control of this territory, later recovered it, and lost it again. What remained of the whole adventure was the title "King of Galicia," a real *Titel ohne Mittel*, as it is called in German.

In 1772 "Galicia" took on meaning. In this year, three great European powers, Russia, Prussia and Austria, decided to annex portions of Poland which had been seriously weakened by internal disorder and which then bordered upon anarchy. The negotiations between the three powers began in 1770. It took less than two years from the beginning of the diplomatic talks until March 22, 1772, when Empress Maria Theresa issued an order to the Austrian army to cross the border into Poland. Austrian historians, realizing that it was not a morally proper step, describe the reluctance of the Empress in giving the order. They claim that she cried bitterly when signing this order. Austria's legal claim to Polish territory was obviously without foundation. However, being also Queen of Hungary, she used the old title of the Kings of Hungary concerning "Galicia" as an excuse. The title suddenly became very meaningful. It was proof that the territory around Halicz did not legitimately belong to Poland. Maria Theresa's conscience was relieved when it was explained to her that she was only taking back what really belonged to her. Within a short time Austrian battalions occupied, practically without opposition, territory inhabited by 3,000,000 people. The territory was called "Galicia."

There is no difficulty in determining when the history of Galicia ended: October 1918. The Austro-Hungarian Empire ceased to exist at the end of World War I, and Galicia was then reunited with its old mother country, Poland.

During the intervening years, some territorial changes took place. The Napoleonic wars, which changed the map of central Europe, also affected Galicia. For approximately thirty years, from the Congress of Vienna in 1815 until 1846, the town of Cracow was formally an independent republic.

In 1918, when the new Poland was reborn, the eastern part of Galicia spent several months as a separate country called "Western Ukraina." In the Spring of 1919, the Polish army put an end to the independent existence of Western Ukraina and all of "Galicia" became part of Poland. At this time the population of Galicia totalled about 9,000,000 inhabitants.

This survey covers the history of Jews in Galicia from 1772 until 1918. The Jewish population constituted a considerable portion of the inhabitants of Galicia, initially eight percent and later as much as ten percent. We know the precise figures as a result of a census made in 1773, which showed that 224,981 Jews came under Austrian domination in the newly acquired territories. The accuracy of the census of the following year is open to question. In 1774 the Jews in Galicia learned that to be counted meant also to be taxed, and suddenly the total was only 171,851 Jews. In 1776, after two more years of burdensome taxes, the count of the population showed only 144,200 Jews. Toward the end of the history of Jews in Galicia, some 850,000 Jews lived on this territory.

II

The 225,000 Jews of the province occupied by Austria in 1772 accepted the new rulers with the hope that they would be treated fairly. On October 4, 1777, Count Pergen, the administrator of the province, received an oath of allegiance from the representatives of the Jews in Lwów (Lemberg). We have, in a contemporary Vienna paper called *Wiener Diarium*, a description of the same event in Brody, where General von Graeven, the military commander, came to the synagogue, which was magnificently illuminated and filled to its capacity. The Jewish leader, Dr. Abraham Usiel, delivered a speech in which he expressed the thanks of the Jewish population to Her Majesty. A prayer for her health and further successes was recited and all dignitaries were invited to a reception where wine, Turkish fruit, and the finest cakes were served.

On July 16, 1776, Maria Theresa signed a decree which regulated the communal life of the Jewish community in her new province. She put at the head of the Jewish community a body called *Generaldirektion der Judenschaft* (General Leadership of Jewry) which was composed of thirteen members: six delegates of Jews living in the respective districts of the province (*Kreisaelteste*) and six special appointees called *Landesaelteste*. The thirteenth member was the chairman, a rabbi, called "*Oberlandesrabbiner*," who had to be appointed by the Empress. She appointed the Rabbi of Brody, Judah Leib Bernstein, to this post at the high salary of 600 guilders per annum.

The main task of the body was to distribute the tax for the Government among the individual communities. Under Polish rule, the Jews had paid a head tax of 2 guilders per annum. Maria Theresa changed both the name and the size of the tax. She felt it should not be called "head tax" but, in keeping with her more humane nature, "payment for tolerance" (*Toleranzgebuehr*). For this delicate touch she doubled the tax from 2 to 4 guilders.

In addition, she stated in her decree of 1776 that "no Jew be permitted to marry, who would not give evidence of his true income, who would not receive a special permission for marriage from the authorities, and who would not show that he paid the tax for that." In other words, a marriage tax was instituted, the stated reason being, as the Governor openly explained, "because Her Majesty wants to prevent with all possible means the growth of Galician Jewry." Only rich Jews were permitted to marry, and they had to pay, if they possessed from 500 to 1,000 florins, ten percent of the value of their property as a marriage tax. Those who possessed less then 500 florins could not even apply for permission. Those who possessed more than 1,000 florins had to pay a progressively higher rate of one half percent more for each 1,000 florins they possessed.

This source proved profitable to the government of Galicia. The total revenue reached 40,000 florins per annum. However, this did not prevent the natural growth of the Jewish population. Jews simply married without obtaining the permission of the authorities. Such non-legally-validated "ritual marriages" were not recognized by the authorities, and they later caused much confusion as to the legal status of Jewish families.

Maria Theresa showed special animosity to poor Jews. Those who could not pay the *Toleranzgebuehr* were simply ordered to leave the country. Poland still existed in 1772; the total disappearance of the nation did not occur until 1795. Poor Jews were, therefore, sent to the Polish border. The Jews soon learned how to counteract the draconic regulation. Since the number of Jews was known to the authorities, and it did not correspond to the number of taxpayers, the Jewish communities presented lists which included fictitious names. It was later explained that the fictitious Jews had been expelled from their respective communities. Authorities soon became suspicious and ordered that all lists be carefully checked by the local officials.

Maria Theresa prohibited Jewish artisans from working for Christians. Jewish surgeons were also not to accept Gentiles as patients. This caused despair among Jews, who suddenly saw themselves deprived of traditional sources of livelihood. The Austrian authorities began to act as enemies of the Jewish population of Galicia. In the official reports, the Jews were called "the corruption of the nation" (*Das Verderben des Landes*) and "the leeches of the population" (*Blutigel der Landes-Insassen*).

III

Maria Theresa was succeeded by her son, Emperor Joseph II (1780-1790). Under his rule, the guiding principle for dealing with the Jews of Galicia became speaking more kindly but acting more ruthlessly. Joseph II was a highly educated man, an admirer of Voltaire and the encyclopedists. He made religious tolerance his ideal. With regard to Jews, his policy also purported to be religious tolerance, culminating in his Patent of Tolerance of May 7, 1789. In practice, however, serious discrimination was practiced against the Jewish population.

Under a decree of January 24, 1785, Jews were completely removed from their positions in the small villages. They were permitted to stay on as farmers, but were required to abandon their age-old role as small businessmen. Thousands upon thousands were left without bread, and they asked to be assigned land for farming. The local authorities refused to let them work on the vast territories belonging to the government because "they are unworthy of this favor" (*unfaehig dieser Gnade*).

On February 18, 1788, Joseph II ordered the Jews to be inducted into the armed forces. This meant, of course, total assimilation for the young men. Jews began to leave the country and many fled across the Hungarian border.

The principle of enforcing restriction on marriages was strengthened by Joseph II. The marriage tax started at 40 florins and ran, in some cases, as high as 300 ducats.

In decrees of 1785 and 1787, Joseph II ordered that Jews adopt family names. This innocent-sounding regulation caused great difficulty to Jews, because it exposed them to the discretion of local authorities with regard to the selection of name. In order to obtain a nice family name with a flower or precious metal or stone in it (like "Rosenthal" or "Goldstein"), a bribe had to be given to the local *Kreishauptmann*. Those who paid less were given names with plain metals in them ("Eisen", "Stahl"). Those who paid nothing were branded with the name of an animal ("Hund", "Stier", "Katze") or a defamatory description (like "Nachtlager"). Through their family names Galician Jews appeared Germanized.

With his decree of tolerance of 1789, Joseph II destroyed the autonomous organization of the Jewish community. The *Generaldirektion* was abolished. Instead, 141 local communities governed themselves separately.

The decree began with eliminating "the differences between the legal status of Christians and Jews" and stating generally that "Jews ought to be granted all freedoms that others enjoy." After this introduction, sixty-four articles followed regulating the status of the rabbis and synagogues (Articles 1-10), schools (Articles 11-14), communities (Articles 15-22), marriages and family names (Articles 23-30), way of life and occupation (Articles 31-40), jurisdiction (Articles 41-47), and taxes and military training (Articles 48-64). In this decree, Joseph II enforced the compulsory assimilation of the Jewish population. Jewish children were required to attend German schools. Graduation from a school was a condition for receiving marriage licenses (as was the tax). Rabbis had to prove that they possessed some secular education. Jews were put under the jurisdiction of state courts. Any change of domicile by a Jew was dependent upon his owning a passport, and no immigration of Jews into Galicia was tolerated. A Jew who came to the country had to pay a special duty (*Geleitzoll*). A special tax was introduced on kosher meat. No Galician Jew was permitted to travel to Vienna, except for a temporary stay of fourteen days upon payment of a tax; the receipt (*Boleta*) was to be returned at the point where the Jew had previously entered Vienna.

The successors of Joseph II—his brother Leopold II (1790-92), his nephew Francis II (1792-1835), and Ferdinand I (1835-1848)—continued in the same vein. The Jews of Galicia continued to be considered a source of income for the State. The most discriminatory tax was introduced in 1800, a tax on Sabbath candles. Every Jewish woman was required to pay a tax for her Sabbath candles at the rate of three kreuzer per candle. Failure to pay was proof that she was "anti-religious" and reason for imprisonment. Other candles, such as *Hanuka* candles, *Yom Kippur* candles, wedding candles, *Yahrzeit* candles, were also taxed. In this way the Austrian Empire received large amounts of revenue from the Galician Jews. The collection was entrusted to individuals who rented the business from the Government. The Sabbath candles alone reaped 250,000 florins in the first year. A new type of despicable official appeared on the horizon; he was called a "candle-renter" (*Lecht-pachter*). An organization of terror was built on the basis of this tax. Very soon the right to vote in elections for the leadership of the *Kehilla* became dependent upon payment of the candle tax. The collector of the tax, the *Lecht-pachter*, almost became a dictator in Jewish communal life. He issued the certificate which entitled one to vote; quite often he himself became the leader of the community because he could control the election.

This horrifying mode of life of Galician Jews existed until 1848, when the revolution caused by the "Spring of Nations" brought about a new constitution for Austria, signed by a new and young Emperor, Francis Joseph I. This constitution, dated March 4, 1849, stated: "Full freedom of creed and the right of domestic exercise of religious confession is guaranteed to all. The enjoyment of civil and political rights is independent of religious confession, but civil duties should not be impaired by religious beliefs." This constitution marked the beginning of the emancipation of Galician Jews.

IV

The process of emancipation of Galician Jews was not an easy one. The discriminatory taxes were abolished but full equality of rights was not yet obtained. When the governor of Cracow sent an inquiry to Vienna asking whether emancipation of Jews was included in the new constitution, he was told that "the Emperor wishes that the equality of rights granted to all religions be soon transformed into reality." This expressed goal was governmental policy until the end of 1851. The constitution of 1849 was then declared invalid.

During the short period between 1849 and 1851, the struggle for emancipation was a very difficult one. Galician Jews had a representative in the parliament of Kremsier, Rabbi Baer Meisels from Cracow, who took his seat on the left side of the house. When a member of the Government asked him why he sat on the left side, his famed reply was, "Because we Jews have no rights."

In many respects restrictions of Jews were renewed after the abolition of the constitution. In October 1853, the Jews lost the right to acquire land. On July 1, 1857, the governor of Lemberg (Lwów) prohibited Jews from employing Gentile servants.

At the same time, however, political emancipation was progressing. Galicia received political autonomy, and elections to the local legislature (*Sejm*) took place in 1861. Jews were originally denied the right to participate in these elections. A protest delegation traveled to Vienna, and the Emperor then ordered that the Jews be accorded the right to vote and run for office—the active and passive rights to participate. Three Jews were then elected.

Finally, in 1867, emancipation became a reality. The constitution of December 21, 1867 proclaimed full equality of rights for everyone. Jews were freed from all restrictions. They were admitted to the universities and could be elected to municipal offices.

The fight for full emancipation still had to be conducted in the local legislature of Lemberg (Lwów), where many members opposed full equality of rights for Jews. Not until October 1868 did this struggle end. A great liberal among Poles, Franciszek Smolka, delivered a speech in the *Sejm* in which he said:

> The book of history is before us but we cannot read it. One word can solve the most difficult problems. This word is freedom. Freedom and equality under all circumstances. Look how complicated the Jewish problem is. There is almost no solution to it. However, it is so easy. One word may solve it: equality for all Jews....

The *Sejm* voted overwhelmingly for the emancipation of the

Jews, who did not fail to show their gratitude to the Poles. A strong assimilationist tendency began to prevail among the Jewish "intelligentsia." Instead of following the trend toward German culture, the young generation of the nineteenth century fell under the influence of Polish romanticism.

Jews in Galicia became an important political group. In many municipalities Jews played leading roles; some Jews were elected mayors. In 1874, 45 of 306 municipalities had a majority of Jewish councilors, and 10 towns were governed by Jewish mayors.

This success brought about adverse reaction. Anti-Semitism became stronger in Galicia, both politically and economically, at the same time, in the last decade of the nineteenth century, a new nationalistic slogan gained popularity among the Jewish population of Galicia: "We are neither Poles nor Germans, we are Jews."

With the advent of the twentieth century, the Zionist movement began to play an important role in Galicia. In the 1907 Parliamentary elections, three Zionist candidates were elected. Together with a Zionist elected in Bukovina, they formed the first Jewish National Club in the Vienna Parliament. In 1911, however, no Zionist was elected to the Parliament in Galicia. The local authorities strongly supported the assimilationist candidates, who won with their support.

In addition, Orthodox Jewish representatives occasionally won seats in the Austrian Parliament. We have already mentioned Rabbi Baer Meisels, who was a member of the Parliament in Kremsier. In 1879, the Rabbi of Cracow, Simon Schreiber, was elected to the *Reichsrat* in Vienna from the district of Kołomyja. After his death in 1883, the Jews of Kołomyja sent to Parliament another Orthodox rabbi, Dr. Joseph Samuel Bloch, who was reelected twice.

V

Galician Jewry wrote a glorious page in the annals of Jewish culture. It produced luminaries in Torah study who not only earned the respect and admiration of their contemporaries but also influenced others many years after their death.

Arye Leib Hacohen, who died in Stryj in 1813, authored a commentary to the Jewish civil code *Ketzot Hahoshen*, which is unparallelled in its logical sharpness. Jacob Lorberbaum, who died in the same Galician town in 1832, wrote one of the most important commentaries to the ritual code *Havot Daath*, as well as another commentary to the civil code *Netivot Hamishpat*. Jacob Meshullam Ornstein, who died in 1839, composed the voluminous work *Yeshuot Jacob*, which influenced many scholars. Salomon Margulies, who died in 1828, was not a rabbi but lived as an ordinary member of the community of Brody; he wrote four volumes of responsa, *Bet Ephraim*, and many other books which are recognized as being most authoritative. Jacob Hirsh Yolles, who died in 1825, wrote an alphabetically ordered survey of Talmudic problems, *Melo Haroim*, a masterpiece of methodology. Salomon Kluger, who died in 1869, wrote several hundred books, all of which enjoy the highest esteem today. Joseph Saul Natansohn, rabbi of Lwów, wrote several volumes of responsa, *Shoel Umeshiv*, and many other highly authoritative works. Hayim Halberstam of Nowy Sącz wrote a collection of responsa, *Divrei Hayim*, which gained world recognition. So did the book *Minhat Hinuch*, written by Rabbi Joseph Babad of Tarnopol. Others on the long list of world-renowned Talmudic scholars who lived in Galicia toward the end of the nineteenth century are: Enzel Tzosmir, Abraham Thumim, Meyer Wittmayer, Meshulem Horowitz, Hirsh Ornstein, Isaac Ettinger, Isaac Schmelkes, and Shalom Mordecai Schwadron. Each of these was a giant of scholarship, a man whose word was accepted as decisive not only in Galicia but all over the world, wherever problems of Jewish religious life required solution in accordance with Jewish law.

The Hasidic movement exerted great influence on Galician Jewry, and many of its most respected leaders lived in Galicia. The founder of the movement, Rabbi Israel "*Baal Shem Tov*," lived for several years in Galicia. The famous Rabbi Elimelech (1717-1786) of Leżajsk, the author of *Noam Elimelech*, a classic in Hasidic literature, resided in Galicia while developing his ideas regarding the *Tzaddik* who can influence the course of the entire universe. His disciples, among them the "Prophet of Lublin," Jacob Isaac Horowitz, who began his career in the Galician town of Lublin, were responsible for building the Hasidic movement of the late 18th century. One of Rabbi Elimelech's students was Rabbi Naftali Zvi Horowitz of Ropczyce, one of the greatest Hasidic leaders of all times. In 1840 Rabbi Israel Friedman of Ruzan settled in Galicia and founded in Sadagóra an enduring Hasidic dynasty. One of his sons, David Moshe, settled in Czortków and another, Mordecai Shraga, in Husiatyn; they became the founders of great Hasidic houses. In Dynów resided Rabbi Zvi Elimelech Spira, the author of the famous book *Bnei Isas'har*. Rabbi Shalom Rokach founded the dynasty of Bełz and Rabbi Chaim Halberstam that of Santz (Sącz). Hasidism began and grew in small Galician towns, such as Rymanów, Strelisk, Przemyślany, Żydaczów, Komarno, Sasów, Bojan. Great *Tzaddikim* lived in these towns, and they were surrounded by countless followers.

Another influential movement in Jewish life which was prominently represented in Galicia was the *Haskala*. Its most prominent spokesman was Nachman Krochmal (1785-1840), who lived in Żółkiew and there wrote his famous book *More Nevuche Ha-Zman*. Salomon Yehuda Leib Rappaport of Tarnopol (1790-1867) became the pioneer of the *Wissenschaft des Judenthums* and authored his famous biographies of Saadia Gaon, Nathan-ben-Yechiel, Elieser Hakalir, and others.

Joseph Perl, Isaac Erter, and Joshua Heshel Schorr head the long list of Galician *Maskilim*.

Galician Jewry reacted vigorously to important issues in Jewish life. In 1825, Mordecai Manuel Noah developed plans for a Jewish State and received enthusiastic support from a physician from Sieniawa, Galicia, Dr. Eliezer Sinai Kirshbaum, who had written a booklet, *Hilkot Yemot Hamashiah*, prior to Noah's appeal and thought obviously the time of the Messiah was approaching.

Dr. N.M. Gelber showed in his book, *Toldot Hatenua Hatziyonit b'Galicia* (Jerusalem, 1957), that on Galician soil the hopes for a Jewish restoration in Palestine existed early in the nineteenth century.

One of the first organizations in the world which fostered the Jewish settlement in Palestine was founded, in 1875, in Przemyśl, Galicia. In 1881 a Jew of Lwów named Moses Shrenzel published a pamphlet called *Die Loesung der Judenfrage* in which he proposed the establishment of a Jewish state. Originally he proposed to build this state in America, but later he selected Eretz Israel. The Jews of Galicia were impressed. The contemporary Jewish press covered Shrenzel's brochure extensively.

Real Zionist activities began in Galicia in 1883, when Dr. Joseph Kobak founded the society *Mikra Kodesh* in Lwów. In this society several young people who were destined to become Zionist leaders—Osias Thon, Mordecai Ehrenpreis, Marcus Braude, Adolph Stand, and Salomon Schiller—made their first appearances.

Sixteen years after 1883 Herzl's *Judenstaat* appeared. Galicia became one of the strongest centers of pro-Palestine activities.

This was Galicia, a real "mother of Israel." From that small province light spread all over the Jewish world. *Ex Galicia lux*.

CHAPTER XIII
On the Protocol Books
of the Jewish Communities
in Rzeszów, Przeworsk, Łańcut, and Kańczuga

I

In old Poland, it was customary for the Jewish communities to record the more important decisions of the *Kehilla* in separate books, called in Hebrew *Pinkas*. These books, which recorded the meetings of Jewish lay leaders, included many documents pertaining to the life of the community. A *Pinkas* also reflected the financial administration of the *Kehilla*, since the treasurer of the community entered a written account of the communities' revenues and expenditures into the *Pinkas* every year. Those who dealt with taxation (*shamaim*) provided a list of taxable persons along with an estimated tax quota. Furthermore, a *Pinkas* served as a registry for ownership of seats in the synagogue.

References to these protocol books can be found in old Polish documents, in which the *Pinkasim* are called *księgi duchowne* (ecclesiastical or spiritual books). For example, in the regulation issued by *Voievode* Jabłoński for the Jews of Lwów on July 20, 1726, we read:

> I have received a petition ["supplication]...telling me that the rabbi has permitted himself something new, which goes beyond the legal stipulations contained in their ecclesiastical books recorded from their ancestors. This was shown to me and translated for me.... I recognize [the petition] to be justified [and order] that the present rabbi and those who will come after him should be governed by this book and its provisions.[1]

Such protocol books were kept not only by the *Kehillot* but also occasionally by special associations and brotherhoods.

The *Pinkasim*, which date back centuries, have perished for the most part. Some were destroyed by fires in the ghettos; others were buried, according to Jewish custom, to preserve them from profanation after becoming unusable, in the corners of the local cemeteries together with remnants of old Torah scrolls and loose pages of used Hebrew books. Unfortunately, the need to preserve these frequently invaluable historic relics was never felt very strongly by the organs of the communities, and few of the *Pinkasim* have lasted to our days.

I have succeeded in obtaining five *Pinkasim* for inspection from four communities in Central Poland (Rzeszów, Przeworsk, Łańcut, and Kańczuga). While copying the important parts of these books for possible publication as source material for the history of Jews in Poland, I had the opportunity to do some research on these books. Their contents are of great historical value.

II

The *Pinkas* from Przeworsk, kept by the town rabbi, is the most comprehensive book of the five. The oldest note dates from the year 1759 (or 5519 according to the Jewish calendar). The new book was begun after a fire had consumed the old protocol book. The fire also destroyed the local synagogue).

The *Pinkas* contains:

a) reports on annual elections of *Kehilla* Elders;

b) the treasurers' closing of *Kehilla* finances, containing the makeup of incomes as well as very detailed specifications of expenditures;

c) registers of taxpayers from both local and neighboring villages;

d) detailed statements on the community's debts and records concerning loans incurred by the *Kehilla* from the neighboring clergy;

e) decisions of the *Kehilla* Elders relating to various questions;

f) copies of contracts concluded by the *Kehilla* leadership with the collectors of taxes (*krupki*);

g) agreements and receipts relating to salaries of local functionaries (rabbis, cantors, etc.);

h) notes pertaining to the collection of state taxes (as, for example, the *Toleranzgebuehr* introduced by Empress Maria Theresa in the year 1776);

i) interesting certificates (a total of sixteen items) for the *gubernium* of Lwów from the years 1777-1782, containing a three-year guarantee by the Elders for the payment of taxes—which was necessary to obtain permission to conclude a marriage, in accordance with the regulation of March 8 and June 28, 1773 and the decree of Maria Theresa of 1776;

j) copies of particularly important rabbinical court verdicts;

k) norms governing taxation;

l) inventories of the office of the *Kehilla* and the synagogues;

m) part of the *Kehilla*'s and rabbi's correspondence with people outside the community on important matters;

n) registers relating to the ownership of seats in the synagogue;

o) registers of all Jewish inhabitants, providing the basis for a "per-capita" calculation of the *pogłowne* tax (from which we learn that in 1774 the Jewish community of Przeworsk numbered, together with its neighboring villages 494 men and 545 women, with specification made for men and women in groups according to age: up to one-half year, five years, fifteen years, thirty years. and fifty years);

p) miscellaneous notes from daily life, which have a great significance for scientific research, especially in ethnology.

The *Pinkas* of Przeworsk was not kept chronologically. Some of the notes, such as the registers of inhabitants or inventories, are placed at the end of the book, in order to facilitate their usage without turning pages. Items with recent notes were inserted here and there by rabbis who did not understand that the *Pinkas* should be used chronologically, and therefore they indiscriminately made entries on blank pages.

III

The Jewish community of Kańczuga, which was located in the immediate vicinity of Przeworsk and which belonged administratively to that town, preserved two protocol books. One concerns the city's synagogue and originates from the end of the eighteenth century. The second, somewhat older, is a protocol book of the charitable brotherhood which provided help to the sick (*Bikkur-Holim*).

Both books were initiated by Samuel Falkenfeld, the rabbi of Przeworsk who was simultaneously the rabbi of Kańczuga.

He signed the *Pinkas* of the synagogues with the abbreviation "F.F." taken from his family name, Falken-feld.

While the first book contains nothing of interest (apart from the first two pages), the second presents an example of the bylaws of an association among Polish Jews. In the first eighteen articles, Falkenfeld specified the rights and duties of the members and gave an outline for the activities of the brotherhood's organs. The next four articles concern another association which joined this brotherhood. The concluding articles again refer to the organization of the brotherhood and contain rules governing election to its leadership.

IV

The *Pinkas* from Łańcut is older than that of Przeworsk, and dates back to the year 1730. It is improperly bound, for the oldest pages are located at the end of the book, and the pages are numbered beginning with 152.

It contains protocols of the elections of the Elders, decrees on taxation, registers of the ownership of seats in the synagogue, notes on important events, and also a list of the appointments of three Łańcut citizens as administrators of Palestinian funds. From these appointments we learn that, on behalf of the *Vaad Arba Aratzot* (Council of Four Lands), these funds were administered in 1750 by the rabbi from the Lwów district, Isaac Landau, and the then-rabbi of Yampol, Ezekiel Landau (who later became famous as rabbi of Prague in Bohemia). This appointment is signed by the envoy from Palestine, Yeruhem Ashkenazy. His letter to a rabbi of Żmigród (in which he informs him that he had remained until the tenth of *Elul* "in the region of Zamość in Jarosław" and had managed in the meantime to attend a session of the Jewish *Vaad* in Konstantyn) is also inserted in the book.

Polish notes can also be found in several places in the *Pinkas* of Łańcut. These are endorsements of certain documents by the superior authority of the castle and court in Łańcut. Thus, on page 2b, there appears the following double endorsement:

> 1) I approve these decisions of the Łańcut *Kehilla* in all their Points and Clauses, so that it remain for all time. Signed in the Łańcut castle on the 26th day of April, the year 1751. Jan Rzymierski.
>
> 2) I approve these decisions of the Łańcut *Kehilla* in all their Points and Clauses, so that it remain for all time. Signed in the Łańcut Court on the 22nd day of April, the year 1754 [1751?]. R. Karnierski.

An endorsement of May 12, 1773 appears on page 64a, whereas on page 98a, after a summation of a series of reductions from estimated tax quotas, the following note in Polish appears:

> I approve all the above-mentioned conditions in Hebrew, and in case a debtor should not be content with the present agreement, and venture to quarrel over this with the Elders and drag it to the Superior Authority—on such a person I hereby impose the fine of 300 grzywna. Dated June 2, 1764. Antony Ptocki [Potocki].

Later was added:

> For future occasions, I recommend to the Jewish Elders that [he] be immediately fined with 300 grzywna, which will together add up to 900. *Datum ut supra*. A. Ptocki.

V

The Rzeszów *Pinkas* is the oldest, for it contains notes from the year 1702. It numbers 449 pages and is actually a combination of two books. The older one is from the first decade of the eighteenth century, and the more recent one dates from the first decade of the nineteenth century.

The first part of the Rzeszów *Pinkas* is a cashbook of the *Kehilla*. Each member of the community has his separate page, on which his estimated tax quota is noted in the first paragraph. Payments made by him and credited to him are then listed.

From specific payments, recognized as tax payments, there resound echoes from the Northern War (1700-1721). Examples are: "to the Swedes," "to the Moscals [Russians]," "to the Royal Germans," "to the Saxons," "as a present to Steinbock," "by the *shtadlan* [representative] in Jarosław for pigs [for the army?]," "to the generals," and more.

A few items testify that when the community needed cash it collected advances on tax payments from its members and settled accounts with them later.

The pages containing the individual accounts are mixed with pages from the second *Pinkas*, younger by one-hundred years, which presents an altogether different image; these are texts of partnership contracts between merchants of a haberdashery residing in Rzeszów. These contracts shed a practical light on the curious realm of legal relations between the Jews at that time; they mostly follow one pattern. It is obvious that this branch of trade was very popular among Rzeszów Jews at the end of the nineteenth century.

Were these two bound together simply by accident?

On a series of pages on which tax accounts from the time of the Northern War are listed, the contracts between the Jewish haberdashers were added later. From this we can conclude that the *Pinkas* was originally exclusively a cash book; only one hundred years later were empty and half-empty pages used to enter concluded contracts of partnership.

Thus a lack of piety for historical documents is old, perhaps as old as the documents themselves.

Note

[1]Zbigniew Pazdro, *Organizacya i praktyka żydowskich sądów podwoje-wodzińskich* [The organization and practice of the Jewish Under-*Voivode* Courts), Lwów, 1903, p. 181.

CHAPTER XIV
The Agudat Ha-ortodoksim
(Union of Orthodox Jews) in Poland

I

The World War of 1914-1918 had a decisive impact on the development of the *Agudat Israel* movement. After the foundations of *Agudat Israel* had been laid in Katowice in the summer of 1912 and preparations were being made for the first *Knessia Gedolah* (World Congress), the outbreak of World War I came as a disruptive blow.

During the course of the war, however, it became evident that military developments were creating new and unexpected possibilities for the activities of *Agudat Israel*. Germany's victories over Russia enabled her to annex the Polish territory which had been part of Russia up to 1914. (It was known as "Congress Poland" because, after the defeat of Napoleon, the

Congress of Vienna of 1815 had given it to Russia.) In this annexed territory the Germans set up a "General Gouvernement" with General von Beseler at the head and began to consider creating a new Poland that would be oriented towards the "Central Powers," Germany and Austria.

Berlin immediately perceived that the Jews (who made up ten percent of the population) played an important role in the annexed territory, and that in some way the Jews of Congress Poland would have to be persuaded to take a pro-German attitude. It was not difficult to recognize that the Jewish community in Russian Poland—the overwhelming majority of the Jews in Warsaw, Łódź, and other (smaller) centers—was religious and observant.

The German Jews, on their part, took steps soon after the outbreak of the war to establish contact with Jews in Poland. The Zionist leaders, Dr. Alfred Klee and Dr. Max Bodenheimer, organized a "Committee for the East" to bring the mission of Berlin to the Jews of Russian Poland. The *Freie Vereinigung fur die Interessen des Orthodoxen Judentums* (Free Union for the Interests of Orthodox Judaism) did not lag behind; it even took the practical step of attempting to obtain permission from the German government to send emissaries to Poland.

The head of the Department for Jewish Affairs in the General Gouvernement office in Warsaw was Dr. Ludwig Haas, a member of the Reichstag; the "Free Union" effectuated the appointment of Rabbi Pinhas Kohn of Ansbach as his advisor. A second official emissary was appointed to be the expert in Jewish educational affairs, Rabbi Emmanuel Carlebach of Cologne, who had also been the principal of the Jewish Teachers' Training College in his city.

The two delegates from Germany arrived in Warsaw in February 1916. The situation of religious Jewry in Poland was politically very complicated. Jacob Rosenheim writes in his memoirs[1] that the appointment of Dr. Haas as "expert in

Jewish affairs" was a "thunderclap" for the religious Jews because Haas was a Reform Jew with plans to make "cultured people" out of the "half-savage" Polish Jews who, in his opinion, were an "offshoot of the ancient Tatars." He planned to close the traditional *cheders* and replace them with German schools.

Accompanied by a delegation from the *Freie Vereinigung*, Rosenheim traveled to Poland and had a long talk with Governor von Beseler. As he reports, a "miracle" happened with Dr. Haas. He became friendly with Rabbi Pinhas Kohn and under his influence was transformed into quite a different person. Rabbi Kohn's influence continued to grow stronger and, when Jacob Rosenheim met with Dr. Haas a few months later, Dr. Haas told him: "It is a disgrace for the Orthodox Jews in Germany that such a figure as Rabbi Pinhas Kohn does not occupy the leading position he deserves." Naturally, the Jews in Poland benefited tremendously from this change in Dr. Haas' attitude.

Rabbis Kohn and Carlebach soon realized that what the religious Jews needed, first of all, was an organization. At that time the masses of Hasidic Jews in Poland had no representative who could speak for them. The necessary steps were taken without delay. About a month after the arrival of the two emissaries in Warsaw, the government granted permission for an "Orthodox *Verein*" to begin its activities. The Frankfurt *Israelit* of March 30, 1916 reported:

> Warsaw, 22 March. The Orthodox organization, which was founded by the local Hasidic rabbis with the agreement of the rabbis and many distinguished laymen of the community, was confirmed by the German authorities. The organization aims to unite all religious Jews into one body which will (a) gain its proper influence in Polish Jewry, (b) watch over all religious matters, and (c) conduct those matters as the official representative of Orthodox Jewry. The organization expects to have hundreds of thousands of members who will give it the author-

ity to speak in the name of a prominent section of the Jewish population.

This is the first report concerning the birth of the independent Orthodox organization in Poland. Among Jews it became known as *Agudat Ha-ortodoksim* (the Union of the Orthodox Jews).

II

In Warsaw, the two delegates from Germany relied primarily upon the *Gerer Hasidim*. The *Gerer Rebbe*, Rabbi Abraham Mordecai Alter (who then resided at 20 Pańska Street in Warsaw), gave the emissaries his full support. Dr. Carlebach, writing about this to his friends, drew a very interesting picture of religious Jewish life in the Polish capital.[2]

Rabbi Carlebach describes several personalities whom he met in Warsaw—for example, the future Bendiner Rabbi, Hirsch Henokh Levin, about whom he says: "He is a wise, splendid man with extraordinary love and goodness." In the home of Rabbi Hirsch Henokh and his hospitable family of ten children, the delegates from Germany were made to feel unusually welcome. Rabbi Carlebach writes about this with great enthusiasm. He also mentions that the eldest son was twenty-two years old, and we may assume that this was the later leader of the world *Agudat Israel*, Rabbi Isaac Meyer Levin. In general, the letters of Rabbi Carlebach describe the leading figures of the Polish *Agudat Israel* in their early roles.

The new organization's path of development was not an easy one. Almost simultaneously, another organization was created—its Hebrew name was *Binyan Haneh'rasot* (The Rebuilding of the Destroyed)—whose founding meeting took place on March 29, 1916 with the participation of the *Gerer Rebbe*. Its aims were: (1) the rebuilding of the destroyed synagogues, mikvas, Talmud Torahs, yeshiyoth, hospitals, and homes for rabbis; (2) relief activity; (3) assistance for *mohelim*, *shokhtim*, rabbis, cantors, etc. It seemed as though a competitor to the newly formed Orthodox organization, *Agudat Ha-ortodoksim*, was in existence.

In the report which appeared in the Frankfurt *Israelit* (April 6, 1916) on the founding meeting of *Binyan Haneh'rasot* there is this interesting comment:

> Mr. Elias Kirshbraun, in order to avoid any impression that there is any intent here to compete with the recently founded Orthodox organization, proposed that there be a clear limitation on the tasks of *Binyan Haneh'rasot*. Around this point a debate ensued in which the *Gerer Rebbe* stressed the necessity for cooperation between the two Orthodox bodies. He demanded that there be complete unity among religious Jews. A committee was then appointed to work out an agreement between the two organizations.

This account in the *Israelit* mentions a name that soon became popular among the Jews of Poland, Elias Kirshbraun (later the *Sejm* Deputy and President of the Warsaw *Kehilla* Council). He was destined to begin his political career by arranging an accommodation between the *Agudat Ha-ortodoksim* and the *Binyan Haneh'rasot*.

This agreement was immediately put into practice. The *Israelit* of May 25 reports from Warsaw that "the lengthy negotiations regarding a unification of both Orthodox groups led to a satisfactory result." On Thursday, May 18, a joint meeting took place at which it was decided to postpone the elections of the leadership until the membership reached at least 10,000. (The total at that time was 3,000 members.) By the beginning of the Hebrew month of Sivan they expected to have enrolled another 12,000 members, at which time they were to elect a leadership. Together with the elections they were also to appoint a Rabbinical Committee which would have full authority in all religious matter of the organization.

The first general political elections for a city council in Warsaw were approaching. Although these elections were hardly democratic—ninety councilmen were to be elected in six electoral groups (in Polish Kuria), and only a part of the population was entitled to vote—interest among the Jews in the city was very high. In some of the groups, elections did not take place at all, because an understanding was reached with the Poles, and only one slate was presented, which was then declared elected. In this manner fifteen Jews entered the city council, among them three Orthodox representatives—Luzer Prives, Joel Wegmeister, and Leibush Davidson.

However, a hard fought contest did take place in the Sixth *Kuria*, where, in addition to two Polish lists, there were two competing Jewish slates—one of the General Jewish bloc, in which Elias Kirshbraun, among others, was a candidate, and one headed by Noah Pryłucki, leader of the Folkists.[3] The struggle was extremely fierce. In the newspaper *Haint*, appeals (even in Polish) appeared several times, signed by Warsaw rabbis and lay Jewish leaders, calling for the election of the General bloc. *Der Moment* (another influential Yiddish newspaper) campaigned for Pryłucki and his slate. The result was a resounding victory for the Folkists, who elected four councilmen with 8342 votes. The General bloc drew a bare 1797 votes and failed to elect even one councilman.

The elections in the Sixth *Kuria*, held July 13-14, 1916, taught the religious Jews a lesson: without an organization they could never hope to compete with the secularists.

It is true that two of the councilmen elected in other *Kurias* belonged to *Agudat Ha-ortodoksim* and were among the most respected personalities in Orthodox Jewry. Luzer Prives was a member of the *Kehilla* leadership in Warsaw for thirteen years, chairman of its Committee on Rabbinical Affairs and very popular among the Jews. Joel Wegmeister had a record of almost fifty years of communal activity. He was president of the "Ezra" Society and also a member of the *Kehilla* leadership

for many years; in addition, he was among the Jewish representatives who had traveled to Petersburg to get anti-Jewish
edicts annulled (such as those relating to *shehita*). But in the
election in the Sixth *Kuria*, the Orthodox candidate Kirshbraun was defeated.

III

After the city council elections, Dr. Kohn and Dr. Carlebach
worked tirelessly and energetically to build the *Agudat Ha-
ortodoksim*. When the number of registered members reached
17,000, the first general meeting was convened (on November
14, 1916) in the Vienna Hall in Warsaw. Two thousand people
filled the large auditorium. On the stage sat a number of
rabbis, leaders of the Ger, Sokolov, Grodzisk, Sochaczow,
Piaseczna, and Novominsk Hasidim, along with several lay
leaders. Nahum Leib Weingot presided, assisted by Dr. Kohn
and Dr. Carlebach.

Rabbi Shlomo David Kahane spoke first, pointing out that
the *Agudat Ha-ortodoksim* signified the liberation of religious
Jewry from the uninvited guardianship of elements alien to
Judaism. Then Dr. Carlebach, who delivered the main address,
held the audience spellbound. The *Agudat Ha-ortodoksim*, he
said, wished to put religious Jewry on its own feet. It would
build Talmud Torahs and educate a generation of whole
human beings, whole Jews. It would also concern itself with
providing aid for trade and handicrafts. Dr. Carlebach's
detailed program for the new organization was greeted with
stormy applause.

The broad scope of this historical event can be seen in the
report which appeared the next day on the front page of *Haint*.
"The audience was so large that it overflowed the hall and
many people had to be turned away." Concerning the election
of leadership for the new organization, *Haint* reported that
there were two lists of candidates—one list including rabbis

and laymen, the other only laymen. Finally, a small committee met and worked out a compromise. The rabbis did not become part of the leadership but they organized a separate *vaad* (committee) with which the leadership agreed to meet regarding all matters of religious observance. At the end of the meeting Weingot reported that the *Agudat Ha-ortodoksim* had already received permission from the government to publish its own daily newspaper and to open a school for girls.

In a letter to his family, Rabbi Carlebach wrote: "Whoever did not see this joy and this meeting has not seen the joy of the world." Throughout the country several branches were already being formed and "everywhere they are inviting either me or Dr. Kohn to the founding meetings." The new newspaper would be called *Dos Yiddishe Vort*. But "where shall we find the time for all the tasks that face us?"

It is worth listing here the members of the first "Executive Committee" of the *Agudat Ha-ortodoksim* as they were reported in *Haint* of November 15, 1916 and in the Frankfurt *Israelit* of November 23, 1916:

Luzer Prives, Isaac Wlodower, Berl Gefen, Abraham Parnes, Abraham Meyer Morgenstern, Berl Zolberg, Baruch Kaminer, Baruch Mordecai Czarny, Bendet Klepfish, Gershon Kasperowski, Nahum Weidenfeld, V. Pashet, F. Tauman, Velvl Welt, Hayim Meyer Heller, Henoch Bialer, Joel Wegmeister, Isaac Meyer Levin, Isaac Meyer Elbinger, Salomon Alter, Rabbi Abraham Perlmutter, Yehiel Rothbart, Joseph Weidenfeld, Joseph Elbinger, Simon Landau, Jacob Gutgeld, Isaiah Zolberg, Joseph Krell, Jacob Trokenheim, Meshulem Kaminer, Michael Eliyahu Rosenstrauch, Rabbi Mendel Alter, Rabbi Naphtali Zilberberg, Nahum Leib Weingot, Nathan Bromberg, Nathan Pinhas Ehrlich, Nathan Spigelglas, Rabbi Salomon David Kahane, Shahna Awrech, Salomon Kaminer and Salomon Rothbart.

Many of the men on this list later played leading roles in the life of *Agudat Israel* in Poland. By that time they could already be called the "cream of the crop" of Orthodox Jewry in Warsaw.

The Executive Committee of *Agudat Ha-ortodoksim* immediately elected officers. Rabbi Abraham Perlmutter was elected chairman; Rabbi Joel Wegmeister, treasurer; and Rabbi Isaac Meyer Levin, secretary. On the Management Committee were Rabbi Salomon David Kahane, Isaac Meyer Elbinger, Berl Zolberg, Nahum Leib Weingot, Henoch Bialer, Meshulem Kaminer, and Nathan Pinhas Ehrlich.

The *Agudat* went to work post haste. It appealed to the Warsaw municipality to permit Sabbath-observing Jews to work on Sunday. It allocated to the Łomża yeshiva a stipend of 2000 marks. It asked the yeshivoth and Talmud Torahs in Warsaw to put together all the material describing their programs. It appointed an *Eruv* committee[4] headed by Joel Wegmeister and placed 3000 marks at its disposal.

The two rabbinical emissaries from Germany, by their representations to the government, placed the *Agudat Ha-ortodoksim* in the front ranks of political activity. Dr. Carlebach, in connection with the *Eruv* issue, wrote to his family:

"The government has permitted us [Dr. Kohn and myself] to reestablish the *Eruv*, exactly as we requested, but in order to raise the prestige of the *Agudat Ha-ortodoksim*, we gave them the credit for it—and we cannot be grateful enough to God for this development."

IV

The political activities of the *Agudat Ha-ortodoksim* soon began to unfold. It became virtually the most significant and most influential organization in the Jewish community.

Early in 1917 Germany and Austria-Hungary appointed a "Council of State" for Poland. This body, which was supposed to be the embryo of a Polish kingdom, consisted of twenty-five members (fifteen from the German-occupied territories and ten from the Austrian-occupied sections of former Congress Poland). It had no Jewish representation. (The one Jew on the Council was Kazimierz Natanson from Warsaw, who was there by virtue of being president of the Warsaw Stock Exchange.) A contact between Jews and the Council of State was certainly desirable. The *Agudat Ha-ortodoksim* provided that opportunity.

The Council opened its deliberations on January 15, 1917. On January 30 the *Agudat Ha-ortodoksim*, in a signed message, greeted the Council as the realization of a hundred-year-old dream for a renewed Poland. Tactfully and intelligently the *Agudat* stressed its religious approach to this event. Its work— to maintain the ancient faith of the Jews—would be a blessing for Poland. It expressed the hope that Poland would have a beautiful future in providing for the well-being of all its citizens.

The message was delivered personally by Rabbis Shlomo David Kahane and Joel Wegmeister to the Council President, Niemojewski. Two days later the Council recognized with deep satisfaction the "patriotic and noble declaration of the Jews." A highly political statement then followed in reply, namely, that the new Poland would again take up the torn thread of a historic tradition "that was characterized by religious tolerance" and would, "as in the past, guarantee to Polish Jews the right to practice their age-old religion." This document, which was published in the press, placed the *Agudat Ha-ortodoksim* in the forefront of Jewish public life.

Alongside organizational work went political activity. A brochure was published in Yiddish—"What Does the *Agudat Ha-ortodoksim* Want?"—which contained a report of the founding meeting and a proposed program of activity. This program was in full agreement with the program of *Agudat Israel*. The *Israelit* of January 25, 1917, in an editorial (unsigned, but its masterful style and splendid logic revealing the authorship of Jacob Rosenheim) dealt with the awakening of Polish-Jewish orthodoxy. It mentioned the similarity of its programs with those of *Agudat Israel* and stressed that the new organization, "being the backbone of Polish Jewry," would be "an independent, united body" for which the Torah would be a "natural spiritual light." The article, which is the first evaluation of the organization of Poland's religious Jews, quoted Rabbi Pinhas Kohn as having characterized the founding meeting as the *Shabbat Bereshit* (first Sabbath of the year) of the *Agudat*.[5]

On February 1 the *Agudat Ha-ortodoksim* began publication of its own Yiddish daily, *Dos Yiddishe Vort*, thereby becoming part of the everyday lives of the masses of Polish Jews. Other Yiddish newspapers—*Haint*, *Der Moment*— beginning to feel the competition, reacted in a none-too-civil manner. Dr. Carlebach reports in one of his letters that the boys who delivered the daily newspapers to subscribers were told bluntly not to deliver *Dos Yiddishe Vort*. This state of affairs lasted an entire week. The vendors who sold the newspapers on the street told customers who asked for it that the paper had ceased publication. That was the situation in Warsaw; in the provinces they simply stole *Dos Yiddishe Vort* from the mail. They fought against this religious organ with poisoned arrows.

The costs of publishing a daily newspaper were enormous, and the subscription price of eighteen marks per year was far from covering those costs. Additional financial resources had to be found. Help came from the *Gerer Rebbe*, who, with his great foresight, spoke out concerning the importance of the newspaper for the community. On the Fast of Esther 5677 (1917) he issued a heartfelt appeal for support for *Dos Yiddishe Vort*, from which we cite the following:

> For a long time now I have striven for the establishment of a newspaper which should walk in the path of Judaism and be managed in a way that is free from irreligious and immoral

ideas. A great many of you have shed tears because you saw
your sons and daughters being alienated from Judaism by the
influence of the newspapers. Now, under the masthead of *Dos
Yiddishe Vort*, a newspaper is being published by people who
belong to a circle devoted to God and the Torah. I urge you
therefore to support this newspaper in every possible way ....
Let this not be taken lightly by you.... I especially request all my
friends who deem it important to carry out my wishes to let me
know that you have subscribed to the paper or that you buy it at
the newsstands. Send me your name and address. Although
other newspapers may contain more news than this one, it is
better, because of its religious character, to be content with a
little less....

With this kind of self-sacrifice, the *Gerer Rebbe* built the
Agudat. The Zionist press, both Yiddish and Hebrew, reacted
angrily and insultingly, but the process of making Polish Jewish Orthodoxy independent was already irreversible.

On Sunday, April 22, 1917 the founding meeting of the local
branch of the *Agudat* took place in Łódź (the second largest
Jewish center in Poland.) In addition to a large audience, there
were also present representatives of the Łódź rabbinate and the
Warsaw *Agudat Ha-ortodoksim*. The meeting was opened by
Rabbi Salomon Woydysławski. Rabbi Moses Elijah Halpern,
who presided, said: "We must unite under one flag—the flag of
the Torah—all sections of our people, high and low, rich and
poor, Hasidim and Mitnagdim."

According to a report in the Frankfurt *Israelit* of May 3, it
was announced at that meeting that out of 120 *shtiblekh*
(Hasidic prayer-houses) in Łódź, 80 had already joined the
Agudat. A debate developed over the issue of whether *Mizrahi*
members could be accepted into the *Agudat*. The decision was
left to a special committee. Meshulem Kaminer, speaking in
the name of the Warsaw *Agudat Ha-ortodoksim*, opposed the
acceptance of Mizrahi members because it might lead to con-

flicts of conscience if the *Agudat* were to take positions contrary to the Zionist viewpoint.

The *Agudat Ha-ortodoksim* grew apace. Branches were also formed in Bedzin, Warta and Kalisz, where Rabbi Ezekiel Lifschitz (author of *Ha-midrash v'ha-maaseh*) became chairman. Soon there was a branch in Pabianice.

Early in November a second meeting took place in Łódź, attended by over a thousand people (according to the Frankfurt *Israelit* of November 15, 1917). Rabbi Treistman of Łódź was elected chairman of the local branch. According to this report Mr. Muntzburg announced that 8,000 people had expressed in writing their solidarity with the *Agudat* and that 1700 had paid dues to the organization. "Mr. Muntzburg" is obviously identical with Leib Mintzberg, who was later elected to the *Sejm* and became head of the Jewish community of Łódź.

V

During the year 1918 the *Agudat Ha-ortodoksim* made great strides forward. It rooted itself more deeply among the devout Jewish masses of Poland, took an active part in all community affairs, and laid the foundation for its role in the new Poland which was appearing on the horizon of Europe.

Germany, losing the war, was forced to make further concessions. A three-man Regency was set up to act as a transition step to an independent Polish state. On February 6, 1918 the Regency created a new Council of State, intended as the nucleus of a parliament of 110 members. Among them were eight Jewish representatives, including Rabbi Abraham Perlmutter of Warsaw, who was appointed as an *ex officio* representative of the Jewish faith. Among the eight were two other Orthodox representatives, Joel Wegmeister of Warsaw and Moses Pfeffer of Kielce.

In this Council of State, struggles took place between the Orthodox representative and Noah Pryłucki (one of the eight

Jewish members). Two schools of thought emerged, which in the new independent Poland later characterized Jewish politics: a moderate tendency, represented by the Orthodox, and a radical tendency, represented by the Folkists and the Zionists. The Zionists had one representative in the Council—Dr. Jerzy Rosenblatt of Łódź—but his voice was very seldom heard there.

The two emissaries from Germany, Rabbi Kohn and Rabbi Carlebach, during the last months of their stay in Warsaw, continued their work for the upbuilding of religious life and for the *Agudat Ha-ortodoksim*. Thanks to their efforts a conference of rabbis was called at which an *Agudat Ha-rabbanim* (Rabbinical Union) was founded.

Dr. Kohn became the target of venomous attacks by the Zionist and Folkists press. In the *Juedische Presse*, published in German in Berlin, it was charged that Dr. Kohn had "informed" on the secularists to the German government and that he had characterized Lithuanian Jewry as a "destructive element" (in contrast to the Hasidim). These and similar allegations were made repeatedly. In the face of such attacks, the Frankfurt *Israelit* did not keep quiet and defended Dr. Kohn on several occasions.

During the latter part of October 1918, the military death-throes of Germany began. They lasted until early November. The new Poland was born. But in the midst of all this, Jewish blood was shed; the nightmare of the pogroms began.

In his notebook, Dr. Carlebach wrote: "The times are so laden with significance that one reverses the words of the psalmist. One day is like a thousand years. Peace is near. By January, with the help of God, and without fanfare, I shall be home."

In the meantime, the *Agudat Ha-ortodoksim* changed its name to *Agudath Shlomei Emunei Israel* (The Union of the Faithful of Israel). This was a transitional step to the final change into *Agudat Israel*.

The last political act of the *Agudat Ha-ortodoksim* may be considered to be the meeting of its official delegation with Józef Piłsudski. When he took over the government in Poland after the collapse of Germany and Austria, he invited a delegation of the *Agudat Ha-ortodoksim* to meet with him. On Tuesday, November 12, 1918, at nine o'clock in the evening, in the Kronenberg Palace, the conference took place between the *Agudat* delegation and the temporary head of the new independent Polish state.

Piłsudski put three questions to the delegation:

(1) What form of government did they wish for Poland?

(2) What method should be used to create that government?"

(3) What special requests did the Jewish people have?

The delegation replied that Poland should be a republic and that the form should be worked out by a parliament (*Sejm*) chosen by the people through general, direct, equal, secret, and proportional elections. The delegation also expressed its deep dismay over the anti-Jewish manifestations in Warsaw—Jews were being beaten in the streets, dragged out of tramways, humiliated, and degraded. It asked Piłsudski to put an end to these outrages.

As a program for the future, the *Agudat Ha-ortodoksim* presented the following five points:

(1) full legal equality for the Jews in Poland, so that they might enjoy all the rights enjoyed by the Christian population, and to the same degree;

(2) religious belief should be no obstacle to occupying appropriate positions in the government apparatus;

(3) broad and free development in all fields of religious, cultural, and social life;

(4) Jewish institutions should be subsidized by the government to the same extent as similar institutions of other faiths;

(5) Jews of all political leanings should be represented in the government, with consideration for the Orthodox in accordance with their large numbers in the Jewish population.

This program was published in the press.

The first issue of a new central organ, the weekly *Der Yud*, appeared on December 5, 1918. Its sub-masthead read: "The Organ of the *Agudat Ha-ortodoksim*." In the second issue that was already changed to "The Organ of the *Agudat Shlomei Emunei Israel*."

The pre-history of *Agudat Israel* in Poland ended at that point.

Notes

[1] Jacob Rosenheim, *Erinnerungen*, Frankfurt, 1970, p. 144.

[2] Some of his letters were published by Alexander Carlebach in an article, "A German Rabbi Goes East," in the Yearbook of the Leo Baeck Institute, Vol. 6, 1961, pp. 60-121.

[3] For this party see Mark W. Kiel, "The Ideology of the Folks-Party" in *Soviet Jewish Affairs*, New York, 1975, Vol. 5, No. 2, pp.76-89.

[4] A committee which took care that the ritually prescribed fencing enabling Jews to carry on the Sabbath from private homes to public roads, and on public roads, be set up.

[5] Rabbi Dr. Pinhas Kohn later became chairman of the Executive Committee of the *Agudat Israel* World Organization. He died in 1941.

CHAPTER XV
The Political Orientation
of Agudat Israel in Poland

I

When World War I ended in October 1918 and the new Polish Republic was founded, the Jewish population of that country was politically unprepared for the new situation in which it found itself. Close to three million Jews, who, up to that moment, had lived under various regimes, were suddenly face to face with the militant nationalism of a freshly established state. Anti-Jewish tendencies became violent as pogroms destroyed Jewish lives in various parts of the country. And the splintered Jewish community, the largest in Europe, had no unified political orientation.

The leadership of the Polish government could not go ahead with its agenda regarding the Jews, who were ten percent of the population in Poland. Józef Piłsudski, the temporary head of the government, who wanted to become familiar with the demands of the Jews, invited representatives of several Jewish groups to meet with him in November 1918. The picture of the forces that were involved was unclear, however, and could not have been otherwise. No one knew who had the right to represent the Jews of Poland.

The first bit of clarity was introduced by the January 1919 elections to the *Sejm* (the Polish parliament). The Jews did not vote as a unit at this election, being divided into several groups, a division which had the political virtue of giving the Jewish political leaders (for the first time in the post-war period) the legitimacy to speak in the name of the masses of Jews.

What emerged in these democratic elections in the new Poland? Three movements in Jewish life found expression: the Zionists, the Orthodox, and the Folkists. The Zionist candidates received a total of 180,234 votes; the Orthodox, 97,293; the Folkists, 59,229. (The Bund received 16,366 votes; the Poale Zion, which ran separately, 27,063.) As in former Congress Poland, nine Jewish deputies were elected. (One of them was added later, in June 1919, in the Białystok district.) A tenth Jewish deputy was elected in what was formerly Galicia to represent the entire Jewish community (he was a Zionist). The nine Jewish deputies thus comprised: four Zionists, two Orthodox, two Folkists, one Poale Zion.

Who were the two Orthodox deputies who now had the right to speak in the name of almost a hundred thousand Jews (one quarter of all the votes garnered by the Jewish slates)? They were: Rabbi Abraham Z'vi Perlmutter (Warsaw) and Rabbi Moses Elijah Halpern (Łódź). Both of them represented *Agudat Israel*, which at that time was called *Agudat Ha-Ortodoksim*, then *Agudat Shlomei Emunei Israel*, and finally *Agudat Israel*. (The name *Agudat Israel* did not appear at first because it was considered inadvisable to give the Polish nationalists the opportunity to accuse the Orthodox of being connected to a central body in Frankfurt.)

For technical reasons, the Jewish deputies formed a voluntary "united front" in the *Sejm*, but the differences in their political orientation constantly rose to the surface.

II

At the session of the *Sejm* on February 24, 1919, three Jewish deputies spoke. The first was Rabbi Perlmutter, who reviewed the newly created situation and suggested that the revival of Poland was divine fulfillment of the prayers of past generations. The new state, he averred, was assured of its future. He cited the verse from Psalms: "God is good to all; His mercy extends to all He created." He stressed the word "all," meaning that for God there are no differences of class, religion, or nationality.

After these friendly sentences, however, came a series of far-reaching demands. Rabbi Perlmutter stated that the Orthodox Jews considered themselves part of the Jewish nationality and demanded religious and cultural autonomy. Jewish communal institutions must be subsidized by the government in the same way as those of other religions. Jewish communal life must have the right to develop, with a legally recognized central organ. The Jewish community must be built on traditional religious foundations. Insofar as general matters go, he demanded that Poland be built on democratic foundations, as a republic, with a government responsible to parliament. The Jews must enjoy full, equal rights, and the government must recognize the uniqueness of the needs and demands of the Jewish people. Religion must not be an obstacle to filling positions in the government apparatus.

When Rabbi Perlmutter finished reading this first declaration of Orthodox Jewry in Poland, voices were heard to say (they were noted in the official record): "This means a government within a government!"

From this beginning of Polish parliamentarianism on Feb-

ruary 24, 1919, up to its end in August 1939, the thorny path of
the Jewish representatives in general and of the *Agudat Israel*
representatives in particular was strewn with much more formidable obstacles. The Orthodox representatives found themselves in an extremely delicate situation.

In the first *Sejm*, at the very outset, two Jewish deputies—
Noah Prylucki (Folkist) and Isaac Gruenbaum (Zionist or
officially, "Club of the Temporary Jewish National
Council")—adopted a very sharp position. This position was
completely understandable. Jewish blood was being spilled in
Poland. Anti-Semitism had assumed violent forms. Polish
soldiers who belonged to the army of General Haller were
beating Jews in the streets and railroad trains, mockingly
cutting their beards. Jews were being harassed economically. It
is therefore understandable that Jewish deputies should have
reacted sharply to all this. The minutes of the first sessions of
the legislative body bear witness to the desperate struggle
which the Jewish deputies led in order to arouse a feeling of
responsiblity in the government and among the representatives
of the people. However, the situation also required a degree of
caution and restraint, so as not to provoke even more damag-
ing consequences.

Such an opportunity soon arose. On February 27, 1919, at
the eighth session of the *Sejm*, Deputy Prylucki spoke in
opposition to a Polish deputy who had proposed that "contracts for Polish military supplies should be given to Polish
handicrafts and Polish trade associations." Prylucki interpreted the word "Polish" here as excluding Jewish handicraftsmen and Jewish trade associations. His brief remarks
stirred up a tempest in the *Sejm*. The leader of the Polish
nationalists, Korfanty, immediately took the floor to protest
this dragging in of anti-Semitism where it did not exist. Prylucki spoke again, accusing Korfanty of "feigning innocence."
The proposal was definitely anti-Semitic, he insisted.

The Jewish deputies themselves were in disarray. Again

Korfanty took the rostrum and declared that the word "Polish" does no more than identify someone who lives in Poland, and that Prylucki was simply engaging in provocation. "We are of the opinion," he said, "that in Poland all citizens must have equal rights and that the Jews in Poland must have the same rights they now enjoy in Western Europe."

This statement by the leader of the Polish nationalists carried great weight. Although Deputy Prylucki's intentions were undoubtedly good, the responsible Jewish leadership should not have permitted such a sharpening of the already strained Jewish-Polish relationships. This task of defusing the situation Rabbi Menahem Halpern, the other Agudat Israel representative, took upon himself. The next day, February 28, 1919, he asked for the floor before the *Sejm* began its regular agenda and declared that the Orthodox Jews do not identify themselves with the views expressed by Deputy Prylucki in "his regrettable speech at yesterday's session of the *Sejm*." The stenographer noted at this point (the first time this had ever happened during a Jewish statement) that the *Sejm* deputies applauded.

Rabbi Halpern then said that he believed Deputy Korfanty's assurances that the Polish people would fulfill the historic necessity—and the justice—of granting full equal rights to the Jews. The misunderstandings that have existed between Jews and Poles up to now are lamentable. "We condemn every act, every word, every political expression that aims to prevent the easing of this tension." He then appealed to "my colleagues, the deputies" to join hands in the reconstruction of Poland.

Rabbi Halpern, in his brief statement, mentioned that although he condemned the worsening of political relationships caused by the tactless remarks of a Jewish deputy, he nonetheless asks the Christian deputies to try and understand the feelings of that deputy, "a son of a people which, for a long time, has been subjected to so much wrong and suffering in Poland." In this way he tactfully reminded the *Sejm* that Jews were suffering in Poland. At the same time, he hinted that Prylucki's remarks were spontaneous, provoked by the difficult situation of the Jews.

He concluded his speech with two quotations, one from *Pirke Abot*, "Nor did any man ever say to his fellow, 'The place is too narrow for me to lodge overnight in Jerusalem.'" Rabbi Halpern wished that this might be said of Poland too, that no individual and no nationality should feel oppressed in the republic. The second quotation was from Isaiah: "For the Lord is our Judge, the Lord is our Lawgiver, the Lord is our King; He will save us." May these words be fulfilled, Rabbi Halpern prayed, when we come to write the laws of the new Poland.

There is no doubt that the statement of the *Agudat Israel* representative which the Polish *Sejm* heard on the 28th of February, 1919, determined the political orientation of Orthodoxy in general and the *Agudat Israel* in particular for years and perhaps for the entire two decades of Independent Poland. And that orientation was: to demand Jewish rights, not to give up anything that was due the Jews, but at the same time to strive for an understanding with the Polish people and the Polish government.

III

On March 8, 1919 Rabbi Perlmutter reminded the *Sejm* that Jews, as citizens of the Republic, demanded full and equal rights, but that they were also aware of their responsibilities especially as regards the defense of the country from attack by the enemy to the east. "Everyone must add his brick to the building of the great social structure," he said, "and no one must exclude himself from the common work on the pretext that his tiny contribution means nothing, because if everyone withholds his contribution, then the great structure will never be built." Rabbi Perlmutter then recalled the situation which was created after the Jews were taken into exile in Babylon. At that time, Jeremiah demanded of them that they look upon the new place as their home:

"Build ye homes and dwell in them, and plant gardens, and eat the fruit of them.... And seek the peace of the city whither I have caused you to be carried away captive, and pray unto the Lord for it; for in the peace thereof shall ye have peace" (29, 5, 7). Even after Cyrus restored Jewish independence many Jews stayed in Babylon, because Jews have a feeling for the countries in which they have settled.

Rabbi Perlmutter also cited the verse from Proverbs: "The King's heart is in the hand of the Lord as the water-courses, He turneth it whithersoever He wills." And he explained the verse this way: When you look at flowing waters, they seem to come from a hidden source. The same is true of the heart of a ruler: he seems to be governing in accordance with his own will, but in reality he is led by the secret plans of God. Therefore everyone must obey the laws of the land, because they stem from God. "I declare categorically that there is among us not one spark of Bolshevism!"

This declaration was important because at that period of the Polish-Bolshevik conflict the flames of anti-Semitism were being fanned by the accusation that the Jews were on the side of the Bolsheviks. Rabbi Perlmutter therefore wanted to show that the Jews were obliged by their religion to obey the law of the land and to defend their country. He concluded his speech with an expression of hope that the prophecy of Isaiah would soon be fulfilled: "And the wolf shall dwell with the lamb, and the leopard shall lie down with the kid...."

But life went its own way. The new Poland was being built, but Jewish blood was being spilled. It was difficult to establish an atmosphere of friendship between Poles and Jews when pogroms were taking lives. Rabbi Perlmutter deemed it necessary to say a word about the impossible situation of the Jews, and on May 27, 1919 he presented a statement to the *Sejm* which was no longer "greeted with applause." He told the

Polish legislators that often, as he walked to the *Sejm* building, people on the street shouted at him: "Better go to the Palestine than to the *Sejm*!" So he had decided to give his answer not to the shouters in the street but to the *Sejm* itself. And that answer was:

> The Jew is not a blade of grass that bends for every wind. No, the Jew is an oak tree that holds its head high. Iron can cut it into pieces; a bolt of lightning can fell it; the wind can tear it up by the roots. But to break our granite will, to crush our tough soul, which are the product of our thousand-year national and social existence—that no storm wind, no iron, and no lightning can do! Israel has been too long in Europe for anyone to tell us to go to another country, even a country that flows with milk and honey, like Palestine, or which has mountains and rivers of gold, like California.
>
> We believe that a time will come when the Jewish state will be rebuilt in Jerusalem. We are strengthened in this belief by the miracle of Poland's regained independence. For 125 years no one believed this was possible, but God's mercy has nevertheless shown that this can happen, not by the power of the sword, but by Divine Providence. It will happen that way with the Jews too. One day the trumpet of the Messiah will be heard calling: "Jews—to Palestine!" Then we shall go, as happened once before in the days of King Cyrus, who himself contributed to the rebuilding of the Holy Temple in Jerusalem. But until that divine summons comes we must live safely and securely in this land, together with its other inhabitants, in the land in which our fathers lived and in which the bones of generations of our families lie buried. We shall eat the bread of this land and drink the milk from the breast of the newly established Mother Poland.

The old rabbi said, tactfully and with dignity, that Jews would not allow themselves to be robbed of their rights as citizens and that they would stay in Poland as long as Providence did not summon them back to *Eretz Israel*.

This was not the militant tone of the other Jewish representatives, but it had the charm of Torah wisdom. Slowly the words of the two Agudist deputies began to break down the wall of hatred that stood between Poles and Jews.

Shortly thereafter, Rabbi Halpern died and in his place Asher Mendelsohn entered the *Sejm* from Łódź.

IV

When the first *Sejm* adopted the constitution of Poland (March 1921) and worked out a new electoral system, the Jewish population was faced with a new test: how to increase the number of Jewish deputies and senators. (The constitution had created a senate in addition to the *Sejm*.) The answer they gave was: no splintering of the Jewish vote. The elections actually took place under the sign of unity. So that in the second *Sejm*, elected November 5, 1922, there were now thirty-five Jewish deputies, among them six representatives of *Agudat Israel*—Rabbi Aaron Lewin, Rabbi Meir Shapira, Eliyahu Kirshbraun, Leib Mincberg, Feilvel Stempel, and Eliezer Syrkis. Elected to the senate from *Agudat Israel* were Asher Mendelsohn and Moses Deutscher. A short time later a third Agudist Isaac Bauminger, entered the Senate to replace a Jewish senator who had died.

The Jewish deputies were united in a closed Club, the *Koło Żydowskie* (with the exception of Noah Prylucki, who ran independently in the elections and remained an independent in the *Sejm*). Deputy Kirshbraun of *Agudat Israel* became a vice-president of the Jewish Club and a member of the Military Committee. Deputy Lewin was appointed to the Education Committee. Deputies Mincberg, Stempel, and Syrkis were involved in economic matters.

The nine parliamentarians of *Agudat Israel* worked intensively on behalf of all the three millions Jews in Poland. They fought for maintaining the religious character of the Jewish community. Deputy Kirshbraun introduced a plan that enabled

Jews in military service to get kosher meals. Deputy Lewin, who took upon himself the role of representing Jewish cultural interests, became one of the most respected members of the *Sejm*. His command of the Polish language soon placed him among the finest speakers in the parliament. The Education Committee appointed him rapporteur for matters pertaining to Jewish schools, and he proposed a formula by which the government would have to subsidize Jewish religious schools. In a speech to the *Sejm* on the abolition of capital punishment he cited the Mishna, Tractate Makkot: "A sanhedrin which executes a person once in seven years may be called destructive. Rabbi Eliezer ben Azariah said: once in seventy years [may be called destructive]; Rabbi Tarphon and Rabbi Akiba said: If we were members of a sanhedrin, no one would ever be put to death."

At every opportunity, Rabbi Lewin illustrated the grandeur and nobility of the Torah. At the same time, he insisted categorically on the granting of Jewish civil rights. He fought against anti-Semitism in the public schools and proved with facts and figures how much anti-Jewish poison was contained in many of the textbooks used in public schools. He arranged for Jewish children attending public schools to be excused on Sabbath and Jewish holidays.

In the senate, Asher Mendelsohn engaged in intensive activity and his two colleagues helped him unfurl the banner of *Agudat Israel*.

However, the mood of unity which had brought about such a victory for the Jews did not last very long. Among the Zionist deputies themselves a deep split occurred when, on July 4, 1925, an agreement was concluded between the Jews and the Polish government. At that time, Deputies Reich and Thon, on one side, and Deputy Gruenbaum, on the other, found a deep chasm between them. The representatives of *Agudat Israel* were in favor of the understanding with the government.

But that government itself was short-lived. On May 12, 1926

Marshal Józef Piłsudski's coup d'etat turned Poland upside-down. A new period began. The *Sejm* lost its power and significance, but held on until the end of 1927. New elections took place in March 1928.

V

In the elections to the third *Sejm*, the Jews were again divided. *Agudat Israel* formed a bloc with the "Economic Groups" but, although that bloc did win about 200,000 votes, it failed to receive a mandate. The Zionists were also disunited; in what was Congress Poland and in the eastern regions they formed a bloc with other national minorities. In what was Galicia they ran alone. The number of their deputies decreased in both the *Sejm* and the Senate.

Nevertheless, *Agudat Israel* was not completely eliminated. One Agudist did enter the *Sejm*—Elijah Kirshbraun, who ran on the government slate. In this way, *Agudat Israel* became, from the parliamentary standpoint, part of the "Non-Party Bloc for Cooperation with the Government" (known under the acronym BB or BBWR, from the Polish words *Bezpartyjny Blok Współpracy z Rządem*).

What did this sudden change signify? Did *Agudat Israel* lose its political independence? Not at all! The presence of Deputy Kirshbraun in the Government Club did not deprive the movement of freedom of action. It meant, of course, that *Agudat Israel* did not follow the path of struggle against the Piłsudski government, but clearly *Agudat Israel* was still able to carry out an independent policy in the defense of Jewish interests. The bloc of *Agudat Israel* and the Economic Groups did draw a large number of votes. It failed to receive a mandate only because the votes were so widely distributed among various election districts that they were nowhere sufficient for a mandate. Had it been otherwise, however, *Agudat Israel* would have been completely free to go its own way. The mandate on the government list was complementary, an additional element. It gave *Agudat Israel* great influence with the government, but it in no way limited its freedom of movement. This assessment was confirmed in the next election in 1930, when an Agudist was elected independently in Warsaw, giving *Agudat Israel* representation in the BB Club also.

Very detrimental for *Agudat Israel* in the 1928 *Sejm* was the fact that its sole representative, Elijah Kirshbraun, became seriously ill and could no longer take an active part in the work. From his sickbed he intervened with government authorities to bring help to thousands of needy people. But in the *Sejm* itself, *Agudat Israel* was virtually without representation, a circumstance utilized by its sharpest opponent, Deputy Isaac Gruenbaum, to make various false accusations against Orthodoxy in general and *Agudat Israel* in particular. He even went so far as to call into question the patriotism of *Agudat Israel*. On one occasion he accused it of going along with every government, including the occupying power. The tribune of the *Sejm* was not accessible to *Agudat Israel* in the period from 1928 to 1930, since when Kirshbraun was ill, there was no other Agudist representative in the parliament.

VI

At the end of 1930 this situation changed. On November 16th, elections were held for the *Sejm*; on the 23rd, for the Senate. *Agudat Israel* again ran a slate in opposition to the Zionist groups. This time, however, it won a great victory in the city of Warsaw, where its list drew a large number of votes and where it elected its candidate—my father, Rabbi Aaron Lewin, of sacred memory. In general, the *Agudat Israel* list (with its partners from the Economics list) drew 149,790 votes. At the same time, from the government bloc two other Agudists were elected: Leib Mincberg as deputy and Asher Mendelsohn as senator.

In the daily practical work it soon became evident that, although Agudists were also elected from the BB list, the political orientation of *Agudat Israel* was still thoroughly independent. The independently elected deputy from Warsaw formed his own club in the *Sejm*. For the first time, *Agudat Israel* appeared in the list of parliamentary fractions. Formally the club consisted of one person—Rabbi Lewin—while the other Jewish group (the Koło Żydowskie) had six members. But at every opportunity, in the budget debates and all other important discussions, the representative of the *Agudat* club took the floor. The deputy and senator from *Agudat Israel* who were members of the Government Club had to observe discipline in regard to the Club authorities. Naturally they cooperated with the official representative of *Agudat Israel*. But the impressive word of Orthodoxy, in general, and of *Agudat Israel* in particular, was presented by my father. He was soon appointed member of the important committee charged with changing the constitution of Poland.

The strong sense of responsibility for *Klal Yisroel* with which he carried out his task can be seen from the very first speech he delivered in the new *Sejm*, on December 16, 1930. In that speech he was responding to the terrible attack upon religious Jewry made by Deputy Gruenbaum in the previous *Sejm*, to which no answer had been given up to that time. With utmost sharpness he rejected the claim that religious Jews had cooperated with the occupiers of Poland. He recalled the heroic figure of Ber Meisels, the Warsaw rabbi who was imprisoned by the Russians for aiding the Polish rebellion of 1863. He recalled the religious Jews who helped Piłsudski's legionnaires in the World War. And then he said:

> Let there be no misunderstanding here. I have not cited all these facts in order to stress the loyalty of Orthodox Jews at the expense of other Polish Jews. No, I will not do as Deputy Gruenbaum did; I will not use this forum to

make accusations against political foes. I say that all the Jews of Poland, without exception and regardless of party affiliation, are loyal Polish citizens and are faithful to the country. I only wanted to make clear to future historians that we were accused here in a most shameful manner. And we find it especially painful that the charge came from a Jew who, instead of defending us in this parliamentary forum, used it to defame us.

After this there was no repetition of the spectacle to which anti-Semites always looked forward eagerly—one Jew fighting another in the *Sejm*. The *Agudat Israel* representative honorably repudiated the attack emphasizing that all Jews without exception were loyal citizens of the country.

At every debate on the budget, the courageous word of the *Agudat Israel* representative was heard demanding justice for the Jews. The years 1930-35 were a shining period in Agudist parliamentary activity. In economic questions too the *Agudat Israel* representative fought for Jews, as well as in general matters where the Jewish standpoint needed to be put forward. On March 16, 1931 the *Sejm* discussed the question of supplying cadavers to the dissecting rooms of the universities. The anti-Semitic proponent of the bill had dared to call Jewish opposition to this procedure a "prejudice." Rabbi Lewin protested vigorously, explaining the law and asking the universities and the students to reflect upon the matter. "We shall never renounce an iota of our Torah," he declared fervently, "and no sacrifices are too great for us in the defense of the laws of the Torah!"

On November 7, 1931, during the debates on the pogroms which Polish students were perpetrating upon Jews, he asked:

Are these the future Polish intellectuals who will one day govern our country? If these students have so much energy, let them use it for other purposes, for the good of the country, and not in beating defenseless Jews!

The word of the *Agudat Israel* representative was always listened to with respect. The *Sejm* held in great esteem the Orthodox rabbi who spoke a masterful Polish and who struck notes that had never been heard before. He told the truth, using so many logical and historical arguments that no one could challenge him.

The three *Agudat Israel* representatives—Rabbi Lewin, Mincberg, and Mendelsohn—were kept busy interceding for people. The period 1930-35 was a critical one, both economically and politically. From the west, evil winds were blowing. The Hitler plague was spreading into Poland. The parliamentary representatives of *Agudat Israel*, who were highly visible in the government, were not given a moment's peace as they served the Jewish community indefatigably.

VII

At the time of the *Sejm* elections, toward the end of 1935, the situation was quite strange. The election law had introduced a new system: in order to be a candidate for deputy, one had first to be nominated by an electoral college, in which the government almost always had the greatest influence. Democratic elections were suspended. When it came to determining the candidates for the city of Warsaw, Prime Minister Walery Sławek disapproved my father's candidacy. Apparently it made him uncomfortable to have a courageous rabbi in the *Sejm* who was ready to sacrifice his life for the Jewish Torah. An order came down to the electoral college not to allow his candidacy. He knew well that if the name "Rabbi Aaron Lewin" appeared on the ballots, the great majority of Warsaw's Jews would again vote for the rabbi of Rzeszów.

Thus in 1935 only one Agudist was elected—Leib Mincberg of Łódź. A second Agudist was chosen to be senator—Jacob Trockenheim of Warsaw. He was among those whom the

President of Poland, in accord with the new constitution, appointed as senator without an election among the voters.

Mincberg and Trockenheim were also the Agudist representatives in the *Sejm* at the last elections that took place in 1938. They wrote a wonderful page in the history of Polish Jewry and unselfishly defended Jewish interests in that final period of Polish independence prior to the Holocaust. Their speeches in the *Sejm* brought credit to the Jewish people as they repelled the countless attacks by enemies of the Jewish people in Poland.

All three—my unforgettable father, Mincberg, and Trockenheim—died *al kiddush hashem*. But the Jewish people will forever remember their leadership of a community of three million people, leadership which they gave in the spirit of the Torah. Like dedicated ships' captains they went down with the community they had served all their lives. May their memory be a blessing to us.

CHAPTER XVI
The Relationship of the Polish Government to the Jewish Population Between the Two World Wars

I

In early November 1918 the Polish Republic came into being.

On November 11, Józef Piłsudski came from his internment in Magdeburg to Warsaw, and two days later the so-called "Regents Council" (*Rada Regencyjna*) turned over the government to him. In a decree dated November 22, 1918, Piłsudski declared himself temporary head of the State and ordered elections to be held for a legislative *Sejm*. Thus began the normal activity of a Polish government, first under the leadership of the Socialist Jedrzej Moraczewski, and from January 17, 1919 under the premiership of Ignacy Paderewski. Elections to the *Sejm* took place January 26, 1919.

From November 11, 1918 to the opening of the first session

of the *Sejm*, the Polish government was engaged in the process of organizing itself. This was the period when the "foreword" was written to the history of the new Poland, a history which falls into two periods: (1) up to the May revolution of 1926, and (2) up to the start of World War II.

With regard to the Jews of Poland, both of those periods can be divided even further. The first half of the first period encompasses the first legislative *Sejm* and the period of the second *Sejm*, which ended December 14, 1923, when the cabinet of Wincenty Witos fell. The second half of this period begins with the government of Władysław Grabski, during which the "Polish-Jewish Agreement" (*Ugoda*) was concluded. The second period began with the government of Kazimierz Bartel, on May 15, 1926. Its first part lasted until June 4, 1936, when Premier Felician Składkowski officially sanctioned the economic fight against the Jews. Then began the final period— in which the ruination of Polish Jewry was prepared.

Here we will describe certain features that characterize all five "chapters" of the history of the Jews in Independent Poland, including the "foreword."

II

While the new Poland was being born and Piłsudski was writing the "foreword" to its twenty-one-year history, Jewish blood was being spilled in all parts of the country.

The newspaper *Haint* of October 22, 1918 reports attacks on Jews in Warsaw, on Kiercelak Square, that had taken place the day before. On October 25, 1918 *Haint* again writes about attacks on Jews in Warsaw.

On October 31st a Jewish delegation consisting of Rabbi Perlmutter and the Vice-President of the *Kehilla,* Stanisław Natanson, handed a memorandum to Premier Świerczyński regarding the handbills being distributed in Warsaw and written in a blatant "pogrom tone." The same memorandum called attention also to the excesses in Chłodna Street, on Kiercelak Square, and in the bazaars in Praga and Mokotów.

The events in Warsaw were child's play compared to what happened in other cities of former Congress Poland and Galicia. When Piłsudski, in the first days of his leadership, received a Jewish delegation, everything was under the shadow of the excesses. The head of the government listened to the Jewish demands regarding cultural and religious autonomy, as well as civil rights, but for the time being the greatest concern was for the protection of Jewish life and property in Poland.

On November 11, 1918 a bloody pogrom took place at Kielce. The front page of *Haint* the next day reported Jews dead and wounded in Galician towns and cities: Brześć, Zator, Pilzno. The following day the same newspaper published details of pogroms in Dynów, Zakliczyn, and Żmigród. And on November 21-23 came the terrible pogrom in Lwów, in which sixty-four Jews were murdered, a great many seriously wounded, and Jewish property stolen. Jewish streets went up in flames. Torah scrolls were violated. That the Polish army had a hand in the pogrom was later confirmed by the report of the Morgenthau Commission, from which these facts were taken.[1]

No wonder these occurrences gave rise to an atmosphere of fear and insecurity among Jews and put their mark on the relationship between the Jewish representatives and the government, a government that was responsible for the safety of innocent citizens. The Morgenthau report, very moderate in tone, mentions other pogroms in Pińsk (April 5, 1919), Lida (April 17, 1919), Wilno (April 19-21, 1919)—where 65 Jews were killed and 2,000 Jewish homes and businesses looted, with material damage of over 10 million złoty—Kolbuszowa, Galicia (May 7, 1919), Częstochowa (May 27, 1919). Everywhere the same facts: dead, wounded, pillaged homes.

The outside world began to protest. There was not yet an American mission in Poland, so the instructions and reports went through the embassies at The Hague and Copenhagen.

Among the Poles, who had lived to see the greatest national triumph in 120 years of oppression, the Jewish protests aroused much resentment. When the *Sejm* convened after the elections of January 26, 1919, an alarming Judophobia was expressed by a majority of the Polish deputies. The eleven Jewish deputies were isolated. They were excluded from all regular committees, and when a special committee of leaders of all the clubs in the *Sejm* was established, the principle was adopted that only clubs with a minimum of twelve members would be invited. Twelve became the minimum because there were exactly *eleven* Jews in the *Sejm*.

The government itself had nothing to say on the Jewish question. Premier Ignacy Paderewski had just arrived from the United States. On February 20, 1919 he delivered the first message in the *Sejm*. It contained not one word about the Jews, who were ten percent of the population and who were struggling to survive in an atmosphere of terror and hatred. When things became so oppressive that one could hardly breathe, an idea was born: the largest club in the *Sejm*, *Związek Ludowo-Narodowy*, introduced a proposal to appoint a special *Sejm* committee on the Jewish Question.

On March 18, 1919 the *Sejm* discussed the matter. Deputy Stanisław Głąbiński, the representative of the National Democratic Party (*Endecja*), spoke calmly, saying that "we wish to solve the Jewish problem on the basis of justice, but we want to solve it ourselves, with no outside pressure."

The government said nothing. The Jewish deputies agreed to the committee, but it did absolutely nothing.

Three days after the committee was appointed, the *Sejm* debated certain occurrences in the city of Dąbrowa. The Jewish representative was not given the floor. A statement was put on the table that in Dąbrowa, Kalisz, Wielun, Stopnica, Busk, Szydłów, Chmielnik, Pacanów, Pinczów, and Klementów anti-Jewish excesses had taken place. But the Jewish deputies were gagged and the government was silent.

This government tactic of ignoring and covering up the Jewish Question continued for a long time. Paderewski resigned and in his place came Leopold Skulski, who delivered his message on December 18, 1919. Again, not a word about Jews. On the other hand, Głąbiński spoke about "nationalizing and unifying the Polish cities." The meaning of this was clear to everyone. The cities, after all, were "too Jewish," so the idea was to "Polonize" them. The government did not say that, but its parliamentary base elaborated upon the idea. Isaac Gruenbaum, the Jewish deputy, exposed this in the *Sejm*, and the official minutes noted what happened: *wrzawa*, "an uproar." They did not want to hear about it.

Władysław Grabski, who followed Skulski as Premier, continued the same tactic: silence about the Jews. In his message on June 30, 1920 there is not a single word about the Jewish Question in Poland, as though the problem never existed. The government was satisfied with replying to interpelations by the Jewish deputies, in most cases rejecting them as unjustified.

Poland had signed the so-called Little Versailles Peace Treaty of June 28, 1919, in which the government assumed a number of important responsibilities regarding national minorities in general and Jews in particular. No discrimination of any kind was to be tolerated. All citizens were to be given full civil rights: "In the cities where there are a significant number of Polish citizens who belong to a racial, religious, or linguistic minority, this minority must be assured of equitable participation in the enjoyment of funds that will be allocated by the government or municipal budgets for educational, religious or charitable purposes."

About Jews specifically the treaty made two decisions: (1) that the Jewish communities, under control of the government, would be responsible for the distribution of the funds which would be allocated to them for their schools, and (2) that Jews must not be compelled to do anything that represents a desecration of their Sabbath—for example, they must not be summoned to appear in court on a Saturday, and no public elections were to be held on Saturday. The Treaty on minorities was not ratified by Poland for a long time, but finally it was done.

Bound by this international agreement to include in the Polish constitution articles guaranteeing equal rights for national and religious minorities, the *Sejm* did so. In the constitution of March 17, 1921 there were several articles (95, 109, 110, 111, 114) which either took over literally the provisions of the Versailles Treaty on freedom of conscience for all citizens or which reformulated them in a liberal manner. Any discrimination on the basis of religion was forbidden.

But events took their own course. Despite the liberal paragraphs in the constitution, dozens of previous discriminatory laws remained in effect. Also, new laws were enacted which violated the religious freedom of the Jewish minority in Poland—for example, the law of compulsory Sunday rest. When such laws were adopted, fierce conflicts sometimes erupted between the majority in the *Sejm* and the small group of Jewish deputies. When the Sunday rest law was enacted and an amendment was defeated which would have permitted businesses closed on Saturday to remain open on Sunday, Deputy Gruenbaum cried out: "At this moment you have lost Mińsk, Wilno, and Eastern Galicia!"[2] The *Sejm* never forgave the Jewish deputy for those words.

The governments which followed Grabski's brought no changes in the Jewish situation. Wincenty Witos, Antoni Ponikowski, Artur Sliwiński, and Julian Nowak were the four premiers who led the Polish government up until the moment when a new *Sejm* and Senate were elected on the basis of the constitution of March 17, 1921. These elections took place on November 5, 1922 for the *Sejm* and November 12, 1922 for the Senate. At that time a large Jewish representation entered the legislative bodies. Thirty-five Jews were elected to the *Sejm* and twelve to the Senate.

Elected as President of the Polish Republic was Gabriel Narutowicz, for whom the Jewish members of the National Assembly (*Sejm* and Senate) also voted. On the streets he was called "the Jewish President" and on his first day in office he was assassinated.

The new President, Stanisław Wojciechowski, a minister in previous governments, appointed General Władysław Sikorski as premier. His approach to the Jewish Question in Poland, which was a continuation of former policy and at the same time a transition to a new one, we shall describe below.

III

Sikorski took into account the strength of the Jewish parliamentary representation. It was no longer possible to ignore the Jewish Question. The government, which had first been appointed by the *Sejm* Speaker, Maciej Rataj of the Peasant Party (*Piast*), during the interregnum period between Narutowicz's death and Wojciechowski's election, had a definite majority in the *Sejm* without the votes of the Jewish Club; nevertheless, thirty-four deputies and twelve senators represented such a strong group that Sikorski had to say something about the Jews.

In his message on January 19, 1923 he said:

> The Jewish minority undoubtedly believes that the rights which Poland has voluntarily granted it will be safeguarded by the government. But a note of warning is necessary here, because too often the defense of its justified interests has been turned by the Jewish side into a struggle for a privilege. Many organs of the international press, which are so eager to attack us, label the equality which prevails in Poland "oppression." There are no rights without responsibilities. The years of existence of independent Poland do not demonstrate that this truth is correctly understood by all Polish citizens.

The tactic of the premier was quite clear. Unable any longer to ignore the Jewish Question completely, he took the offensive. What the Jews are demanding, he said, is simply a privilege. Poland is a country with full equal rights. It is no more than an attack by the international press against Poland. The Jews want rights—without corresponding duties.

This official approach of Premier Sikorski spelled danger for the three million Jews of Poland. In the infested atmosphere of hatred toward Jews, such a voice from the rostrum of the *Sejm*—not from a party leader but from the head of the government, a general—could have terrible consequences.

A brilliant reply, superb in its wisdom and style, was given to Sikorski by the leader of the Jewish Club, Dr. Osias (Joshua) Thon, of Cracow, at the meeting of January 22, 1923.

First of all he contended that the statement "Poland gave the Jews rights" is false. There are no "givers" and no "takers" when it comes to rights; we are all equal. Jews are included when the rights of all citizens of the country are established. He then expounded on the matter of "rights" and "privileges." When the Jews demand safety of life, limb, and property, this is a right, not a privilege. Here the Jewish deputy skillfully took advantage of the opportunity to enlighten the parliament on the situation of the Jews in Poland—how they were being thrown out of trains, how they were being attacked on tramways, how they were being kept out of certain cities. He mentioned the legal discrimination against Jews. He spoke about the Jewish communities that were fighting for a broader area of effectiveness and how the government appoints commissars instead of letting them function democratically. He spoke of schools that the Jews should have. And with each of these points he asked: "Is this our 'right' or are we here demanding a 'privilege'?"

Dr. Thon responded sharply to Sikorski's allusion to "the international press," which allegedly was inspired by Jews. He denied this categorically. Regarding the aphorism that there are no rights without duties, he observed that, when young Polish Jews enlisted in the army in order to fulfill their first duty to the state, a special camp was set up for them in Jabłonna. He spoke of the assassination of the "Jewish President" (Narutowicz)—was this not an attempt to create a situation where some sixty percent of the members of parliament would have full rights, while the representatives of the minorities would be deprived of their right to vote for a president?

"No, we shall not allow ourselves to be thus demeaned!" Deputy Thon insisted. He concluded with the statement that the Jewish Club would continue to be critical of a government which proposed such a plan that contravened the Polish constitution.

Thon's speech made a powerful impression, so that the next day, in his reply, Premier Sikorski devoted a great deal of his time to the deputy's remarks. The Jewish deputy, he said, had "with real Talmudic shrewdness" posed several excellent questions, to which he wished to respond. Although he was being accused in some newspapers of building a "Jewish Poland," he was nevertheless a pure Pole and would not be a party to such cleverness. "In Poland, people persist in posing certain questions which are not asked in other democratic countries."

To the question whether the protection of life and liberty is a right or a privilege, the Premier replied that this is a right. "It is bad that such things happen in Poland, but it is your privilege to make of every tiny adventure an anti-Jewish pogrom."

Concerning the Jewish communities, the Premier replied: "To have equal rights with all other citizens in the cities is a right, but to create a separate Jewish community is a privilege." He added: "It is possible that you deserve this." Challenged from the floor that "this is in the constitution," Sikorski realized that he had made a mistake and replied extemporaneously, "I don't deny this and I don't question it. I'm only responding to the Talmudic philosophizing about rights and privileges."

Again the Premier referred to the "international press." He mentioned Georg Brandes, who (he said) had been warmly welcomed in Poland and then made unwarranted attacks upon her when he returned to Copenhagen. In America "your circles" are leading a bitter struggle. He mentioned Jewish interventions with the government for "every Jew who will come from Russia." Is this not a privilege? Sikorski concluded his reply to Dr. Thon with the comment that the government, in its program, was attempting to bring the laws into agreement with the constitution.

This was the first time in the history of Independent Poland that there had ever been an exchange of opinions between a head of government and the official Jewish representation. It was not merely an exchange of opinions; it was a duel. Both spokesmen used sharp swords. With General Sikorski, however, there was another interesting circumstance. He was not a party leader, not even an elected deputy in the *Sejm*. He was a "stranger" who had come to power in a moment of crisis, when the parties in the *Sejm* were faced with the nightmare of decline. Dr. Thon alluded to this in his speech when he said that he had looked for "the prompter" who had coached General Sikorski to say what he did about the Jewish Question.

The "prompter" did not stay concealed for very long. On May 26th the Sikorski government was overturned. The rightist parties in the *Sejm* formed a united front with the center and the Peasant Party (*Piast*) and took power into their own hands. Wincenty Witos, leader of the *Piast*, became premier. In the cement that held together the new partners—the *Endecja*, the *Chadecja*, the *Piast*—there was a good portion of anti-Semitism. At the end of October 1923 the new government was strengthened in its anti-Jewish position by the addition of Wojciech Korfanty, one of the most virulent anti-Semites in the *Sejm*, as Vice-Premier.

When Witos took over the government and, on June 1, 1923, presented himself to the *Sejm* as head of the government, he returned to the old tradition of ignoring the Jewish Question. He said only that "as in every other sphere, so in the area of education, the government will take into account the needs and the just demands of the national minorities." In the debate that followed, Deputy Gruenbaum asked: "What are these just demands?"

He then stressed that the Jewish representatives had helped to overturn the government of General Sikorski because they wished to put an end to his "progressive anti-Semitism." "Let anti-Semitism," he said, "be that which it should be— reactionary, regressive, and let it not cover itself with the figleaf of progress and social radicalism.

Wincenty Witos, however, soon had an opportunity to state his position on the Jewish Question. In October 1923 a debate took place in the *Sejm* on the budget. On October 16th Dr. Leon Reich described for the *Sejm* the difficult, almost desperate situation of the Jewish population. The next day, Premier Witos took the podium and said:

> Dr. Reich again has found it necessary to tell us that in Poland conditions are bad for the minorities in general and even worse for the Jews. Here, with full responsibility, I must say that Polish society in general is, in many areas, still a long way from possessing what the Jews in Poland possess. Constitutional rights apply to everyone equally, and if the honorable deputy were to review all the areas of life and objectively draw the conclusions, he would arrive at the conviction that Poland ranks first in Europe in tolerance; it is a country where Jews, above all others, fare best.

It should be clear why we place the first year of the first normal *Sejm* in the first half of the first period of Jewish history in Independent Poland: the government of Wincenty Witos certainly belonged among those who treated the Jewish Question as non-existent, just as Paderewski and Skulski had done. This first half ended with the fall of the Witos government, which represented "*Chieno-Piast*", the right wing of the *Sejm* and of Polish society.

IV

Witos fell because of the economic crisis and the currency chaos. His successor was Władysław Grabski, who had previously been premier for a brief period. Grabski was supposed to save the Polish currency—and he partially succeeded. About the Jewish Question he thought little and did even less.

In his message to the *Sejm* on December 20, 1923 he confined himself to economic matters. He said not one word about the Jews, who were very critical of the new premier. On December 21, Deputy Leon Reich spoke with bitterness about the presence of General Sosnkowski in the cabinet as Minister of War. It was Sosnkowski who, as soon as Poland won her independence, set up the camp in Jabłonna for Jewish soldiers. At that time he also suggested that Jews should be excused from military service and instead pay a special tax. This shameful provocation was never put into effect, but the Jews remembered it and voted against Grabski's government in the *Sejm*.

Still, in historical perspective, Władysław Grabski's government was a positive interlude. On the one hand, the stabilization of the złoty was of great significance for the country and consequently for the Jews. On the other hand, the Grabski period was one of severe economic pressure against the merchant class in Poland. The tax screw was tightened even more, and for the Jewish merchants this was like draining the blood out of their veins.

After his success in stabilizing the currency, Grabski turned to other problems. First he tried to create a *modus vivendi* with three territorial national minorities—the Byelorussians, the Ukrainians, and the Lithuanians. In July 1924, on Grabski's initiative, the *Sejm* adopted several laws which would have introduced the language of these minorities into government administration, schools, and courts. It was decided that in geographic areas where the national minority comprised twenty-five percent of the population, if parents of at least forty children requested it, a school must be opened in one of the three languages. In regard to the Jews, however, who comprised more than twenty-five percent of the population in a number of areas, there was no mention in the laws passed in 1924.

Minister of Foreign Affairs in the Grabski cabinet was Aleksander Skrzyński, a man of high culture and a first-rate diplomat. Skrzyński took it upon himself to negotiate an agreement with the Jews. In this he was assisted by another minister, Stanisław Grabski, who happened to be the Premier's brother. Himself an active politician in the rightist camp, Stanisław Grabski, a professor of economics at Lwów University, had a broader view of Polish-Jewish relations than his brother. Stanisław had Jewish acquaintances abroad, among them Lucien Wolf of England. With the help of Stanisław Grabski and Lucien Wolf, Skrzyński began talking with Jews, particularly Dr. Osias Thon and Dr. Leon Reich, concerning an agreement.

deteriorate. It simply drove the Jewish parliamentary representatives to acts of desperation. On the basis of an order issued December 27, 1924 by the President, concessions for state-monopoly-controlled articles were revised, which meant that tens of thousands of Jewish merchants would lose their livelihood. The Jewish Club in the *Sejm* demanded that this order be revoked. After going through all the parliamentary procedure, the *Sejm* voted down the Jewish proposal.

At the June 3, 1925 session, the Jewish deputies engaged in an unprecedented act of obstruction: using all the means available to them, they prevented the session from proceeding with its business. They banged on the podiums, they whistled, they cried aloud to heaven. Never before had the *Sejm* witnessed such a scene. The desperation of the representatives of ten percent of the population was here expressed more dramatically than it had ever been before or ever could be again, because that was the only time the *Sejm* had a group of thirty-four Jews (thirty-five, with the independent Folkist deputy, Noah Prylucki). Physically they were able to carry through such a demonstration. But in vain. The *Sejm* Speaker called the shouting Jewish deputies to order and the session was forced to adjourn.

This sort of atmosphere provided a favorable opportunity for reaching an understanding. The Jewish representatives wanted to achieve at least something that would ameliorate the lot of their constituents. The government wanted to show its good will, in order to prevent further desperate acts by the Jews and in order to show the world that something was being done for the Jews too. Thus was born the mysterious document known as *Ugoda*—the Polish-Jewish agreement. It is dated July 4, 1925.

In this agreement the leadership of the *Koło Żydowskie* affirmed its loyalty to the Polish government as well as its readiness to vote for the government's budget; the government, for its part, pledged to carry out forty-two Jewish demands. Only twelve of these demands were made public, all in the areas of religion, culture, or organization of Jewish communities. The provisions that had an economic character remained secret.

The twelve public points of the Polish-Jewish agreement were:

(1) Jewish communities had the right to unite organizationally;

(2) the law that had been adopted by Piłsudski for the Jewish communities in Congress Poland would be broadened to include the eastern border areas;

(3) the election system for the Jewish communities in Galicia would be made more democratic;

(4) joint conferences of Jewish communities would be permitted;

(5) Hebrew and Yiddish could be used at public meetings;

(6) Jewish students could, to a degree, observe the Sabbath;

(7) the Jewish *hadorim* would be given public rights;

(8) the Jewish trade schools would receive support from the government;

(9) rights would be granted to a certain number of elementary schools, high schools, and seminars that use Hebrew as their language of instruction;

(10) all Jewish students in government schools would be excused from writing on Saturday;

(11) Jewish students in government schools would be given the opportunity to worship on Saturday, inside the school building;

(12) Jewish soldiers in the army would be given kosher food.

Jewish and non-Jewish opinion alike received the twelve published points of the *Ugoda* with understandable skepticism. Although the principle of an agreement between the Jews and the Polish government was a constructive one, the twelve points themselves were clearly disproportionate to the seriousness of the Jewish situation. This was confirmed in no uncertain terms by one of the authors of the agreement, Dr. Reich, after the fall of the Grabski government.

On November 13, 1925 Władysław Grabski resigned and Aleksander Skrzyński was appointed premier. In his program message to the *Sejm*, the new premier stated:

I am happy that I take office following a government under which a declaration was given by the President of the Jewish Club to my predecessor, a deed which promised a favorable change in the relationships that previously existed. In the area of politics, as in the area of economics, we need to make the same discoveries several times; nothing can hold back the development of an idea once it has been awakened. I do not doubt that the spirit which initiated the talks between the presidium of the Jewish Club and Premier Grabski will again be alive and effective.

It is easy to recognize in these words the skepticism on the Polish side toward the *Ugoda*. Skrzyński wished to comfort himself with the thought that "an idea once awakened cannot be held back in its development." The Jewish side expressed its skepticism in even clearer terms. Dr. Reich spoke in the *Sejm* on November 26th, and after describing the situation of the Jews in Poland, he said:

> A certain degree of understanding was shown for the tragic situation of three million Polish Jews by the government of Władysław Grabski, which obligated itself, after the conference with the presidium of the Jewish Club...to fulfill a number of Jewish demands that had been recognized as justified. Unfortunately, this government did not carry out their obligations, except for issuing the orders concerning Jewish communities and kosher food for Jewish soldiers; but with the intensification of the quota system against Jewish students, it then violated the constitution.

Dr. Reich underscored the disappointment of Polish Jewry which had now turned to "resignation, almost despair." However, he also expressed satisfaction that the new government had come into office under circumstances that aroused no distrust. The fact that it contained important Polish groups, as well as the Premier himself, gave hope that the Jewish demands would be taken into consideration "very soon." Dr. Reich mentioned several of them: to wipe out the disgraceful stain of *numerus clausus* in the universities; to enable observant Jews to work or do business on Sunday, so that they would not lose two or two-and-a-half days work every week; to eliminate the threats to Jewish handicraftsmen and their work opportunities. The sum total was that the Jewish Club was taking a position of "friendly waiting" toward the Skrzyński regime.

The "friendly waiting" did not last long. Aleksander Skrzyński resigned on May 5, 1926. Wincenty Witos was named to succeed him, but failed to form a government. Józef Piłsudski appeared once more on the political arena. Revolutionary winds began to blow in Poland. The government structure that had been erected by the political parties and which had a clear anti-Semitic coloration now began to totter.

V

Without any doubt, the May revolution began a new period in the relationship between the Polish government and the Jews. The Jewish population, which had seen in the governments up to that time either outspoken enemies or leaders without the courage to oppose the waves of anti-Semitism, now hopefully greeted the return to power of the national hero Piłsudski, whose views were liberal and who himself was a target of the anti-Semitic right and the Peasant parties.

After Piłsudski's rebellion was legalized by his election as President (an office which he did not accept, indicating Professor Ignacy Mościcki as a suitable candidate), Kazimierz Bartel was named premier. The new head of government soon made his position on the Jewish Question clear. On July 19, 1926 he spoke in the *Sejm* during the debate on a proposal to enable the new President to issue orders with the power of law. This is what he said:

> Proceeding from the standpoint that economic anti-Semitism is harmful to the country, the government deems it necessary, in the sphere of its activity, to safeguard the principle of impartiality and justice, mindful that especially in regard to taxes and credits (including production credits) we must be guided solely by existing circumstances, not by national or religious considerations.
>
> The government will not make any secret agreements with the Jewish population, but will stand firm on the ground of implementing the constitution. The government takes the posi-

tion that the conditions of commerce must be regulated, that the obligatory work-norms must be safeguarded solely from the standpoint of the interests of both the buyer and the seller. In an appropriate way, the government will make certain that all legal restrictions on Jews that were ordered by the occupying powers shall be nullified and not enforced against the Jewish population.

This kind of "revolutionary" declaration concerning Jews gave rise to a mood of optimism among the Jewish population in general and its parliamentary representatives in particular. At the July 20, 1926 session of the *Sejm*, Isaac Gruenbaum (who had before opposed the leadership of the Jewish Club because of its *Ugoda* tendencies) spoke in the name of the Club. He explained that the Jews would vote for the powers requested by the government. He underscored that this was the first time any Polish government had had the courage to brand economic anti-Semitism as harmful to the country and the first time that a Polish government ever publicly expressed a willingness to do something about correcting it.

In his enthusiasm for the Bartel government, Gruenbaum went so far as to engage in a polemic with the leader of the Ukrainians in the *Sejm*, who opposed giving these powers to the government. Gruenbaum was always a protagonist of the idea that all minorities should cooperate to assure proper parliamentary representation for themselves and should together struggle for national rights. This time, however, there was an open split between him and the Ukrainians.

But Gruenbaum's enthusiasm did not last long. The fine words of Premier Bartel were not followed by deeds. The Jewish population waited for them impatiently, but in vain. Bartel resigned on September 30 and his place was taken by Piłsudski himself. The government of Piłsudski carried out new elections for the *Sejm* in which not only was the Jewish representation drastically reduced, but a new direction in Jewish politics was also taken. Two members of the Jewish Club, Elijah Kirshbraun (*Agudat Israel*) and Wacław Wiślicki (Jewish Merchants Association), were elected on the list of the "Non-Party Bloc," which was the official support of the government in the parliament.

The Jewish representation was thus split and two groups became evident: one which at first was bound to the government and a second which did not have a firm position in regard to the government. In the latter, since there was no unified position, internal disagreements were frequent: part of the Jewish Club believed that they should go over to outright opposition to the government and vote against the budget, another part held that they should abstain from voting.

These divisions continued at the next elections to the *Sejm*, which took place on November 16, 1930. At that time, there were in Warsaw two independent Jewish lists, from which were elected Isaac Gruenbaum (Zionists) and Rabbi Aaron Lewin (*Agudat Israel*). Five other Jewish deputies were elected on independent lists, as well as three from the Non-Party Bloc. In this way, Jewish political life was badly splintered.

No new declarations on the Jewish Question in Poland were made by the various governments that held office after Piłsudski resigned from the premiership on June 27, 1928. Bartel's message of July 19, 1926 was delivered to the *Sejm* in the name of the first Piłsudski government and therefore it at least placed a moral obligation on the governments that followed him—Kazimierz Switalski, Walery Sławek, Aleksander Prystor, Janusz Jędrzejewicz, Leon Kozłowski, and Marian Kościałkowski—until General Sławoj-Składkowski changed this policy with his statement on June 4, 1936.

Up until that time the *Sanacja* governments took certain steps to implement Bartel's assurances. Thus on March 23, 1931 the *Sejm* abolished the discriminations that remained from previous eras and which were based on origin, nationality, language, race, or religion. On this matter the Jewish deputies had fought for many years without success until the government, with the votes of the Non-Party bloc, pushed it through. In the autumn of 1931, when the "excesses" of the Polish students took place in Warsaw, Wilno, and other cities, the government took stern measures against the perpetrators. On November 9, 1931 Minister of the Interior Pieracki told the *Sejm*:

> In recent days, regrettable excesses are being committed by some of our young people in Warsaw against citizens of Jewish nationality. We cannot place the responsibility for this on our entire student youth or on Polish society, which is far from condoning such criminal excesses. This is only the activity of a group under the unsavory influence of hoodlum party elements and on whom falls the entire responsibility for the provocations—which are in complete contradiction to the culture and tradition of the Polish people. As to the position of the government, that is expressed in the fact that, in this instance, as in similar instances, the organs of power that are under my jurisdiction did everything possible...to assure the safety of the citizens and put a stop to the criminal excesses.
>
> The security organs, however, were thwarted by the autonomous position of the universities for as long as the events took place on the university grounds. As soon as they spread beyond that area, however, they were energetically dealt with. Several score people were arrested on suspicion of having taken an active part in the excesses. The university authorities, for their part, suspended classes and instituted a disciplinary procedure. The government is determined to put down relentlessly any attempts to renew the excesses if feelings of justice, dignity and the welfare of the country do not prevent the young people from again succombing to the mindless agitation.

On the other hand, the governments from 1930-36 did nothing to lighten the economic pressure upon Poland's Jews. In the general debate on the government budget in the *Sejm*, on February 4, 1932, Rabbi Aaron Lewin said:

The position of the Jewish merchant has completely broken down. He is breathing his last.... The onerous tax burden has deprived him of any possibility of surviving the hard times.... The Finance Minister recently estimated the delinquent taxes to be 1,200 million złoty. These must be written off as soon as possible.... The Jewish population is suffering painfully from the reduction of almost 1,300 state monopoly concessions carried out on January 1, 1932.... Jewish merchants are being excluded from government and state trade. The Jewish handicraftsmen, with their long and honorable tradition, are at the end of their rope.

During those years a situation was created in which the government was speaking beautiful words but the three million Jews were barely able to stay alive. The agitation of the anti-Semitic parties, who were in opposition to the government, continually used the Jews as a scapegoat. In its editorial of November 23, 1933, the *Gazeta Warszawska* wrote: "If we are to fulfill the tasks that stand before us, we must get the Jews out of Poland. That is the only solution to this burning problem which threatens the internal equilibrium of the life of our people."

In the face of such open calls by the *Stronnictwo Narodowe* (as the "*Endecja*" was then officially called) for the destruction of Polish Jewry, the government grew more and more powerless. When Marshal Piłsudski died on May 12, 1935, the strong hand went with him, as well as the strong moral authority which had held the Polish government together. The constitution of Poland was soon amended; the articles concerned with civil rights for all citizens remained in the document, but there was no one now to enforce them.

VI

On May 15, 1936 the government of Kościałkowski resigned and General Felicjan Sławoj-Składkowski was named Premier. On June 4 the new premier, in his message to the *Sejm*, said: "My government considers that no one in Poland should be wronged. An honest host does not allow anyone in his home to be harmed. But an economic fight? That is in order (*owszem*)!"

The Polish word *owszem* became a symbol. An economic fight against the Jews was permitted. Contrary to what Bartel had said about economic anti-Semitism, Składkowski plainly had given permission for an anti-Semitic economic campaign against Jews.

Premier Składkowski later interpreted his own words. In a speech to the *Sejm* a year and a half later (January 24, 1938), when the *owszem* policy was at its height, Składkowski declared that the problem of the minorities in Poland was not dependent on the government but on the relationship of the dominant nation to those national minorities. He warned against manifestations of hatred and intolerance toward the minorities, which can avenge themselves on the Polish state. But the conflict between Jews and Poles stemmed from economic forces; competition was based on social and economic changes which were driving the peasant into the city. This process was an economic necessity. Not only must it not be obstructed by the government, it must be supported by the government. This the Jews must understand, he said, just as they must understand that the economic campaign against them is in no way an attack on their rights as citizens of the state. As citizens the Jews are entitled to live in peace. The government will treat them well and will see to it that they have equal rights.

In a speech to the Senate on February 9, 1938 General Składkowski justified the anti-Jewish economic fight even more clearly.

It is no surprise, then, that when the reorganized government party (now called "The Camp of National Unity"—OZON, *Obóz Zjednoczenia Narodowego*) formulated its policy on the

Jewish Question, it did so in the following manner. At a meeting of its central council on May 22, 1938 it adopted a resolution which first of all declared that the Jews constitute a group with loyalties to world Jewry and with its own national aspirations. For that reason they were considered to be a factor which would weaken the normal development of Polish national and state forces. In a word, the Jews were seen as a hindrance to the social evolution then taking place in Poland. The strength and greatness of Poland was taken as dependent on the solution of the Jewish problem, which could only be solved by reducing the number of Jews in Poland through emigration to Palestine and other countries.

Furthermore, the participation of Jews in the economic life of Poland had to be diminished by intensifying the economic activities of Poles and by reconstructing Polish social and economic life. The Jewish influence on Poland's cultural and social life had to be eliminated. Jewish participation in schools, universities, and other educational institutions had to be regulated.

But all of this had to be done by legal means. Demagogic acts which attempted to make the Jewish Question a football for political parties were condemned, as were acts of violence and barbaric treatment of Jews. The Jews, however, had to display absolute loyalty to the state and to the Polish people. International contacts with Jews outside of Poland were not to be used to damage the interests of the Polish state. It was not an objective of Polish policy that the Jews should assimilate, although individuals of Jewish origin who deserved to be regarded as Poles must be accepted into Polish national society.

Several months later, on December 3, 1938, the head of OZON, General Stanisław Skwarczyński, delivered an address to the *Sejm* in which he referred to this ideological declaration and said that the direction of government policy on the Jewish Question had been delineated therein: "The Jewish problem can be solved first of all by substantially reducing the number of Jews in Poland." Therefore, he added, the trend toward emigration among Jews must receive the most far-reaching assistance from governmental authorities. The Polish population in the village and the city must become economically independent. The large number of Jews in some professions had to be reduced. Polish culture had to be freed of Jewish influence, which was foreign to the Polish psyche. But in no way must the Jewish Question be made an instrument of partisan conflict, because this creates anarchy in the life of the country, it demoralized the youth, and it is in contradiction to the beautiful Polish tradition of chivalry.

This was the official Polish government policy in the last years prior to the outbreak of World War II. In accord with this policy, the *Sejm* and the Senate, where the government had a strong majority and could carry through whatever it pleased, adopted certain laws. For example: the law of March 25, 1938 which revoked the citizenship of individuals who lived abroad for five years and lost touch with Poland. In October 1938 this law led to sending back Polish Jews from Germany and interning them in a camp at Zbąszyń because Germany did not want them and Poland would not admit them. On May 4, 1938 a law was passed to regulate the legal profession. Thousands of young Jewish students were thereby left without any prospect of ever becoming lawyers. The *Sejm* also adopted a law to prohibit Jewish ritual slaughter, but this step the government opposed. Consequently a complete ban on *Shehita* was not passed by the Senate and the law was never put into effect.

During the years immediately preceding World War II anti-Jewish excesses were not infrequent in Poland. The government condemned them and fought them, but the rightist parties could not live with the fact that the government had taken over the economic fight against the Jews. They therefore agitated the population to go at least a few steps further. The result was the pogrom in Przytyk on March 9, 1936. In Brześć there were bloody excesses on May 13, 1937, in Częstochowa on June 19, 1937. "Minor incidents" took place in the hundreds.

One can safely say that after the OZON government submitted to the anti-Semitic slogans of the rightwing camp, it could no longer control the situation surrounding the Jewish Question. The terrible example of Poland's western neighbor undoubtedly had an effect on the position of the government toward the three and one-half million Jews in Poland. It did not understand at first that the destruction of Polish Jewry must bring with it a collapse of the newly established state. When it finally realized this, in the last days before World War II, it was too late. Events then moved with fearful rapidity. The resulting chaos consumed everything. Nothing remained but the hand of history, carefully noting everything that had happened.

Note

[1] *The Jews in Poland, Official Reports of the American and British Investigating Missions,* The National Polish Committee of America. Chicago, Ill., (1920?). pp. 4-9.

INDEX

Also available at the Polish Institute of Arts and Sciences of America:

Polish Civilization, Essays and Studies
  edited by Mieczyslaw Giergielewicz in cooperation with
  Ludwik Krzyzanowski

The Beginning of Cyrillic Printing in Cracow, 1491, From the Orthodox Past in Poland
  by Szczepan K. Zimmer
  edited by Ludwik Krzyzanowski and Irene Nagurski
  with the assistance of Krystyna M. Olszer

The Origin of Modern Russia
  by Jan Kucharzewski and Pindar Epinicia
  edited by Alexander Turyn

The Polish Institute of Arts and Sciences of America, Inc.
59 East 66 Street, New York, N.Y. 10022